Following I

Following Isabella

Travels in Colorado Then and Now

ROBERT ROOT

UNIVERSITY OF OKLAHOMA PRESS : NORMAN

Also by Robert Root

Library of Congress Cataloging-in-Publication Data

Root, Robert L.
    Following Isabella : travels in Colorado then and now / Robert Root.
        p. cm.
    Includes bibliographical references.
    ISBN 978-0-8061-4018-6 (pbk.: alk. paper)   1. Colorado—Description and travel.   2. Rocky Mountains—Description and travel.   3. Bird, Isabella L. (Isabella Lucy), 1831–1904—Travel—Colorado.   4. Root, Robert L.—Travel—Colorado.   5. Colorado—History.   6. Natural history—Colorado.   7. Bird, Isabella L. (Isabella Lucy), 1831–1904 Lady's life in the Rocky Mountains.   8. Travelers' writings—History and criticism.   I. Title.
    F776.R74 2009
    917.8804'02—dc22

                                                         2008034326

The paper in this book meets the guidelines for permanence and durability of the Committee on Production Guidelines for Book Longevity of the Council on Library Resources, Inc. ∞

Copyright © 2009 by the University of Oklahoma Press, Norman, Publishing Division of the University. Manufactured in the U.S.A.

1 2 3 4 5 6 7 8 9 10

For Zola, Ezra, and Louis,

With whom I hope to wander many trails,

And for my brother, David,

who made our emigration easier

One advantage of retirement is that it gives you time to open yourself to your surroundings. There is always something that transcends the immediate. You seldom escape the pressures of our world and its murderous news (count no day lost in which you have no idea of what is going on), but there are other voices to listen to.

John Hay, *A Beginner's Faith in Things Unseen*

The difference between landscape and nature is the difference between separation and inclusion.

Reg Saner

Contents

Illustrations

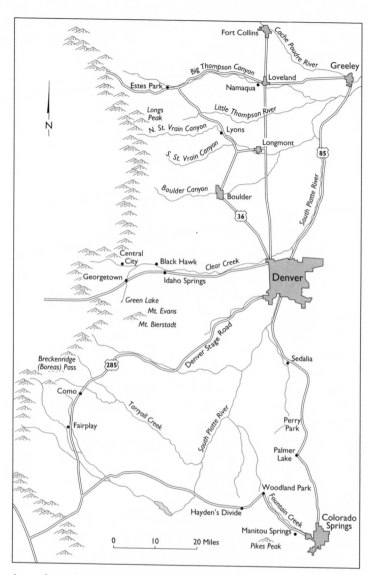

Area of travels in Colorado 1873 and 2004–2005

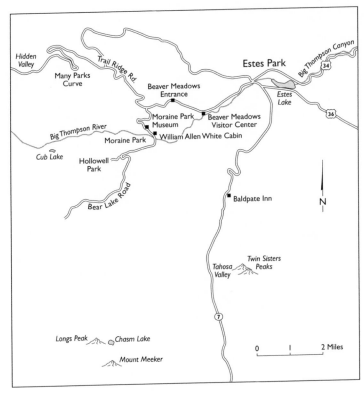

Rocky Mountain National Park

Following Isabella

Arrival

The mountains startled me when they appeared across the plains one Sunday morning in September. It was as though I'd never seen them before. I'd taken my wife to catch an early flight and, as I drove away from the Denver airport, I mused idly about the white meringue peaks of its multi-tented roof and silently began listing chores for the coming few days of solitary living. I was vaguely aware that I was the only one heading west on the toll road. The sky was cloudless and the air clear; the plains northeast of Denver were bathed in sunlight and, for a very short stretch, seemed uninhabited and empty. I value those moments when, as I ride the crest of a ridge, the land around me is too flat to expose landmarks anywhere ahead and I'm aware only of an expanse of dry tan grasses meeting an expanse of cobalt blue sky. Here, at such a moment, I was lifted out of listmaking and suddenly alert to the sensation of terrain.

Then the road rose to the top of another low ridge and the mountains appeared, spread out all across the horizon. I live much closer to the mountains than this, see them every day, if only for a few moments, hike in them as often as I can. By now they're familiar sights to me. But some-how, though I'd traveled this route often for more than a year, this view of the mountains was unexpected. It caught me by surprise. I checked my mirrors—the tollway was still empty behind me—and slowed the car to concentrate on the view.

Had I truly not realized that the entire expanse of the Front Range of the Rocky Mountains was visible from certain points on the plains? It was, and even I, who can never quite sort out the names of the mountains visible from my apartment balcony—even I could identify Pikes Peak, far to the south, and Longs Peak, the northernmost 14,000-foot summit in the range. A multitude of mountains rose between them in the distance, like an upright row of uneven sawteeth, some dingy white, some dark gray, separating unbroken beige earth and unblemished blue sky.

At that moment, my unexpected view of the mountain panorama, together with my location on mostly empty plains, jolted me with a frisson of frontier déjà vu. Suddenly I sensed the surprised consternation that westward-bound travelers must have experienced, after days on seemingly limitless rolling prairie, to discover a definite boundary lying up ahead, across the whole length of the horizon—a boundary that grew larger, more imposing, the nearer they came to it. And yet, unnervingly insurmountable though the mountains may appear, they are also riveting and magnetic; once seen, that first view is impossible to forget and the next view, eagerly anticipated.

A few minutes later I rounded a bend or topped a ridge and suddenly there was Denver in the distance, the sprawl of suburbia racing to fill all the empty spaces between the tollway and the city, and even more metropolitan development forming a line between the mountains and the plains. And then a descent or another curve cut off the chance for vistas and I became aware of the highway again.

Nonetheless, I'd had that one spellbinding moment of beauty and awe. I'd also had a glimpse into how that view might have affected those early adventurers and explorers and entrepreneurs who were lured west by the promise of new beginnings. Though I had some kinship with them, as someone who had also come to Colorado in search of new beginnings, I especially appreciated being able to see the Front Range anew, as if for the first time, because I suddenly realized how, in September 1873, the Front Range might first have appeared to Isabella Bird.

The Approach

These letters, as their style sufficiently indicates, were written without the remotest idea of publication. They appeared last year in the *Leisure Hour* at the request of its editor, and were so favourably received that I venture to present them to the public in a separate form, as a record of very interesting travelling experiences, and of a phase of pioneer life which is rapidly passing away.

I. L. B.

Tobermory, Argyleshire
October 1879

Prefatory Note, *A Lady's Life in the Rocky Mountains*,
1st Edition

Here is the itinerary for Isabella Lucy Bird's three months in Colorado. She came on the Denver-bound train from Cheyenne, Wyoming, on Friday, September 9, 1873, and disembarked in Greeley. For nearly two weeks she failed in her attempts to reach Estes Park, a valley surrounded by mountains of the Front Range. She finally reached Estes Park on Sunday September 28, and boarded at a ranch run by Griffith Evans, a Welshman. A few days later she climbed Longs Peak. After three weeks in Estes Park, on Monday, October 20, she left on horseback for a solitary tour of Colorado Territory (it would not become a state until 1876). She rode south as far as Colorado Springs, then west over the Rampart Range through the broad valley known as South Park up to the Continental Divide, then northeast back to Denver. After a sidetrip through the major mining district to Georgetown and visits to towns then called Golden City and Boulder City, she returned to Estes Park on Thursday, November 20. She remained there until Tuesday, December 9. It took her three days to make it over to Greeley, and the train to Cheyenne carried her out of Colorado on Friday, December 12.

I can be this precise about her itinerary because, as she remarks in her Prefatory Note, while she traveled she wrote a series of long journaling letters to her younger sister, Henrietta, then living in Scotland; some years later those letters, much edited and revised, formed the basis, first, for a series of articles titled "Letters from the Rocky Mountains," published in 1878 in *The Leisure Hour,* a British magazine, and subsequently for a book titled *A Lady's Life in the Rocky Mountains*, published in London and New York in 1879. The original letters to her sister that still survive—the ones from the earliest weeks apparently no longer exist and the rest were censored by Isabella herself—were published in 2002, in *Letters to Henrietta*, edited by Kay Chubbuck. *A Lady's Life in the Rocky Mountains* ran through three editions at the end of 1879 and the beginning of 1880, and many more editions followed. My most recent review of seventy-one listings for Isabella Bird in *Books in Print*, after eliminating books out of stock or available only on demand or edited from her writings by others, found thirty-seven editions of nine of her books still available at the beginning of the twenty-first century—thirteen of those are editions of *A Lady's Life in the Rocky Mountains*.

The daughter of a clergyman and a Sunday school teacher, Isabella Lucy Bird was born in North Yorkshire,

England, in 1831. She suffered from ill health throughout her youth, particularly from back problems; she had a fibrous tumor surgically removed when she was eighteen and frequently wore a brace to support her spine. Although her physical ailments were real enough, she toured and wrote about Australia, Hawaii, Japan, China, the Malay Peninsula, the Sinai, Persia, Kurdistan, Tibet, and Korea between 1873 and her death in 1904 at age seventy-three. Some biographers and commentators, noting her active life on and off horseback all over the globe, suspect her complaints were more psychosomatic than physical. Certainly she had a "high-strung temperament," and her health curiously bloomed while she traveled and wilted when she returned home.

It was her health, and perhaps her depression, that motivated her parents to send her to North America at age twenty-three. Her tour of eastern Canada and the northeastern cities of the United States resulted in her first book, *The Englishwoman in America*, published in 1856 by John Murray, her publisher throughout her life and still the major repository for her letters. A second trip in 1857 led to a second book, *Aspects of Religion in the United States of America*, published in 1859. Following the death of her father, Edward Bird, in 1858, Isabella, Henrietta, and their mother, Dora, relocated to Edinburgh, where Bird's life revolved around charitable work and familial obligations, with intermittent bouts of ill health (though she managed to get out a book on Edinburgh). After Dora Bird died in 1866, the sisters lived together in a flat in Edinburgh until 1872, when Henrietta moved to a cottage in Tobermory and Isabella launched herself on another journey.

By the time Isabella Bird reached Colorado, she had been traveling for over a year. She sailed from Liverpool in July 1872, landed in Australia in October, departed for New Zealand at the end of November, and set off for San Francisco on January 1, 1873. Her landing and subsequent stay in Hawaii was another act of inadvertence, but it says something about her burgeoning talents as a writer that her travels in a single year would lead to two remarkable and still readable books, *The Hawaiian Archipelago* (published in 1875 and also known as *Six Months in the Sandwich Islands*) and *A Lady's Life in the Rocky Mountains*. Both books were fueled by letters home to Henrietta (as were her other books before Henrietta's death in 1880), and I suspect that the habit of recording and reflecting upon her experiences in Hawaii primed her for her writing about Colorado.

The title is a little misleading. She may have been a lady in her deportment, but a three-month visit doesn't really make up a "life," and it would be more accurate, if clumsy, to describe the book as "Letters from an Englishwoman Traveling along the Front Range of the Rocky Mountains." Although Bird's book is the best known and the easiest to find, travel writing about Colorado by women authors abounded in the 1870s. Bird's friend and countrywoman Rose Kingsley spent a considerable amount of time in the territory in 1871, accompanying her brother Maurice, then assistant treasurer of the Fountain Colony in Colorado Springs. Kingsley's book, *South by West, Or, Winter in the Rocky Mountains and Spring in Mexico*, was published in 1874, but Bird was in correspondence with her before then and relied on Kingsley's recommendations about whom to contact and where to go in Colorado. Grace Greenwood (the pen name of Sarah Jane Lippincott) was also in Colorado in August and September of 1871 and November of 1872. Well-established as a poet, lecturer, and journalist by then, she traveled around the country writing what she referred to as "light letters" for the *New York Times*, which she later collected in *New Life in New Lands: Notes of Travel* (1873). Greenwood returned to Colorado in summer 1873 and, from a base in

Colorado Springs, toured the southern part of the territory with a large party of affluent tourists, one of whom
was the artist Eliza Greatorex. Greatorex's book on *her* travels, *Summer Etchings in Colorado,* with an introduction by
Greenwood, was published within months of her trip.
Another writer, Helen Hunt (later Helen Hunt Jackson),
advised to visit Colorado Springs for her bronchitis, arrived
in Colorado around the time Isabella was leaving it. She too
was a well-established poet and travel writer (as H. H.) and
later wrote the enduringly popular California novel
Ramona. She married a Colorado Springs businessman
named William Sharpless Jackson and settled in Colorado
Springs, publishing her observations on the territory and
other sections of the United States in *Bits of Travel at Home*
(1878). In addition, the orator/actress Anna Dickinson,
who climbed Longs Peak shortly before Bird did, was also
making well-publicized lecture appearances around the
territory; she briefly summarized her travels in *A Ragged
Register (of People, Places, and Opinions)* (1879).

In Colorado in the 1870s, then, a woman writer was
hardly a rare species, but Isabella Bird, alone of all these
writers, is the one whose Colorado book a modern reader is
most likely to find and most likely to enjoy. Companionable, observant, self-effacing, and wry, she managed to create what she termed "a faithful picture of the country and
state of society as it then was." Changes in the country and
the state of society haven't made her prose outdated. Perhaps equally important for me, her path around the territory was the broadest in scope and the one least centered
on seats of commerce and development.

The interests of editors and biographers and storytellers
in *A Lady's Life in the Rocky Mountains* vary a good deal.
Some are concerned with what they might glean of her personal life in its pages, particularly alert to the hints of incipient romance between Isabella and the trapper Jim Nugent,

or focused on the air of high adventure in her climb up Longs Peak and wild rides rounding up cattle, or hoping for (or against) confirmation of her attitudes about women's liberation. Others have studied her life and writing to discover more about her attitudes and observations and to contemplate her contributions to social history, natural history, and women's literature. As a "Victorian lady traveler," a clergyman's daughter, an invalid whose health improved whenever she left for foreign climes, an apparent spinster until the age of fifty, a small, well-mannered woman who traveled alone and mostly rode astraddle in an age when ladies rode side-saddle, a cultured representative of a specific social class and a particular nationality, a prolific and well-read writer, and the first woman elected as a fellow of the Royal Geographic Society, she has proved to be of enduring and varied interest in a number of academic fields, not the least travel literature, geography, anthropology, history, and women's studies.

My interest has been most sympathetic with those determining her contribution to what would now be termed "ecoliterature" or "environmental writing." In his highly useful annotated edition of her Rocky Mountain book, Ernest S. Bernard asserts, "As the first major chronicler of the region that later became one of America's most important wilderness and scenic areas, Bird clearly deserves recognition both as a figure in preservation politics and as a contributor to the literature of the early national park movement." Histories of Rocky Mountain National Park routinely quote from *A Lady's Life in the Rocky Mountains,* and those of us who have benefited from artist-in-the-parks programs often find her, along with painters such as Thomas Moran and Albert Bierstadt, held up as an early example of how conservation in general and national parks in particular have been served by art. Her comments on landscape in the book reflect familiarity with writers on nature and theorists on landscape—we know she met Emerson and Thoreau earlier in life, and clearly had read William Wordsworth and William Gilpin. It says something about the book's richness that, though popular tastes and academic interests continually shift, it has not grown irrelevant or outmoded.

* * *

I first became aware of Isabella Bird some twenty-five years ago, when I encountered an excerpt from *A Lady's Life in the Rocky Mountains* in *The Wilderness Reader*, edited by Frank Bergon. I doubt that I read the excerpt, which was the account of her climb up Longs Peak (as I learned this morning when I pulled the anthology from a bookshelf). In those days I read very little about the West, since I never expected to be in the West. The name of the book and its author were mere items of literary trivia stored in memory until a few years ago, when circumstances raised both to the center of my consciousness.

I'd been teaching at a university in Michigan for over twenty-five years when a friend and colleague in the English department invited me to co-chair and keynote a conference on nonfiction she was organizing. The conference, titled "Mapping Nonfiction," would highlight varieties of creative nonfiction, with emphasis on the nonfiction of place, and be held at the YMCA Center of the Rockies in Estes Park. I eagerly accepted. Determined to localize my talk by quoting a relevant piece of literary nonfiction, I quickly stumbled on Isabella Bird's book. It was a serendipitous discovery, not simply for the keynote I would give but also for the life I would soon be living.

With our children grown and gone to three separate coasts, my wife and I had decided to change our lives and leave our teaching jobs—I would complete unfinished books and essays and start new ones, she would join an educational research firm in Denver. She began her job a year before the conference at Estes Park and the date I could leave my university. From time to time, though she was able to work from Michigan most of that year, she would fly out to Denver for a week and a couple of times, when my schedule allowed, I joined her to scout out locations where we might begin living that following June.

Colorado was virtually a new world for me. I'd spent most of my life near the Great Lakes, from my childhood in western New York through my teaching career in Michigan; the farthest west I'd ever lived had been in Iowa, during graduate school, only an hour's drive west of the Mississippi. I was a midwestern flatland boy through and through. To give up the Great Lakes and the North Woods for the Great Plains and the Front Range dislocated me in every sense of the word, and I cast about for a way to gain a sense of place.

One August day I drove from Denver to Boulder to meet Reg Saner, a writer who'd be presenting at the conference the following June. I took a somewhat circuitous route and, having maneuvered for days through dense Denver traffic to get to central-city houses and outlying suburban housing complexes, I finally found myself in open country. At last. I followed Colorado Highway 93 north from Golden toward Boulder, the road dipping and rising and curving through rangeland and open space. I couldn't take in all the changing landforms and shifting vistas as I hurried along the highway.

Reg lived up on Table Mesa, on the very last street before the houses gave way to steep slopes of grassy open space and the road continued arching up to the top of the mesa. He was cheery and welcoming. He'd packed us a lunch and put it in the cooler in the bed of his well-worn white pickup truck and offered to show me something of the terrain. He asked if I wanted to borrow one of his hats. "The sun is more intense out here because the air is thinner. You think your hair will protect your scalp but it won't. Skin cancer is more common here than in the Midwest." He had grown up in Illinois but had been in Colorado for over forty years and couldn't imagine living anywhere else. Each morning he took a walk across the mesa to collect the dawn.

We drove up the mesa to the National Center for Atmospheric Research (NCAR), housed in a faux-pueblo-styled building designed by the architect I. M. Pei. From a distance it looked like a natural formation of stark sandy rocks. Reg noted a spot along the road where, a day or two earlier, he'd spoken to a fallen bicyclist who'd passed him earlier as they both ascended the hill. A slender man, with a lean wiry carriage, short straight white hair, and the tanned leathery look of a lifelong outdoorsman, Reg was ten years older than I. I tried not to react as he told me of climbing the slope, where the angle of ascent gained 600 feet of elevation in about a mile. Granted, this was Colorado, mile-high altitude, something he'd lived in for decades, and I was only a visiting near-sea-level midwesterner, but I felt winded sitting in the passenger seat and couldn't help wondering what kind of world I was moving into—one where I doubted my ability to keep up with my seniors.

Strolling a short trail behind NCAR, an informational loop with signs discussing terrain and weather, we paused on one side of the mesa to look off at the Flatirons, nearly upright triangular slabs of reddish-grey rock standing in a row to the south at an angle of repose over 50°. Devoid of vegetation, seeming to lean against the foothills, they were sections of horizontal sedimentary rock uplifted to nearly vertical by the rise of the Rockies. "A lot of people around here climb the Flatirons," Reg said. "It's a good place to learn climbing because of the angle and the hand and foot holds." He told me of someone climbing the Flatirons alone at night, creeping up a sharply inclined slab of rock in the moonlight. I added it to the growing list of things I would not be doing in Colorado.

From Table Mesa we descended to Highway 93 and headed south, turning off to pass through the town of Eldorado Springs and enter the state park at the mouth of Eldorado Canyon. The canyon walls rose sharply on either side of the narrow dirt road, as much as a thousand feet above the creek tumbling over boulders at the bottom of the canyon. "If you look up as we go through, you'll probably see some climbers," Reg suggested. "I've got to go slow because so many people climb right along the road."

Soon we passed small groups of people wearing helmets, carrying ropes over their shoulders, strapping on harnesses, and scanning sheer rock walls intently. Across the creek I could see a few small figures high up on the nearly vertical canyon walls, clinging to the rock and pulling themselves slowly upward. A twinge of acrophobia chilled me. What in Michigan I would have found foolhardy was here, I already understood, a popular sport.

Past the narrowest and most precipitous part of the canyon, we turned off into a picnic area among the trees along South Boulder Creek. The creek gurgled past with mountain water still frigid in August, but children from the crowded picnic spots still played along its banks and waded in its shallows. We had lunch at a table not far from the creek, listening to the water and talking about writing, teaching, and books. The sky darkened and a gentle rain began that we thought would quickly pass. Reg explained the dangers of lightning on exposed mountaintops while sunshine occasionally sneaked under the rain and glinted off the persistent raindrops. Watching the play of sunlight on rain, we found it easy to ignore how wet we were getting.

We dried out driving back to Boulder, through town, back out of the houses into more open space, and up a paved mountain road. Switchbacks twisted and turned up 1,100 feet or more in about a mile and a half. At one point we left the truck to wander up to a place where we could see both the Continental Divide off to the west, nearer than I'd seen it from Denver, more immense, more stunning, more alluring, and also the high plains off to the east, so far below us, so vast and limitless. It was hard for me to take in the scale of what I was seeing but not hard to feel awe at what I beheld. Lightning flashed brilliantly nearby and from its thunder Reg estimated it struck only a mile away. We retreated into the truck and descended to the city.

Back at his house, the rain having cleared again, we sat outside and talked about writing and the environment and the nonfiction of place. Shortly before I left, Reg observed quietly, "The difference between landscape and nature is the difference between separation and inclusion." The remark stayed with me, not only in the context of the conversation we were having but also in light of the way I'd felt before in the wilderness, the way I was beginning to feel about the terrain of Colorado.

In Denver I felt the alienation of urban life, the isolation of the perpetual stranger, contracting myself to withstand the buffeting of overcrowded and confining space. There, the Front Range was simply backdrop to a life indistinguishable from that of any other large city. But in the canyon and on the mountain, I felt the pull of inclusion, an innate promise of connection, felt myself expanding to breathe more deeply, more freely, of unrestrained existence.

Driving back from Boulder that afternoon, I realized that Isabella Bird, in her own way, had also felt this sense of connection, this awareness of being where it was sufficient to know you were alive, existing here and now. I thought how magnetic the pull of the mountains was for her and understood that I was feeling drawn in the same direction.

* * *

Isabella Bird approached Colorado from the west and the north. Except for the title, her book, in its early chapters, gives no indication that Colorado will be her destination. Her first letter is datelined "Lake Tahoe, September 2." It opens with a description of Lake Tahoe, then backtracks to tell how she left "the clang of San Francisco" and crossed California by train to Truckee. There she rented a horse and rode alone up to the lake. Along the way she encountered a bear and was thrown from her horse. She rose "covered with dust, but neither shaken nor bruised. It was truly grotesque and humiliating. The bear ran in one direction and the horse in another." Only the intervention of some teamsters let her catch up with the horse and resume her ride. She spent the night at Lake Tahoe and in her second letter recounts returning to Truckee the next day. In Letter III she takes the train across Nevada and Utah to the Great Salt Lake and to Cheyenne, Wyoming. There she switched trains and, on September 9, 1873, arrived in Colorado.

I approach Colorado from the east, the direction of origin more traditional for migratory Americans. In the 200th anniversary year of Lewis and Clark's great expedition of discovery and in the manner of those settlers who emblazoned "Pikes Peak or Bust" on the canvas of their Conestoga wagons, I come in a large rental truck with all our worldly possessions behind me, sharing driving duties with my brother, David. Unlike the globetrotting Isabella Bird, who moved from one fresh discovery to another, I uproot myself (the term is loaded but inevitable). To fit the furnishings and paraphernalia of our lives into a single cargo space, I have had to donate and recycle and pack and discard books and papers and memorabilia from an office I have occupied for twenty-seven years, donate and recycle and pack and discard the contents of the century-old house where we and our children have lived for twenty-one years. Isabella Bird was a body in motion tending to stay in motion; I am a body at rest tending to stay at rest but now in the process of not so much setting myself in motion as transplanting myself—uproot indeed!—into unknown and alien soil.

Our final two weeks in Michigan are a frenetic farce of almost willfully complicated hyperactivity; our first few weeks in Colorado are a bewildered immersion in sorting out the belongings we kept and finding our way around unfamiliar streets and towns. I persistently focus on micro-management of our space and our movements, too preoccupied to think long about the office I cleared until one o'clock in the morning, the empty rooms of the house I walked through alone, my footsteps clattering hollowly, before locking it one last time and driving away.

For the first few weeks, unable to figure out mass transit in a metropolitan area, I drive Sue past the bus stop she could be using and take her all the way into Boulder, ten miles away, to catch the express to Denver. Each morning we head west, the Rockies ahead of us, visible with varying clarity depending on the atmosphere, the morning sun behind us, like us rising early. From the intersection of McCaslin Boulevard and South Boulder Road, where we begin the long descent into Boulder Valley, the panorama of the mountains, the red upraised Flatirons with the massive, snow-covered, remote peaks of the Continental Divide beyond them, comes into view—a spectacular vision that startles and enthralls me every morning.

One morning, after Sue gets on the bus, I keep going. I follow Boulder Road until it becomes Table Mesa Drive, continue up past Reg's street and across the open space, and park in the NCAR lot. Slowly, alone, I wander the loop behind the building, my first brief outing in my new surroundings. The day is dry and cool and when I reach the limits of the trail I simply stare at the mountains rising beyond the mesa. I have no concrete idea about how to get into them or beyond them. Now that the apartment is in order, our routine is established and the frantic pace of relocation chores has subsided, I realize, uncomfortably, that sometimes I don't recognize the person sitting on our balcony, driving to and from the bus stop, listening to bird-call and windrush on this mesa. I feel completely adrift, uncertain about what to do next and how to start doing it. I don't seem to know how to become the person who does these things.

Then I remember the upcoming conference in Estes Park and Isabella Bird's account of her rambles there and throughout the Front Range. Isabella was an outsider too, but she entered each new world with an openness to experience and an intention to record what she encountered. She was well aware of how quickly the world changes, reporting in the note to the third edition of her book the word of friends "that things are rapidly changing, that the frame house is replacing the log cabin, and that the footprints of elk and bighorn may be sought for in vain on the dewy slopes of Estes Park"; nonetheless the freshness of the world she explored is still there on her pages. It can be recaptured there.

Wherever Isabella Bird went on the Front Range I can go in a day's drive. I can push myself out in search of her world and see how much remains beneath the world that replaced it. Using her travels as a template for my own, searching for the remnants of the world preserved in her writing, as well as in the writings of her contemporaries and the writings of those who came after Isabella, I may come to understand—and in my turn, perhaps, somehow, preserve—the world in which I find myself.

A few of the writers who will be my textual companions on my travels will be long-time Coloradoans, residents, not ramblers, but most will be transients, tourists and travelers who go back to where they came from when they've seen enough. I seem to be somewhere in the middle. Even as I set out, I realize that whatever world I discover will be the world that replaces the one I left forever. It's not enough for me to have arrived in Colorado; I have to learn to live here.

And, with that realization, I begin.

The Plains

It gave me a strange sensation to embark upon the Plains.
Plains, plains everywhere, plains generally level, but elsewhere rolling in long undulations, like the waves of a sea
which had fallen asleep. They are covered thinly with buff
grass, the withered stalks of flowers, Spanish bayonet, and
a small beehive-shaped cactus. One could gallop all over
them.

Isabella Bird, Letter III, September 10

We don't know when Isabella Bird first resolved to visit
Estes Park; certainly Rose Kingsley and other English
friends had recommended places for her to go in the territory and she expected to meet people whom Kingsley knew
and visit places Kingsley had gone. In the book the choice
of Estes Park seems more spontaneous than deliberate, as if
inadvertence played a greater role than design—after all,
Kingsley had never been there.

As the travel diaries and correspondence of other writers
do, Isabella's letters to Henrietta, composed and sent regularly, give her writing a trajectory ruled by chronology and
event. Although she didn't know it until after she arrived
there—and lets her readers make that discovery with her
by recounting her slow progress towards it—Estes Park is

the core of her book and the central element of her experience of Colorado,

I come to realize this later than I should, and at the same time realize that my plans for following her trail have centered on Estes Park as well. In the year before our final move to Colorado, I applied for and received an artist's residency in Rocky Mountain National Park in hopes of approximating Isabella's experience in the area. That residency was the most exciting prospect of the project. For Isabella the world outside Estes had its limitations; plotting my trajectory along her path in that world, I discovered limitations of my own.

Isabella used her letters not only to entertain and inform her sister but also to record her experience and observations immediately after they occurred. My notes and journals and chapter drafts have similar goals—they are first of all letters to myself as well as, in an entirely metaphorical sense, letters to Isabella, to bring her up to speed on what's happened since she left and to report what a traveler on a similar venture today encounters. But if her core is my core, much of what was peripheral to her is, I quickly find, even more peripheral to me.

The California to Wyoming leg of her journey, including Lake Tahoe and Cheyenne, wasn't pertinent to my intention to tour the Front Range, and Isabella's comments on the first communities she visited on the plains are limited. She referred to Cheyenne as "this detestable place" and hurried to the post office to pick up "a circular letter of recommendation from ex-Governor Hunt, procured by Miss Kingsley's kindness," and another from Samuel Bowles, editor of the *Springfield Republican* and author of popular books on Colorado and the West. "Armed with these," she declared, "I shall boldly plunge into Colorado." On September 9 she "took the cars [*i.e.* boarded the railroad] for Greeley," which she identifies as "a settlement on the plains, which I had been recommended to make my starting point for the mountains." This is the first indication the reader is given that Isabella has a specific destination in mind.

Bird had little to say about the plains, only a paragraph of description about the vegetation and another about prairie dogs. Those travel writers about Colorado who were her predecessors and contemporaries tended to write at greater length about the crossing to Denver—Bayard Taylor came by stagecoach from Kansas in 1866, Samuel Bowles by coach from Cheyenne in 1868, Grace Greenwood and Rose Kingsley by train from both directions in 1871—and most were alert to the unfamiliar fauna, if not the flora, particularly the "antelopes," prairie dogs, owls, and rattlesnakes. At the time these writers were touring the West, pronghorn—not actually antelope but still the species celebrated for playing where the buffalo roam—were nearly as plentiful as bison, particularly in the plains and deserts where they thrived. Bayard Taylor, crossing eastern Colorado, near the Big Sandy, noted, "The country swarms with antelopes, which provoked several shots from the coach, but without effect." The desire to shoot animals from moving vehicles, apparently to credential marksmanship or merely indulge the joy of killing, seems to have been habitual among travelers. Grace Greenwood, traveling by train from Cheyenne, noticed "an antelope, standing at a respectful distance, and watching with mild curiosity the passing of the engine" and overheard an exchange about it between a passenger she identifies as a "young Nimrod," who regretted not having his rifle handy, and an older hunter, who pointed out that the animal was shrewdly out of range.

But it was the prairie dogs that seemed to provoke the most speculation. Taylor, Kingsley, and Greenwood all discussed them at length, and Greenwood rode the train from

Cheyenne "directly through a large old dog-town" that Bird must have traversed as well. Bird's account of the "large villages of what are called prairie dogs" seems indebted to earlier accounts; her observation that they were called dogs "because they utter a short, sharp bark, but the dogs are, in reality, marmots," may have been taken from Rose Kingsley (black-tailed prairie dogs and marmots are, in reality, both members of the squirrel family). She also repeats the notion reported by others that prairie dogs have neighborly, "fellow-lodger" relationships with burrowing owls and prairie rattlesnakes. But she was considerably more descriptive than opinionated: "We passed numbers of villages, which are composed of raised circular orifices, about eighteen inches in diameter, with sloping passages leading downwards for five or six feet. Hundreds of these burrows are placed together. On nearly every rim a small furry reddish-buff beast sat on his hind legs, looking, so far as head went, much like a young seal. These creatures were acting as sentinels, and sunning themselves. As we passed, each gave a warning yelp, shook its tail, and, with a ludicrous flourish of its hind legs, dived into its hole. The appearance of hundreds of these creatures, each eighteen inches long, sitting like dogs begging, with their paws down and all turned sunwards, is most grotesque." In this passage Isabella's powers of observation are well displayed.

In *Land of Grass and Sky: A Naturalist's Prairie Journey*, Mary Taylor Young, a modern nature writer, tells of a researcher who, in 1901, rode for "most of a day through one continuous prairie dog complex"—it's been estimated that over five billion prairie dogs inhabited the continent before the advance of European-American civilization. It is now hard to imagine the landscape filled to the horizon with a prairie-dog village, or for that matter with extensive herds of bison or pronghorn, but I can appreciate how prairie dogs are a kind of marker of having reached the western prairies. Like squirrels and chipmunks back in Michigan, prairie dogs are still hard to avoid. They occupy an open space next to a baseball field across the street from my apartment complex, and Sue and I encounter them as we pass patches of land on our regular biking paths. Other bikers, I notice, pay little attention to them, except when they scurry almost under the wheels of their bikes, and their abrupt piping calls seem to go unheard, except by other prairie dogs. I admit that I'm often tempted to stop, sit down at a little distance, and watch them for awhile—in Michigan squirrels in the trees outside my window often kept me from my work—and I tend to notice when a colony suddenly disappears about the time a new housing development breaks ground in our area. I've yet to see an owl or a snake anywhere near the prairie dog villages scattered around the suburbs.

In more remote and less populated counties perhaps some portion of the prairie dog world that Isabella Bird and other early travelers noted can still be found. But along the Front Range all I've seen are remnants and isolated and constrained communities surrounded by development, squeezed between housing and highway. If I need an indication of what I'm likely to see still surviving from the Colorado landscape after Isabella Bird's passage through it, the vanished world of the prairie dog towns might be one key example.

* * *

Isabella Bird spent little time describing the territory between Cheyenne and Greeley that she observed from the windows of the Denver-Pacific Railway, and yet I think I ought to see the terrain for myself. I decide to drive up to the Wyoming border just south of Cheyenne. U.S. 85 north from Greeley parallels for a long way the railroad bed of the Union Pacific, which had superseded the Denver

Pacific; to get back home I would take Interstate 25 south, past Fort Collins and Longmont. The loop would take only three hours or so.

Highway 85 takes me through mostly dead flat land. When I peek west I see mountains in the distance, a long stretch of blue haze and white-capped peaks all the way along the horizon, but when I glance east I can see only as far as I can see, no end to the horizon, except distance disappearing beyond itself and that limitless blue sky over everything. I pass through little agricultural towns, Lucerne and Eaton and Ault ("*A Unique Little Town*," according to a sign) and Pierce and Nunn, with the railroad tracks running near the highway all the while and the towns barely noticeable except for signs that randomly catch my attention ("The Booze Barn," one liquor store frankly labels itself; "Bill Jerke Republican," a billboard heralds, triggering imaginary headlines and campaign slogans for the next few miles). The land on either side of the road is almost entirely cultivated and long distances separate buildings except near the towns and crossroads.

All along the highway I scout out places where the prairie dog town described by Greenwood and Bird might have been. But cultivation has leveled everything in the service of farming. I see no prairie dogs, only from time to time the raised openings of their burrows set in confined spaces between plowed fields and paved highway. Eventually, in a stretch of fallow farmland reverting to the wild, I finally locate a sizable field of burrows, but as I pass, a golden eagle swoops down, lands gently near an opening, and begins surveying the deserted village. If prairie dogs are there, they've prudently dropped to the lowest levels of their burrows.

I don't expect to see pronghorns but near the boundaries of the Pawnee National Grasslands a flicker of movement in cultivated fields to the west catches my eye and I pull onto the shoulder. At a distance three pronghorns in a line, the first I've ever seen outside a zoo, step slowly across a field. The one in the lead is calm and concentrates on foraging but the two in the rear are skittish and tend to retreat and advance sporadically, glancing in my direction. One paces up to the wire fence, seems to survey the cattle grazing in the middle of the field on the opposite side of the road, but pays no attention to the trucks that flash by and disrupt its vision. I try to memorize the white and reddish-tan patches of their coats, their large dark eyes, their pointed ears and straight black horns, their white rumps as they pivot and trot lightly away from the road. Their departure makes me recall Grace Greenwood's story of a little boy who reports seeing antelopes and is accused by his mother of imagining them; the boy retorts, "I guess my imagination isn't white behind."

Over the next several miles pronghorns show up again from time to time, singly or in pairs or trios or, once, in a string of a dozen or so. The pronghorn population was decimated by young and old overeager nimrods and by the loss of open range, but conservationists helped bring them back to numbers higher than they'd had at the beginning of the last century. Though they aren't exactly abundant here, they're plentiful enough that I feel with somewhat less force the sense of absence and loss that extinction and decimation usually inspire in me.

Absence and loss. For mere moments the highway is empty in either direction and I sit in my car by the side of the road, alternately watching the retreat of the pronghorn across the open fields to the west and gazing into the wide expanse of the Pawnee Grasslands to the east. I am aware of how solitary I am, how only the road makes me feel I have a sense of direction—without it I wouldn't know which way to go. For an instant my isolation is emblematic of the psychic space I've been occupying lately as well. Unlike the historic or contemporary travelers I've been reading, who temporarily left home to wander for a while, Sue and I had divested ourselves of everything they'd left behind, every-thing to which they intended to return. When my wife went off each day to wrestle with the challenges of her new job, I sat alone in our apartment wondering what was replacing my jettisoned career. In time I would tell a few friends that I didn't just retire—I seemed to have vanished. Some days the sense of disappearance—of being cut off from my own identity—was very strong.

So here on the plains, the horizon stretching off in every direction around me, the sky limitless and empty above me, I feel a flash of uncertainty about whether I'm really here, about where I am. I wonder if I should feel all this emptiness as erasure or opportunity, and it strikes me almost at once that I'm not the first person on the plains to wonder that. I remind myself that this little tour is part of my effort to *learn* where I am and that I have much farther to go. I put the car in gear and move off the shoulder of the road.

The terrain turns into undulating landscape, no longer flatland but rolling prairie, rising up on either side of the road, which itself dips and rises. The mountains to the west have disappeared; so have the long distances to the east. I pass through a kind of trough and am surrounded by land, my horizon narrow and limited on the ground, the bright blue sky overhead a contrast to the brown earth and incred-ibly open, as if nothing else is beyond the hills but sky. This is the place where, in *Magpie Rising,* Merrill Gilfillan says that "you reach a point where the plains rear and assert them-selves, lift toward piedmont, almost crackle. . . . Then, just as you settle into a steppe frame of mind, you crest a ridge and there is Cheyenne, Wyoming." Exactly so.

I turn off on a side road that takes me west to the inter-state and start back south. Heading north on 85, I couldn't see beyond the highest point of the plains and was channeled toward Wyoming, but heading south into Colorado, the end of the plains rise on the east and the foothills leading to the mountains open up the view to the west again. I now have the mountains almost constantly in sight.

The railroad had coursed across the plains to the east of me. Isabella Bird wrote, "After running on a down grade for some time, five distinct ranges of mountains, one above another, a lurid blue against a lurid sky, upheaved themselves above the prairie sea." I am only half a dozen miles or so from the Wyoming border and the "Welcome to Colorful Colorado" sign. I see the mountains rise up, the white of their peaks seeming to come out of the blue of the sky, the lower, snowless ranges a deeper, darker blue. Grace Greenwood thought the mountains the only thing that redeemed the trip across the plains; Isabella Bird, though she complained that an "American railway car, hot, stuffy, and full of chewing, spitting Yankees, was not an ideal way of approaching this range which had clearly impressed itself upon my imagination," nonetheless concluded that "it was truly grand." By the end of the train trip, she could declare that the mountains "are gradually gaining possession of me. I can look at and *feel* nothing else." I drop briefly into another trough and the mountains disappear, but then I crest another rise and have another chance to glance off into the distance and there they are. Each time I rediscover them I'm granted a sudden insight into what Isabella Bird and Grace Greenwood saw from the train. If you hadn't seen them before, they would be pretty hard to believe—pretty hard not to *feel*.

Though the pronghorn are here in fewer numbers and the prairie dogs are barely here at all, though the shortgrass prairie has been converted into ranchland or farmland or, not far down the road, the sprawling housing developments that reach epidemic proportions closer to Denver, it is still possible, gazing at the long line of the Front Range, to be intrigued, even awed, by their scope and their splendor and to intuit what drew Isabella Bird so magnetically toward them over the weeks after her first sight of them. I feel that I am seeing—and to some extent comprehending—where Isabella's time in Colorado began.

*   *   *

If you tour cities like Rome or Venice, you encounter layer after layer of history; some neighborhoods in Paris and London give you a sense of how life was lived there two or three centuries ago. If you visit the Pueblo "Sky City" of Acoma, the oldest continuously occupied site in North America, you get in touch with a culture dating back a millennium. But Colorado, despite earlier Indian and Spanish populations, dates its development from the Gold Rush of 1859 and became a state only in 1876, one hundred years after the Declaration of Independence; here, the artifacts of culture have been steadily in flux, continually building and rebuilding.

In 1873, Isabella Bird visited very few places that had been continuously occupied for even the fourteen years since the gold rush. Many of those would vanish in succeeding years, and some of the Front Range's most substantial communities hadn't been started yet. All along the Front Range, in any of the towns or cities and most of the empty spaces she passed through, change has been constant and obliterating.

Just north of where I live in Lafayette are four communities lightly connected to Isabella Bird's time in Colorado. Geographically, they can be charted along the lines of a plus sign (+). At the bottom of the vertical line (U.S. 287 on an actual map) is Longmont, and at the top is Fort Collins; at the intersection of the vertical line and the horizontal line (U.S. 34 on a map) is Loveland; Greeley is at the right tip of the crossbar, out on the plains, and out on the left tip is the entrance to the Big Thompson Canyon; extend the crossbar to the canyon's western end and you reach Estes Park. Fort Collins and Greeley are connected diagonally by the meandering course of the Cache la Poudre River, which flows through them both and, in linking them, gives the figure the general shape of a backwards 4.

Greeley, where Isabella spent her first night in Colorado, was a stop on the Denver-Pacific Railway and the most substantial town between Cheyenne and Denver. It was three years old when she arrived, founded in 1870 as a planned community known as the Union Colony, its members adhering strictly to principles of hard work and abstinence from alcohol. Their ambitious scheme provided for a business and civic center around a central park, wide tree-lined streets, house lots with room for ornamental gardens and private orchards, a fifty-mile-long fence keeping stray cattle out of streets and gardens, and irrigation ditches exploiting the Cache la Poudre and South Platte Rivers.

Grace Greenwood, coming upon the place in August 1871, only a year after it began, found it full of promise. She envisioned its population "transforming a barren region into a vast garden of verdure and bloom and fruitfulness" and asserted that "the inevitable glare and unsightliness of newness" was outweighed by its "peculiarly cheerful and spirited look." Positive, supportive adjectives tumble out of her: the irrigation ditches are "really very pretty," their currents of "clear, cool water" flowing "on blessed errands to the generous, responsive soil," a "ditching-plough" being pulled by "noble oxen," the trees and the crops growing "astonishingly." She declared, heartily, "Were I a man, I would rather give my name to a town like this, and teach such a brave colony what I knew of farming, than be President of the United States." (It wasn't simply an off-hand remark—Horace Greeley, the well-known advocate of western settlement and the man for whom the town was named, ran for president in 1872, the year Greenwood's book was published. He died a few weeks after he lost the election to Ulysses S. Grant.)

Isabella Bird, arriving in September 1873, was less enthusiastic. In Letter III she identified "the Greeley Temperance Colony" as composed of "an industrious class of emigrants from the East, all total abstainers, and holding advanced political opinions." Though she credited them with industriousness, their success at increasing the population from 742 to 3,000 in three years, and the absence of crime, drunkenness, and squalor, she was skeptical of their circumstances: "Their rich fields are artificially productive solely; and after seeing regions where Nature gives spontaneously, one is amazed that people should settle here to be dependent on irrigating canals, with the risk of having their crops destroyed by grasshoppers." Bird's comment was particularly pertinent—the issue of irrigation on the arid high plains is still a contentious one.

Grace Greenwood kept on to Denver the same day she visited Greeley; Isabella Bird spent the night at the Colorado House and complained that her room was set off "with only a canvas partition . . . and every place was thick with black flies." Of supper she noted that the "chief features were greasiness and black flies. Twenty men in working clothes fed and went out again, 'nobody speaking to nobody.'" In bed she was awakened "by crawling creatures apparently in myriads" and slept propped up on wooden chairs the rest of the night.

The next day, unable to find a suitable horse, Bird accepted a ride by wagon to Fort Collins with a man from Vermont. They traveled from 10:00 in the morning to 4:30 in the afternoon, the journey notable for "the fierce, ungoverned, blazing heat of the sun on the whitish earth." Though the heat was "terrible" and "sickening," and the lack of greenery made her restless, she admitted that "the view in front was glorious . . . not only do five high-peaked giants, each nearly the height of Mont Blanc, lift their dazzling summits above the lower ranges, but the expanse of mountains is so vast, and the whole lie in a transparent medium of the richest blue, not haze—something peculiar to the region."

She arrived in Fort Collins "sick and dizzy with the heat of the sun, and not disposed to be pleased with a most unpleasing place." She noted that the town, begun as a military post in 1864, "at present consists of a few frame houses put down recently on the bare and burning plain. The settlers have 'great expectations,' but of what?" The house where she spent her second night in Colorado—very likely the hotel run from the home of the widow "Auntie" Elizabeth Stone—was "freer from bugs than the one in Greeley, but full of flies" and the first story of the inn "swarms with locusts in addition to thousands of black flies." The evening meal in Fort Collins was dismal: "the beef was tough and greasy, the butter had turned to oil, and beef and butter were black with living, drowned, and half-drowned flies." The conditions provoked a rare outburst of disdain: "These new settlements are altogether revolting, entirely utilitarian, given up to talk of dollars as well as to making them, with coarse speech, coarse food, coarse everything, nothing wherewith to satisfy the higher cravings if they exist, nothing on which the eye can rest with pleasure." Worse, the mountains seemed to her no nearer than they were in Greeley and the higher peaks were no longer visible.

After these few days in frontier communities and an interval in Big Thompson Canyon attempting futilely to reach Estes Park, Isabella hitched a wagon ride into Longmont. It was another planned community, created in 1871 by the Chicago-Colorado Colony, a group of prominent and wealthy Chicagoans, and, like Greeley, it was founded on confidence in the prospects for Colorado agriculture.

Isabella Bird noted its flour mill and inevitable irrigation ditches harnessing the St. Vrain Creek. She thought Longmont to be "as uninviting as Fort Collins," made up of "dust-colored frame houses set down at intervals on the dusty buff plain, each with its dusty wheat or barley field adjacent, the crop, not the product of the rains of heaven, but of the muddy overflow of 'Irrigating Ditch No. 2.'" She stayed in the St. Vrain Hotel, a "two-storey house, one of the whitest and most glaring," and in her room she found the "heat within was more sickening than outside, and black flies covered everything, one's face included." Despite her scorn for the place, through the agency of her genial landlord, Captain William Beach Sigley, she finally reached Estes Park and, from that point on, Longmont would serve her as a way station in her travels around the Territory.

By my count, Isabella Bird spent only seven nights in those four communities over the ninety-three days she spent in Colorado Territory. Her September nights are merely stages in her efforts to reach the mountains, but they rouse my curiosity about the towns. Surely some portion of her response to the mountains, once she was among them, was influenced by her reactions to the frontier towns. Perhaps they will have the same effect on me; perhaps they will have no effect at all. But I can tour them all in a day's drive.

* * *

If you read Isabella's account, and perhaps those of other travelers and inhabitants, and if you let their descriptions fill your thoughts as you sit quietly with your eyes closed, you find it possible to envision what was there when they were there.

Long stretches of shortgrass prairie rolling from Cheyenne south, the terrain flattening out by the time the first significant signs of civilization appeared, the buffalo grass and the blue grama thick on the ground except around the prairie dog villages, where the black-tailed prairie dogs had thinned it with foraging and their own unique cultivating and interrupted the flatness with open-topped cones of tan earth leading to their burrows. On the flattest, most level sections of the high plains the earth seemed, in Willa Cather's phrase, simply the floor of the sky, instead of the sky being the ceiling of the earth, and the room you gazed on was made up of walls of sky and ceiling of sky and that flat earthen floor, and the room stretched limitlessly, far beyond as far as you could see. *This House of Sky*, Ivan Doig memorably titled his memoir of Montana. Because you thought of landscape in terms of limits, in terms of identifiable features, in terms of trees and hills and rivers and distant formations of stone and grass, this landscape was troubling in its featurelessness, its emptiness, in the mere idea that so much space could be so devoid of everything you looked for in a landscape. That the plains were the home of all kinds of creatures would have been harder to recognize in passing unless you stopped and paid close attention. Here were not only the somewhat exotic bison and pronghorn and the somewhat comical prairie dogs: here were a panoply of birds—meadowlarks, lark buntings, horned larks, grouse, prairie chickens, longspurs, mountain plovers, savannah sparrows, ferruginous hawks, prairie falcons, golden eagles, burrowing owls: here were an assortment of mammals—mice, voles, gophers, jackrabbits and cottontails, coyotes, foxes, black-footed ferrets, badgers—and reptiles—prairie rattlesnakes, bullsnakes, yellowbelly racers, coachwhips. All of these were easy to overlook in that vast rolling terrain. Only to the west would there be relief from the scope of that room of sky, with a long jagged blue line of foothills and lower mountains and a white jagged backdrop of snowclad summits rising beyond them, but nothing between the mountains and whatever point you viewed them from on the plains.

And then you reached Greeley, where a sizable group of people were diligent and purposeful as they strove to keep tight control over almost every aspect of their lives, to plan for every contingency and march determinedly toward the fulfillment of their plans. Here were frame houses constructed along a carefully laid out grid of 100-foot-wide streets, trees conscientiously planted to eventually provide shade, space conscientiously allotted on each plot for gardens and decorative landscaping; here a fifty-mile-long fence closed off the town from the plains and the plains from the town, and the prairie was broken in neat rows for miles, and ditches ran into the fields the plows created. Here the nights were quiet because everyone sought well-earned rest after long laboring days and, unlike the mining towns elsewhere in the Territory, here no saloons and no brothels did business—Greeley was a town almost fanatic in its fealty to temperance (though the rumor was that its citizens could be intemperate in their behavior towards those who flouted their adherence to temperance). It was a place where people believed in the promise of their future, in the possibility of perfecting their lives through communal planning and common purpose.

As industrious as it was, it didn't take long for the evidence of community to fall out of sight on the plains as you followed the winding Cache la Poudre River northwest toward Fort Collins. Looking west, the plains were just as open and empty as they had been looking east, but here they were finite, bounded in the distance by the mountains, a threshold to a place where the sky was a ceiling again, raised high above the blue and white of the Front Range. Looking about you on the plains, you could have no certainty that other communities existed—Fort Collins to the northwest, Longmont to the southwest were mere rumors for all the evidence you had of them—but the mountains were solid, massive, material proof that all this space had an end and you could have a destination if you wanted it.

Fort Collins, incorporated as a town that very year, the push for township coming from people who had settled in Greeley only two years before, was less organized, less determined about its destiny, than Greeley, but where the fort had briefly been there were indications of a settled town—businesses like a hotel, a livery stable, a general store, a mill, a brickyard, and two hallmarks of established community, a post office and a school. The territorial legislature had approved the creation of an agricultural college, still to be started, and the farming, aided as in Greeley by irrigation ditches connected to the Cache la Poudre, was suffering from a plague of grasshoppers.

If you left Fort Collins, you were back on the plains; to travel thirty miles back to Greeley or twenty-five miles south to Longmont or sixty-five miles south to Denver, you were back crossing the open spaces with only the distant mountains for orientation. If you veered southwest, toward the opening in the foothills where the Big Thompson River rushed out of its canyon, you faced a destination awesome in its scale and confounding in the complexity of its terrain. But it wasn't empty, and that's the destination Isabella Bird chose.

* * *

It's a different matter to leave imagination behind and strike out into the actual terrain, to tour locales you've only reconstructed in your mind out of memoirs and travel literature and see them as they are on the day you make the circuit.

I drive the backwards 4, from the bottom to the top and out to the eastern end of the crossbar, in a matter of hours, setting out from Lafayette on the multilane highway to Longmont late on a pleasant March morning. I like to think that somewhere around here is the track Isabella Bird would have followed to get down to Denver from Longmont. Glancing off to the west, I see Longs Peak towering snow-covered and magnificent above the virtually snowless foothills, all the peaks of the Snowy Range, as Isabella called it, white and treeless above timberline, the native forests still thick on the mountainsides between tundra and plains.

Imagining Isabella Bird on horseback gazing at those mountains takes little effort, but imagining her on horseback alone on a vast prairie devoid of landmarks is almost impossible here. The topography is largely unchanged but the habitat is utterly altered. Nowhere along 287 is there any sign of prairie; open spaces are all pastures and farmlands and occasionally a spacious house and yard with aspirations to be considered an estate. So it will be between the cities, wherever the outskirts of town give way to definite countryside.

Harder still is it to imagine the cities the way they were in 1873. Longmont had a few hundred people then, Fort Collins likely less than a thousand, Greeley no more than a few thousand, and Loveland didn't exist but for a stage stop outside where the city would eventually emerge. In contrast, the census for the year 2000 gives Longmont over 71,000 inhabitants, Fort Collins roughly 119,000, Greeley nearly 77,000, and Loveland, which had 238 people in 1880, over 50,000. By now these four cities alone have a combined population ten times that of the entire Colorado Territory in 1870 and their populations are increasing rapidly, Greeley's doubling and the others tripling since 1970. These kinds of increases demand a subsequent rise in infrastructures—roads and houses and apartment/condominium complexes and shopping centers and strip malls and parks and civic buildings and schools and industries.

And so you have communities begun along rivers—Greeley and Fort Collins on the Cache la Poudre, Loveland on the Big Thompson, Longmont on the St. Vrain—where most of the citizens and visitors seldom see the rivers, communities where "Historic Business Districts" preserve in more or less faithful fashion buildings from the end of the nineteenth century or the beginning of the twentieth but draw far fewer shoppers than do the malls and plazas of the decentralized city, new subcenters of population creating new subcenters of business and government. Of the earliest history in any of these towns, little remains. The restored whitewashed cabin that Mariano Medina maintained at his Namaqua stage stop, west of where Loveland sprang up, is preserved inside the Loveland Museum. The oldest cabin around Fort Collins, built by pioneer Antoine Janis in 1859, and the Auntie Stone house, constructed in 1864, have been moved to an enclosed courtyard outside the Fort Collins Museum, in Library Park. Greeley has transported a number of buildings, including one from 1870 now converted into a museum store, from various locations to create a "Centennial Village" and has lovingly preserved on its original site the homestead of the Union Colony's founder, Nathan Meeker. In Longmont a hundred buildings have been designated as historic but only three date from 1873. One is grateful for these preservations but well aware that the contexts for any of them have irretrievably disappeared.

Eventually, I feel a sense of déjà vu each time I enter any of these cities. It always begins with an approach down a four- or six-lane highway, through outlying districts of still spreading housing developments and strip malls and shops of one kind or another, the urban and suburban enterprises incrementally converting the agricultural circle at which the city had been the center. Depending on the city's size, it takes me varying lengths of time to reach the city's center—the center is a long way from the edge in Fort Collins and I'm not completely certain I really find the center in Greeley; in Longmont the highway leads me up the middle of Main Street, and in Loveland the road converts to a multilane northbound one-way that zips me past the center of town—but it was merely scale and length of time that differentiated them. Again and again I drive through a big, sprawling area with no easily identifiable center, just multitudes of randomly placed repetitions of standard franchises and fast food places and familiar retail chains.

The same signs show up everywhere, for the same supermarkets (Safeway and King Soopers), the same pharmacies (Rite Aid and Walgreen's), the same discount department stores (Target and Big K and Wal-Mart), the same restaurants (all four cities have Arby's, Dairy Queen, Domino's, IHOP, Johnny Carino's, KFC, McDonald's, Papa John's, Papa Murphy's, Quizno's, Taco Bell, Taco John, and Wendy's, and often the chain outlets have multiple locations—eleven Subways in Fort Collins, six each in Greeley and Longmont, eight in Loveland, while Starbuck's has twenty locations in these four cities). Even Greeley, the Temperance Colony at its outset—Grace Greenwood joked once that "feeling in need of a little dissipation, I ran up to Greeley for a three days' visit," but later asserted it was "a model temperance town"—nowadays has nineteen liquor outlets, one for every four thousand citizens, usually close to supermarkets. From city to city not only are the strip malls and discount outlets anchored by the same stores, but the architecture and décor are also virtually interchangeable. To an outsider, each city seems all but indistinguishable from the others.

Whatever they might have been in the past, however they started out, the cities are merely generic American communities now, hard to distinguish from the cities and towns I knew in Michigan or New York or Iowa. I wonder, given how late in history Colorado developed, whether there isn't a kind of permanent present here, rather than a real sense of past, something endemic to all cities in flux that standardizes them in service to the corporate homogenization of retail franchising.

What was on the plains when Isabella Bird passed through is long gone—you have to think that, before long, the populations of Fort Collins, Greeley, Loveland, and Longmont will have doubled and tripled and expanded right up to each other's doorsteps, one massive conglomeration of communities occupying the plains; they are already the same place in terms of what it's like to be in any of them, their identity transformed by proliferating franchises and retail chains into nowhere in particular and everywhere else, no matter their physical location and historical origins.

This is a familiar lament, I know. It's one that might be made by any moderately observant tourist who isn't comforted or relieved by being in the same place wherever he goes. I made just such laments while living in the Midwest. But I'm dismayed to think I might have written about *this* Colorado while still in Michigan. My wife and I had been securely anchored in the Great Lakes for decades; we thought our launching ourselves west was uncharacteristically daring, because we would be adapting to a different world. Instead, my little tour of the cities on the plains finds me a thousand miles from where I was but still where I started out, encouraged to be either an undiscerning tourist or an indifferent inhabitant. Neither role tempts me as a new identity. Here in Colorado I may be unclear about who I am, but at least I'm certain about who I'm not.

The Canyon

The solitude was becoming sombre, when, after driving for nine hours, and travelling at the least forty-five miles, without any sign of fatigue on the part of the *broncos*, we came to a stream, by the side of which we drove along a definite track, till we came to a sort of tripartite valley, with a majestic crooked canyon 2000 feet deep opening upon it. A rushing stream roared through it, and the Rocky Mountains, with pines scattered over them, came down upon it. A little farther, and the canyon became utterly inaccessible. This was exciting; here was an inner world.

Isabella Bird, Letter IV, September 12

If a flatlander, having departed the glacier-leveled terrain of the upper Midwest and crossed the vast flatness of the Great Plains, first reached the Front Range by following the Big Thompson River upstream through its canyon, he would have such an introduction to western geology that he might well ride through with mouth agape and senses reeling. The plains convince you that the earth is stable, settled, virtually uniform, sometimes level, sometimes given to broad rolling swells, like the crests and troughs of waves frozen into place on a placid sea of grass. Rivers and creeks, all winding toward eventual confluence with the

Platte and the Missouri and finally the Mississippi, confirm in their watercourses that erosion changes the landscape; they give you the impression that whatever changes, changes slowly—the present here, you think, is very much like the past, however long the past might extend. The plains, it would seem, result simply from dust falling on dust, layers of dirt building up over time, and it's hard to imagine that all this was once sea bottom, that layers below layers below layers were deposited by the sedimentation of waves and the sedimentation of rivers running off mountains that existed and eroded away before the Rockies came into being.

But then the flatlander approaches a ridge with slopes having the same soil as the plains, and beyond the ridge suddenly the terrain changes. If you want proof of the variety of layers deposited ever deeper below the surface, here it is, startlingly exposed. Generally speaking, the younger, more recent deposits begin on the east, where Loveland rests on Pierre shale, and the farther west you go the older and more ancient the deposits are—first, a hogback of Dakota sandstone; then a little farther west a sharp fold in the sandstone weathered away into a row of thin upright rocks called the Devil's Backbone; beyond that, the foothills made up of Fountain formation sandstone. The western side of the ridge is steeper and more exposed than the eastern side. The tilting of the earth's surface is clear in inclined layers of the western bluffs differentiated by varying shades of red at distinct levels in the sandstone. Sedimentary deposition and uplifting are obvious.

And then you come up to the high walls through which the Big Thompson River has carved its canyon. These walls, the oldest in this part of Colorado, are made up of Precambrian material that, rising from below the plain, pushed aside and upended the younger rocks on top of it. The traveler has crossed more easily weathered sedimentary rocks, largely sandstone and shale, to reach the canyon, but the rocks in the canyon, geologists tell us, are much harder, more resistant to weathering, made up of banded gneiss and shiny schist. In *Time, Rocks, and the Rockies,* Halka Chronic has described them as "standing on end like books on a shelf."

The flatlander enters the Narrows here, where the river, ever resourceful, followed the path of least resistance through highly resistant rock, and subsequently twists and turns constantly with no possibility of a floodplain on either side. David McComb, writing of the historic and devastating 1976 Big Thompson flood, describes "the strat-ified brown and rust colored walls stretch[ing] 500 feet per-pendicularly from the edge of the road" and observes, accurately by my lights, "It is easy to become anxious and nervous here. Human beings are dwarfed at the bottom of this chasm. It is claustrophobic; there is no quick escape."

The Narrows extend for only a few imposing, sharply winding miles. Then the valley opens up into a long, more easily eroded section with open land on either side of the river. Here the Utes often wintered; here the first settlers in the canyon set up their cabins and barns; here Isabella Bird stayed with the "Chalmers" family and made her failed first attempt to cross over into Estes Park. Today the area, known as Cedar Cove, still has its share of settlers.

The canyon narrows and widens intermittently as you follow the river upstream. About ten miles in, where the North Fork of the Big Thompson meets the main channel, the settlement of Drake still stands. A flatlander driving through the entire canyon from Loveland to Estes Park finds a long stretch of summer homes, rental cabins, resorts, and recreation businesses fairly thick on the west end. Although intermittent stretches of canyon have no buildings whatever, people seem determined to scratch out space on the rocks and the riverbanks, sometimes building their own bridges in order to cross and perch there, close to the river. For someone who has recently caught up on the history of the canyon, the density of habitation is a little surprising, particularly when you consider that the best histories of the canyon are usually in books about the Big Thompson Canyon flood of 1976.

In the beginning of the westward movement, the only trail through the canyon was one blazed by the Utes. David Thompson, a Northwest Fur Company agent and explorer, visited the area in 1810, and the frontiersman and scout Kit Carson passed through the canyon in 1840, wintering in what was later named Estes Park. Passage through was possible but difficult. Hard though it may be for the modern traveler to imagine, the canyon beyond the narrows seldom gave room for a trail along the river; crossing and recrossing the stream was both necessary and dangerous. Over time a road was developed and from time to time improved, especially after Loveland had become a railroad stop and Estes Park a resort destination—to reach the Stanley Hotel, the resort built by E. O. Stanley, coaches and early automobiles, particularly Stanley Steamers, needed easy passage. People could spend two days getting through the canyon—they stopped midcanyon at a hotel in Drake—until the road became a national highway in 1938 and was improved enough to reduce the time to half a day; today it takes less than an hour. By 1976, the canyon had around 1,400 buildings; over 9,000 automobiles drove through each day.

Between 1864 and 1976, the canyon flooded twelve times, often washing out dams and bridges, stranding visitors at the Forks Hotel, killing people and destroying homes. The Big Thompson rises on the Continental Divide and is joined by a number of tributaries before it reaches or passes through the canyon. The 1976 flood was the worst deluge on record, scouring the canyon nearly clean of human habitation. It moved twenty-foot boulders, rose from the average two feet to as high as nineteen feet in places like the Narrows, killed 145 people and destroyed 418 houses and 152 businesses. But Halka Chronic comments, "Houses on the river floodplain have been built, rebuilt, or extensively repaired since the flood. Memory of the terror in the night and the tumultuous power of the floodwaters has been surprisingly short-lived."

The canyon had felt the force of such floods many times before European-American settlers and even Native American peoples had come along to record them. The chaotic results of such events—the debris of devastated timber, the jumble of rolling boulders and fallen stone slabs, as well as the relentless and resourceful river itself nimbly leaping over and around the debris to stay on its own course to the plains—had occurred with only the changes inherent in erosion, weathering, and decay to alter the terrain. No semblance of development, of settlements and roads, except where Isabella Bird was staying on the east end of the canyon, just after the Narrows, and only a game and Indian trail to follow if one could find it. This is the situation Isabella Bird found herself in as she continued hoping to find a way to cross into Estes Park.

* * *

Isabella Bird only ever calls the area "Canyon" or, later on, after she moved to a different location, "Lower Canyon"; at one point, trying to get from the homestead where she's been staying through the canyon to Estes Park, her entry is datelined, "Nameless Region." We now call all of this the Big Thompson Canyon, the gorge carved by the Big Thompson River running from Estes Park on the west to Loveland on the east. When Isabella Bird was here, neither town existed and "Estes Park" referred only to a large valley surrounded by mountains.

Someone in Fort Collins suggested she might go into the canyon to stay with a settler who "had a saw-mill and took boarders." Unable to get a horse and travel alone, she rode there "in a buggy drawn by light broncos and driven by a profoundly melancholy young man." From Fort Collins they crossed trackless prairie, which she likened to "being at sea without a compass." She paints a somber picture of the drive, with a cloudy sky overhead, "the air hot and still," vultures feasting on the carcass of a mule, houses few and either overcrowded or in mourning, the driver morose and confused about his destination. Eventually, to her considerable relief, they reached the canyon's mouth. When, soon after, "the canyon became utterly inaccessible," she observes, "This was exciting; here was an inner world."

I've always been struck by that statement, those seven words in two sentences neither narrative nor descriptive but instead declarative and revelatory. After all the details of travel and terrain, here she seems spontaneously responsive: this was exciting *to her* because *she* had arrived at the threshold of an inner world that promised something different from the outer world of settlement and development, of commerce and community, of narrowly focused industriousness and shortsighted squalor. Her arrival at Canyon is a significant turning point for her interest—and frankly, for mine—in what she will encounter in Colorado.

The distinctive quality of her writing may be identified by this particular moment, when she exclaims her exhilaration at the prospect of transporting herself beyond the familiar and the relatively settled, out of an "outer world" and into "an inner world." While most of the other Colorado writers of her time have moments, some more than others, in which they appreciate the terrain they travel through, Bird is the only one who seems more interested in the landscape and its prospects than in the society emerging on and spreading across that landscape and its potential.

In Big Thompson Canyon, Isabella Bird found a scattered society of homesteaders and convalescents. She and her driver pulled up at a broken-down cabin, not a boardinghouse, and located the people she had been urged to contact. The couple—their family name was Alexander, but Bird called them Chalmers in the book—were not particularly welcoming or, for that matter, competent at homesteading, but they agreed to let her board with them for five dollars a week. Though she was put off by the roughness of their living conditions and "repelled" by the "faces and manners" of the family, she gambled that, somehow, from here she might "get over canyons and all other difficulties into Estes Park, which has become the goal of my journey and hopes." She decided to stay.

Because her entire purpose in coming to the canyon was to gain access to Estes Park, Isabella was soon frustrated with her residency, declaring after five days, "I am weary of the limitations of this existence" which she felt was "a life in which nothing happens." The Chalmers family was a hapless and unhappy crew, their living quarters in disarray, their sawmill nonfunctioning, their ability to cope with their circumstances inadequate. The cabin where she slept—the family slept outside—was open at one end and had holes in the roof; her days were taken up with washing, mending, knitting, writing, "and the various odds and ends which arise when one has to do all for oneself." She tried to make herself "agreeable" to the cheerless members of the family and "made the acquaintance of all the careworn, struggling settlers within a walk," people traveling and roughing it to improve their health in the restorative Colorado climate. She pushed herself to become more involved with the family, with the result that they were somewhat less sour and indifferent to her, but she found it "a moral, hard, unlovely, unrelieved, unbeautified, grinding life" filled with "discomfort and lack of ease and [lack of] refinement."

In time Chalmers agreed to take Isabella through the canyon to Estes Park, and she and he and his wife set off on what turned out to be a fruitless expedition through an area that was, in her words, "unsurveyed, and mostly unexplored." Though frustrated by the incompetence of her guide and the rugged conditions he continually tried to lead them through, she was highly pleased with her surroundings. She thought the scenery was "glorious, combining sublimity with beauty," and claimed that "in the elastic air fatigue has dropped off from me." Like the settlers homesteading for health, she thought this was "no region for tourists and women" but "its unprofaned freshness gives me new life." In spite of the futility of their efforts to get through the canyon, she reveled in the changes in the terrain. "Deep, vast canyons, all trending westwards, lie in purple gloom," she wrote, and the mountains she could see provided "the frame out of which rises . . . the splintered, pinnacled, lonely, ghastly, imposing, double-peaked summit of Long's Peak." Even while their efforts were getting them nowhere, the attempt was strengthening her resolve.

Generally ill-equipped for their outing, the trio really had no sense of where they were going and, after reconnoitering, Chalmers led them "into a steep, deep, rough ravine, where we had to dismount, for trees were lying across it everywhere, and there was almost no footing on the great slabs of shelving rock. . . . Ah! it was a wild place." The horses began falling and the women were bruised and knocked down. Eventually, they reached an open space, built a fire, and, with snow flurries and gusty winds blowing around them and without food, slept through a cold night and awakened to discover that the unhobbled horses had wandered off. The second day's outing was as futile as the first and by the end of it they were back at the wreck of a cabin. Isabella was grudgingly forgiving in her remarks:

"Yet, after all, they were not bad souls; and though he failed so grotesquely, he did his incompetent best." Near a blazing fire and with her eyes on the stars and her thoughts on Longs Peak, she "resolved that, come what might, I would reach Estes Park."

* * *

Determined to be neither detached nor disoriented in the canyon, I study my passage through it. Several times I drive its twenty-five-mile length both ways, hoping the drive one way will catch something I missed driving the other way. Other times I simply roam around different sections of the canyon. Each time I find myself in the Narrows, I feel the thrill of being enclosed in "an inner world." It is the most imposing stretch of canyon I've yet seen along the Front Range, with its absolutely vertical walls, the strata upended as if by a cataclysm. Twisting along the confined path of the highway, just above the boulder-strewn riverbed, I remind myself that, though canyons usually get worn away speck by speck, grain by grain, sometimes they get flushed and scoured, and this is a canyon where that's happened.

Some of my explorations are on foot. I take a short hike on the Foothills Nature Trail because it begins just past Cedar Cove, across from a city park straddling the river. It follows a narrow dirt road originally installed to maintain a waterline feeding a power plant down on the river. I benefit from numbered markers along the trail which correspond to sections in a pamphlet that help me identify yucca, prickly pear, bitterbrush, common juniper and Rocky Mountain juniper, an introduction to widespread western flora. I learn something about soil formation, erosion, and the effect of south- and north-facing slopes on tree and plant growth as I climb.

The trail winds upward through open, quiet Ponderosa pine forest, along steel water pipes and occasional power lines and poles, the recreational and utilitarian uses of nature placidly evident side by side. It ends at a stone shelter overlooking the canyon. I hoist myself into a sunlit window, hoping the sun's warmth will fend off a cool breeze. Melting snow drips off the roof while I scribble notes and gaze at the Big Thompson River winding a long way below me. Through the haze to the west I discern the snow-coated mountains of the Continental Divide, where the Big Thompson River begins, and in the intervening terrain appreciate the complications of trying to get through the canyon without the benefit of a road.

My solitary excursions, whether motor tours or hikes, take place on weekdays; my wife and I hike together only on weekends or holidays. Her shift from higher education to the corporate world has made her time more regulated and rigid; my shift to nominal retirement has given my schedule nothing but flexibility, unless I want to hike with my wife. Sometimes my weekday outings serve as scouting expeditions for future weekends.

A few days after my solitary walk, from the same Round Mountain Trailhead, my wife and I climb another, longer trail to the summit of Sheep Mountain. A continually ascending footpath follows east- and southeast-facing slopes through Ponderosa pine, providing ever more panoramic views of the canyon and the plains. The day is clear, and most of the snow from days earlier is already gone. As we cross a long talus slope I note lichen so bright green that I bend close to the rocks to make certain I'm not seeing splashes of Day-Glo paint. In a rocky section about two and a half miles up, boulders pile on top of one another, separated by innumerable joints and faults and eroded into sometimes startling shapes—a Hershey's kiss, a penis, a deep bowl in the center of a thick cylinder. One narrow cleft in the rocks, which reminds us only of a narrow cleft in the rocks, makes us scramble a little to get through. Hopscotching across several seasonal rivulets fed by snowmelt, we encounter one very pronounced spring, the slope below it richly verdant, with green grasses and plentiful young trees, a contrast to the dry, gravely slopes we've been climbing.

We cross a little creek and ascend a north-facing slope through a long lush stretch of purple pasqueflowers, fully in bloom and beautiful. Pink wild geraniums and white star lilies appear intermittently along the trail. From time to time we pause to identify some Townsend's solitaires, a northern flicker, dark-eyed juncos, and, rummaging amidst fallen trees on a shady slope, a blue grouse. We have climbed high enough, gone deep enough, that we hardly notice the trail and stay alert for whatever inhabits or occupies the terrain. At the summit, the end of the trail, stones have been piled onto a cairn taller than either of us. The altitude gives me the chance to observe a distant open space, a "park" in the parlance of the mountains—according to my topo map it's likely Rattlesnake Park—and I'm aware of how much canyons restrict our awareness of what they're connected to, the less limited world that stretches away from them on all sides. To appreciate that, you have to rise above the canyon walls.

On the way down I concentrate on the contours of the land on either side of the canyon, thinking about Isabella Bird and her party choosing among all those promising ravines, all those elk and mule deer trails. Picking your way over rough terrain is a challenge. If "Chalmers" tried to make it through on guesswork and no trail sense, it's no surprise they got lost. Trudging silently behind my wife, I try to remember where Bird said they wandered and wonder where I can get a better awareness of that terrain.

Isabella, of necessity, is vague about the specifics of their wanderings, but she does describe riding through a pleasant, open park with clear views of the plains in one direction and the Snowy Range in the other; if I strain to read my topo map carefully, I might be able to locate such a parklike meadow or openings. She also mentioned ending up close to Storm Peak—the nearest likely location is a nearly 10,000-foot summit on the north side of the canyon, above the confluence of the Big Thompson River and the North Fork Big Thompson. Called Storm Mountain, it can be accessed through a meadow known as Cedar Park. Midweek following our Sheep Mountain hike, I set off alone by car.

The canyon of the North Fork Big Thompson River is narrower than the Big Thompson Canyon, not precipitous like its Narrows but not as open and broad as the big canyon in the stretch leading to Drake. Local rivers have been high from the rapid snowmelt of the past week, and talk of flooding has abounded, but the waters on the Front Range, though turbulent and tumultuous, are not much beyond bounds. At an elbow in both river and road, I notice a place to park and swing the car around to pull in. For awhile I sit in a cold wind and listen to the continuous rush and gush of the rapids, the river pulsing and plunging and pumping over, around, and through the boulders in its bed. I watch the ceaseless contortions of the coursing water. The force of it, the volume in both quantity and sound, is something in nature I never tire of. If I were less inclined to be text-bound, continually setting out with purpose like a literary researcher bound for a library—old habits die hard—I could envision myself as someone willing to wander in search of sites for quiet moments of meditative calm. But imagining myself even for a moment as a wilderness contemplative makes me think at once of studying haiku and reading up on Bashō, as if I can't really act in life except on projects arising that I deem worthy of pursuing. I shake off these thoughts and try to concentrate on the sound of mountain water a moment longer.

When I check my map I realize I missed the turnoff to Cedar Park. It turns out to be a dirt road marked only with a small sign indicating "Forest Access." I turn onto it and see another sign warning me I should use a four-wheel-drive vehicle. I compensate for my subcompact sedan by moving slowly up the long, steep climb. If this is indeed the place Isabella Bird mentions, I can't blame her for being daunted—the uneven dirt road passes through very rough terrain, walled in by rocks and forest, its switchbacks often steep and sharp; on the lowest levels boulders and cliffs line one side of the road and a drop-off to the North Fork parallels the other side. Then both sides of the road close in. I ascend slowly, up any number of switchbacks, no view on any side of me but of canyon walls, and emerge gradually onto open space where several intersecting roads seem to have been worn down into the soil. The flat shoulders on either side are higher than my car. The land here opens up into an extensive rolling meadow, clear and broad, its grass lush and long. If this is the park she mentioned, I understand her thrill at finding it.

I follow the road towards Storm Mountain. The farther up I go the more I find myself in an extensive burned-over area, trees blackened and dead, rock naked and exposed, ground cover gone and the bare contours of the slopes revealed, some patches with the ever hopeful return of green and some trees surviving next to others devastated and dead. Houses appear in the middle of the burn, perhaps saved from the fire, perhaps already replaced. A friend of mine once said, as we drove through a different canyon, that he thought people were crazy to build on a wooded slope—"It isn't a question of whether a fire will happen; it's a question of when." The houses here look cheery and complacent, untouched by the forest fire that must have burned right up to their doorways. It's hard to believe they survived unscathed; harder still to imagine what their owners make of the view from their windows. I think of the homes down along the floodplain of the Big Thompson River. The housing market here seems to depend a great deal on a concentrated communal amnesia.

I go higher than I need to go—narrow dirt roads with high shoulders switching back and forth and curving around hillsides make it hard to turn around; they deceive you into thinking you're almost "there," at some spot that will give you a sense of arrival at a destination you didn't know you were striving for. Sometimes I have a clear view down onto a vast open park, which I soon realize is that Cedar Park I left behind. I've been ascending awhile and decide not to go as far as the road might take me—Isabella Bird didn't summit Storm Mountain, after all, and I already have an appreciation of the terrain she encountered after leaving the canyon floor.

I descend slowly through the burned-over sections, through the grassy park, along the rocky switchbacks. The hiking and the driving have altered my perception of the canyon, I know, but I wrestle with *how* I know it's been altered. Maybe it has to do with how I think about canyons.

The canyons of the Front Range are impressive geological features in their own right. I've been on the lip of canyons elsewhere, where the canyon seems to have dropped below the surface of the earth and you feel as if you're encountering an impressive feat of natural engineering. Canyons of that kind are holes in the ground you could fall into; the wonder about them is how far down they go and how difficult it would be to climb up out of them. The Front Range canyons all carve their passages through the foothills of the Rocky Mountains and generally, when you approach them from the east, you find the surface of the earth on the level with the mouth of the canyon and the canyon walls rise above you. The canyon is a place you have to enter into if you want to reach the mountains across the barrier of the foothills set up against the plains. This is what I think Isabella Bird was driving at when she declared at the mouth of Big Thompson, "Here was an inner world." On the plains the space is so vast that the horizon simply drops away rather than reaches its limits; in the canyon the horizon is overhead and the limits of space can be measured in a few minutes' brisk strides. Which makes you feel smaller? Which is more intimidating, more menacing? In the canyon there are distinct limits to freedom of movement, to hours of daylight, to hours without shadow, to sightlines and perspective, to proximity to other people. The canyon has very finite boundaries but to get to the deep inner world of the mountains, where space is felt differently than on the plains, one has to pass through the long, roofless tunnel of the canyon, paying the toll of compression and enclosure to trade one kind of expansiveness for another. It's only when you climb the canyon walls to their limits and angle back beyond the canyon to the heights from which the canyon walls began that you see the way the canyon is connected to the rest of the landscape, that you see how far beyond the canyon the world runs. But even if you know all that, for a while in the canyon, especially in a part of it like the Narrows, you forget how large the world really is and think only of the confining closeness and imposing height of the canyon walls.

It may be that, when Isabella Bird spoke of "an inner world," she felt as if she were, at last, *entering someplace*, leaving behind what was, to her, as good as nowhere, progressing into somewhere *else*. Perhaps she sensed that she might feel a place *within* her, rather than *beyond* her. Though I can't know if that was true for her, it feels true for me. The canyon provides not only a physical passage into Estes Park—I know other, more convenient ways for me to get there—but also a psychological passage. It feels like an immersion experience from which I will emerge . . .

where? Somewhere other than on the vast empty plains through which I've been drifting.

What an inner world the canyon can be. How grand it would feel to make the passage through and to emerge once again in unlimited space, in a place that might fill me.

The Park

i

We have received a call from Miss Bird of Edinburgh, Scotland, who is traveling not only across the continent, but across the world from the West. She is a literary lady, comes with high testimonials from distinguished men. She is just from the Sierra Nevada Mountains, which she traversed on horseback, and she came to California from New Zealand and Australia, which countries she traveled on horseback, at the rate of forty to fifty miles a day, and yet she calls herself an invalid. She is stopping at present at the Colorado House, and will soon take a horseback trip to the mountains.

Greeley Tribune, September 10, 1873

A Scotch lassie named Miss Bird, all the way from "Edinburgh Town," literary in tastes, adventurous in travel, and withal an invalid in health, is now in this Territory, en route round the world, from the west. From Australia to California, by steamer; across the State of California on horseback to Nevada, at the rate of forty miles a day, she is now ready and willing to ride up and through our Rocky Mountains, for the fun of it. And yet she isn't happy, because she's an

58

invalid. Here's a hint to American girls, who are hale, poor, and prudish.

Rocky Mountain Herald, September 13, 1873

One day, while visiting an English doctor and his wife in what she calls "Lower Canyon," Isabella Bird was thrown from her horse. The "Hughes" (or Hutchinson) family encouraged her to recuperate from her fall with them. Offered more comfortable surroundings and more congenial companionship, Bird transferred her belongings to their homestead, but soon decided that the canyon was a dead end for her travels. "Dr. H." drove her by wagon to Longmont, a journey that took two days because he had difficulty finding the way. In Longmont, when Captain Sigley, the "jovial, kindly" landlord of the St. Vrain Hotel, learned that she had given up hope of reaching the mountains and was planning to depart for Denver and New York, he quickly found her a horse to ride and two young men to accompany her to Estes Park. Isabella was a little nervous about the horse, still "shaken by my fall at Canyon," and wrote, "I earnestly wished that the *Greeley Tribune* had not given me a reputation for horsemanship, which had preceded me here." She probably had not seen the *Rocky Mountain Herald*'s version of the item, which took a jolly tone and admonished American women for not being as plucky. The horse, to her pleasure, "in gait and temper turned out perfection—all spring and spirit, . . . a blithe, joyous animal, to whom a day among the mountains seemed a pleasant frolic."

The trio's passage across the prairie from Longmont followed the course of the St. Vrain Creek and eventually traced its north fork, crossing and recrossing it as they entered its canyon. Isabella was delighted by the change from the "brown and burning plains" to "green and bright" cottonwood trees and "aspens shiver[ing] in gold tremulousness." They often found themselves "wedged between [the creek's] margin and lofty cliffs and terraces of incredibly staring, fantastic rocks." She reveled in the colors on the rocks—"carmine, vermilion, greens of all tints, blue, yellow, orange, violet, deep crimson, coloring no artist would dare to represent"—and in "the blue gloom of the pitch pines." Eventually, she writes, they "left the softer world behind, and all traces of man and his works, and plunged into the Rocky Mountains."

Isabella Bird's prose undergoes a transformation as she describes her journey into Estes Park; her language is invigorated by her surroundings. She details her route vividly, and captures features of the route most visitors to the area take today. In the celebratory September 28 section of Letter VI she writes of "great brick-shaped masses of bright red rock," "passes dark with shadow, and so narrow that we had to ride in the beds of the streams which had excavated them," "colossal pyramids of rock crested with pines," and "parks so beautifully arranged by nature that I momentarily expected to come upon some stately mansion, but that afternoon crested blue jays and chipmonks had them all to themselves." Descriptive phrases tumble out of her pen and her sentences lengthen cumulatively trying to get everything in, cataloguing "chasms of immense depth," "the indigo gloom of pines," "mountains with snow gleaming on their splintered crests," "still streams and shady pools, and cool depths of shadow," "and so, on and on through the lengthening shadows, till the trail, which in places had been hardly legible, became well defined, and we entered a long gulch with broad swellings of grass belted with pines." She is virtually breathless at the sights she's taking in.

It's at this moment in her narrative that Isabella Bird describes the log cabin at the head of the gulch and her first meeting with Jim Nugent, also known as Rocky Mountain Jim. Nugent was to become an important character in the Estes Park portions of her narrative, making certain she achieved the summit of Longs Peak and initiating a relationship that has since provoked a good deal of speculation, not to mention fantasizing. Because most of Isabella's original letters to her sister are lost and all we have are her revised and published accounts, we have little way of knowing how much of what she says about Jim and her reaction to him is retrospective rather than immediate. Certainly her feelings toward him grew complicated over the following weeks.

Jim Nugent was a colorful figure. She describes him as thickset, about middle height, clad in an old cap, a tattered grey hunting suit with a scarf at the waist, "dilapidated" horsehide moccasins, and armed with a knife and a revolver. She thinks of him as strikingly handsome—grey-blue eyes, aquiline nose, "smooth shaven except for a dense moustache and imperial" [pointed beard], long curly "tawny hair"—but one side of his face had been mauled by a bear, and it was scarred and missing an eye. She thought "one side of the face repulsive, while the other might have been modeled in marble," and claimed, "'Desperado' was written in large letters all over him." He made sufficient impression on her that her report of their initial encounter interrupts the account of her entrance into Estes Park for roughly two and a half printed pages.

The moment when she first beheld the valley is a memorable one. She tells of standing on a ridge at the end of Muggins Gulch and seeing "at last Estes Park, lying 1,500 feet below in the glory of the setting sun, an irregular basin, lighted up by the bright waters of the rushing Thompson, guarded by sentinel mountains of fantastic shape and monstrous size." She exclaims, "Never, nowhere, have I seen anything to equal the view into Estes Park." Then "mountain fever seized me, and, giving my tireless horse one encouraging word, he dashed at full gallop over a mile of smooth sward at delirious speed."

Her arrival marks a turning point for her book because it is a turning point for her feelings about Colorado. Estes Park is central to everything Colorado comes to mean for her and eventually comes to earn her exuberance on first encountering it.

* * *

My own first approach to Estes Park is more prosaic. From Boulder I take U.S. 36 north, a portion of which follows the route taken to Estes Park by Isabella Bird. Her route and mine intersect where the road from Longmont and the road from Boulder meet, just across the St. Vrain River, a little east of Lyons, a town that didn't exist in 1873. I'm familiar with the town only because, everywhere I go in Colorado, I see, in front of businesses and public buildings and suburbs, upright red stone markers formed from the distinctive Lyons sandstone quarried here. I pass quickly through a strip of restaurants and bars and the quaint downtown, aware that the open space of the high plains I've been crossing is closing down and the hills are rising around me.

My route from Lyons to Estes Park, the one Isabella Bird took (more or less) years before, parallels North St. Vrain Creek and climbs through its canyon, then leaves it to descend into and across a long valley, rise over a low divide to follow the bed of the Little Thompson River, and finally pass along Muggins Gulch and descend into Estes Park. Once, Lyons was a depot on the Chicago, Burlington & Quincy Railroad. Visitors to Estes Park would leave the train at Lyons, then travel this overland route by stage. Now the road is swift and well maintained, and the traffic on summer weekends is often continuous and crowded.

From exploring Big Thompson Canyon farther north and noticing the terrain around Boulder, I recognize familiar landforms as I travel through Lyons. I've also been consulting two texts on local geology: *The Geologic Story of the Rocky Mountain National Park Colorado*, the 1917 report for the National Park Service by Willis T. Lee of the U.S. Geological Survey, written soon after the creation of the park, and *Time, Rocks, and the Rockies: A Geologic Guide to Roads and Trails of Rocky Mountain National Park*, a dandy little 1984 book by Halka Chronic, whose various books on western geology are standard sources. Isabella Bird didn't have much interest in the science of the landscape, and reacted more to the mood it created in her or the circumstances under which she encountered it. Although I sometimes— well, frequently—struggle to grasp the information, I find the tumult of rocks and the changes in texture and form fascinating, and often wish I would spend more time trying to better comprehend what I'm seeing.

I generally understand that the Rockies arose at least twice, raised by forces of plate tectonics and affecting the surface of the earth on either side of them. The various layers of sedimentary rock had been laid down by periods when the central part of North America had been inundated by shallow seas. The mountain range that scientists refer to as the Ancestral Rockies had not only risen but been ground down and washed away by erosion. The mountains had been leveled into a broad plain before. "Rising from the plains," as John McPhee titled his Wyoming book of geological history, they had tilted the various and distinct layers of sedimentation that had been deposited on top of them. Traveling from the east, you pass through stages of the history of the earth, generally speaking, from the most recent to the most ancient, as if you were burrowing straight down into the horizontal strata of the earth. So the upended hard shale of the Dakota hogback running east of the Front Range is more recent than the soft fossil rich Morrison formation sandstone farther west, which is more recent than the "thick cross-bedded flaggy layers" (as Lee describes them) of the Lyons sandstone, which is more recent than the layers of the Fountain Formation, which is more recent than the Precambrian granite of the mountains. Geologists make finer distinctions, but that's the general order in which I see things while heading from Lyons to Estes Park.

Just west of Lyons, where the road turns north, Steamboat Rock, also called Steamboat Mountain, rises directly ahead, standing, according to Lee, "like a domination headland overlooking the valley." The western edge of its top is exposed layers of dark red sandstone, but the mountainside from the valley floor upward is entirely eroded talus. As prominent as the formation is, I've seen similar structures near the mouth of Big Thompson Canyon. The road soon curves west, enters the granite walls of the North St. Vrain canyon, and begins rising along the north wall, with the canyon floor dropping away to the south. Unlike a good many of the other canyons linking the Front Range with the plains, the North St. Vrain is not particularly narrow or enclosing, and the highway allows for comfortable passage.

Driving so high above North St. Vrain Creek, I have no sense of when the highway stops paralleling it, but soon I sweep down through the little town of Pinewood Springs, mostly a couple of restaurants and a plethora of mailboxes close to the road in a wide valley known as Little Elk Park. Across the valley the road enters the canyon of the Little Thompson River and continues along the bottom of a narrow V-shaped valley, Muggins Gulch. The highway rises again as it passes through the gulch. Lee points out that the road follows "a winding course through forested hills, which assume huge proportions as we approach Estes

Park." Mount Pisgah (8,630 feet) and Mount Olympus (8,808 feet) are on the right side of the road and Kruger Rock (9,355 feet) is on the left, and the road aims toward a passage through the hills that lie below these summits. Somewhere at the top of the divide, I reach the area where Isabella Bird first topped the rise and gazed into Estes Park. I suspect that the view was somewhat less obstructed in her day and, because of road building, more open in Lee's time thirty years later, and even in Chronic's, nearly seventy years after Lee's. Even so, and even with the trees thicker and taller on the slopes along the road, we reach consensus: it's a splendid view.

Because the traveler is moving through deeply forested hills with mountains rising above, closed in to varying degrees for so much of the passage, the sudden emergence into the top of a broad valley—Chronic identifies it as "one of the largest valleys along the east slope of the Front Range"—can be startling. I gasp the moment I first glimpse it and pull off at the first overlook I come to. As Chronic points out, "the valley shows in its entirety, from the narrow river passage at its upper end, west of the town of Estes Park, to Olympus Dam at its lower end." I find it hard to pick out individual features; instead, I am filled with the impression of openness, the distant circling mountains and ridges and the space between them on the valley floor so far below. Estes Park, at an elevation of 7,522 feet, is one thousand to two thousand feet lower than the surrounding summits and, after miles and miles of granite slopes and steep forested valley walls, seems a broad, inviting open range. The entrance point at the top of Park Hill, where the sign carved on a mountain-shaped slab of Lyons sandstone welcomes you to Estes Park, positions you for an overview of valley floor, open sky, and encircling mountains that seems like a panorama of unlimited possibility.

* * *

So in this glorious upper world, with the mountain pines behind and the clear lake in front, in the "blue hollow at the foot of Long's Peak," at a height of 7,500 feet, where the hoar frost crisps the grass every night of the year, I have found far more than I ever dared to hope for.

Isabella Bird, Letter VI

According to the timetable we glean from her letters, Isabella Bird achieved Estes Park on the evening of September 26. By the time she wrote the letter datelined "ESTES PARK!!! September 28"—"I wish I could let those three notes of admiration go to you instead of a letter"—she was already settled in and, except for her memorable excursion to Longs Peak, had begun to see her life there in terms of an exhilarating routine. Her enthusiasm for her location was unrestrained. She regarded it as " everything that is rapturous and delightful," by which she meant: "grandeur, cheerfulness, health, enjoyment, novelty, freedom, etc., etc." It's an interesting list, particularly since it includes so much that is indicative of her feelings and state of mind rather than simply aspects of her surroundings.

Grandeur, of course, refers to landscape—she wrote, "The scenery is the most glorious I have ever seen, and is above us, around us, at the very door."—and she expressed her proprietary feelings about the place with vivid description of its natural features. She claimed (in Letter VIII, October 2) that Estes Park was "mine by right of love, appropriation, and appreciation," and catalogued all the aspects of the area that delighted and amazed her—light, air, landforms, fauna, sounds. She tended not to make much of wildlife and seldom mentioned what she may have seen or heard herself, except for the bear that startled her horse near Tahoe and the occasional screams of cougars and howls of wolves and coyotes, so we don't know how much of her catalogue is the result of actual sightings and how much is hearsay. But wapiti (elk) and bighorn sheep and coyotes still make tourists stop and gape in Rocky Mountain National Park, and sunlight behind the mountains at the end of day still invites skywatching.

Scholars of nineteenth-century nature writing have made much of her awareness of and apparent allegiance to standard ideas of the picturesque and the sublime: "Here and there the lawns are so smooth, the trees so artistically grouped, a lake makes such an artistic foreground, or a waterfall comes tumbling down with such an apparent feeling for the picturesque, that I am almost angry with Nature for her close imitation of art. But in another hundred yards Nature, glorious, unapproachable, inimitable, is herself again, raising one's thoughts reverently upwards to her Creator and ours." She concludes, "Grandeur and sublimity, not softness, are the features of Estes Park," and offers such evidence as "glades . . . soon lost in the dark primëval forests," "granite blocks piled and poised by nature in some mood of fury," "canyons nearly or quite inaccessible, awful in their blackness and darkness; every valley ends in mystery. . . ." Readers cannot mistake what she means by grandeur, nor should they doubt the sincerity of her awestruck appreciation of what she beheld. She was in a long narrow valley surrounded by mountains and virtually unpopulated, except for the few people around her on Griff Evans's ranch. As she noted, after Jim Nugent's cabin in Muggins Gulch, there was "not another cabin for eighteen miles toward the Plains. The park is unsurveyed, and the huge tract of mountainous country beyond is almost altogether unexplored." This was a very impressive expanse of wild country. If, as Reg Saner observes, "the difference between landscape and nature is the difference between separation and inclusion," then Isabella's difficulty was using the familiar language of landscape to expound upon the unfamiliar experience of nature. Here, she was immersed for the first time in almost total wilderness.

Grandeur can go a long way toward filling both rapture and delight departments, but the other items on her list are considerably more personal. "Cheerfulness" and "enjoyment" were attributable not only to her surroundings but also to the people she interacted with daily at the ranch where she stayed. "Health" might well have been less noticeable to someone who didn't think of herself— and describe herself to newspapermen—as an invalid; like so many others who sought respite from their respiratory problems in the thin, dry mountain air, she had begun to feel more robust in her short time in Colorado. "There is health in every breath of air," she wrote. "I am much better already, and get up to a seven o'clock breakfast without difficulty." She doesn't emphasize the possibility but it seems like that the last two items on her list—"novelty" and "freedom"—may have had something to do with the improvement in her cheerfulness and enjoyment as well as, yes, her health. She wrote, in Letter VI, "This is perfection, and all the requisites for health are present, including plenty of horses and grass to ride on." Horses and grass would not be everyone's "requisite for health." It seems, rather, that Estes Park fulfilled desires she may not have fully recognized in herself: the need for novelty, for a world that challenged her resourcefulness and curiosity, and the need for freedom, for a world where she was largely unfettered by her duties to her family and her society. Isabella Lucy Bird was about to turn forty-two on October 15, 1873. She'd honored family obligations and chafed quietly but obediently under the restraints of her upbringing by pious, church-centered parents and the proprieties of her Victorian society, but here in Colorado, in spite of her regular letters to her sister Henrietta, she was completely independent and self-reliant. That, too, may have been a destination she had been seeking.

*   *   *

I have just dropped into the very place I have been seeking, but in everything it exceeds all my dreams. It is quite comfortable—in the fashion that I like.

Isabella Bird, Letter VI

The place Isabella Bird had dropped into, "a glorious region" where both "the air and life are intoxicating," was a small community in a vast, unpopulated region. Within a week of her arrival she would claim, "I live mainly out-of-doors and on horseback, wear my half-threadbare Hawaiian dress, sleep sometimes under the stars on a bed of pine boughs, ride on a Mexican saddle, and hear once more the low music of my Mexican spurs." Riding was very much a central activity to this life with which she was so delighted; Griff Evans often asked her to ride out and round up cattle, which were grazing freely, unfenced, throughout the valley and up the side canyons. Many of the cattle were his own but most of the thousand head he tended belonged to other ranchers wintering their cattle over in Estes Park. Whenever she wasn't helping herd cattle, she was free to ride wherever her fancy took her.

She lodged at the ranch run by Griffith Evans and Sam Edwards, another Welshman, for eight dollars a week, "which includes the unlimited use of a horse, when one can be found and caught." The cost included daily meals, breakfast at seven, dinner at twelve, tea at six, all repetitions of one another in terms of food—beef, potatoes, "delicious bread baked daily" that she proclaimed to be "super excellent," tea, coffee, butter, and milk. In addition to Evans and Edwards and their wives and children, the community included an American couple, Mr. and Mrs.

Dewy, a young Englishman, a silver prospector, a consumptive young hunter, Evans's adult niece, and a hired man. Mountain Jim Nugent was a frequent visitor, and occasional passersby out hunting or prospecting would drop in. Bird thought of the place as her "cheery mountain home" and, in Letter VIII, which provides her most extended explanation of her circumstances, she presented a picture of idyllic camaraderie—songs and laughter before a blazing fire, snow blowing through the chinks in the walls, the wind "rav[ing] and howl[ing]." Isabella was happy to have "a log cabin, raised on six posts, all to [her]self" and "a clean hay bed with six blankets" free of bedbugs and fleas.

Evans's ranch was located near the confluence of Fish Creek and the Big Thompson River, just above Mirror Lake, on a site originally settled in 1860 by Joel Estes, for whom the area was named and who moved on in 1866. The central building, "Queen Anne Mansion"—Isabella kept her allusions to English country estates running throughout her description of the park—was a large log cabin, unchinked, with a flat roof of "barked young spruce," hay, and mud and "roughly boarded" floors. The main room, with a stone fireplace, was "about sixteen feet square" and smaller rooms branched off from it, including a bedroom, two "bed-closets," a small dining room "at the table of which we feed in relays," and a kitchen. The central living room was where all the socializing, conversation, and singing, as well as Isabella's letter writing, occurred. In addition to the main cabin and Isabella's small cabin, set a little way off, the property had a two-room cabin, a log dairy, a wagon shed, a separate room for the hired man, a livestock shelter, and a corral.

Other than this ranch, a small homestead elsewhere in the valley, and Jim Nugent's cabin, the valley was entirely open range surrounded by mountains. In this place

Isabella Bird was serenely contented, although she resented the encroachment of civilization and the incursions of wandering hunters, killing game for sport or for transport to the mining camps and developing cities on the plains, and single-minded prospectors hoping to exploit mineral wealth. Later, after she left Colorado, the Earl of Dunraven bought out Evans as part of a scheme first to turn the valley into a private estate and hunting reserve and later, when that failed, to develop it for tourism by building the first hotel in Estes Park. When Isabella published her description of Estes Park in 1878, she claimed in a footnote that she would not have revealed its location had not others already "divulged the charms and whereabouts of these 'happy hunting grounds,' with the certain result of directing a stream of tourists into the solitary, beast-haunted paradise." Like other travel writers and nature writers before and after her, she was torn between sharing her rapture at an idyllic location and risking its ruin by encouraging others to trample through it.

* * *

When I descend from Park Hill on a warm August day, I first pay attention to the tight curves of the highway and then to the expanding view of the valley below me. Closing in on the valley floor, I realize how fully settlement and development have altered Estes Park. My hope of determining the location of Evans's ranch evaporates by the bottom of the hill. Instead of open land, I find a broad lake divided by a long two-lane causeway, Lake Estes, the reservoir behind Olympus Dam. The sites of Evans's ranch and Isabella Bird's cabin are well underwater. Past the smaller arm of the reservoir the highway expands into multiple lanes tracing the main body of the lake and arcing toward the intersection of the three major approaches to the center of the city. It is soon joined by Colorado Highway 7, which travels up the

South St. Vrain Canyon from Lyons, and then meets Highway 34, which runs through Big Thompson Canyon from
Loveland. At the intersection the traffic thickens, not only
from the convergence of highways but also from the crowd-
ing at the shopping center on the slope to the northeast.
Straight ahead, Wonderland Avenue leads up the hill to the
huge white, historic Stanley Hotel. I turn west onto a four-
lane running through the center of the business district,
dense with auto traffic on the road and foot-traffic on the
sidewalks. A side street leads me to a tightly packed parking
area, and I disembark to explore on foot. Walking should let
me move more slowly and absorb more fully what has
become of Estes Park.

The Big Thompson River still runs through Estes Park,
relegated in the city to the back side of businesses. For
much of its run, the river is remote from tourists. I follow it
east, a pleasant stroll, especially since I avoid the storefronts and crowded main sidewalks that abut the constantly flowing lanes of traffic on Elkhorn Avenue. I drift
along a section of river with a sizable stretch of undeveloped slope over on the south bank. Occasionally, I stop and
stare across the stream and try to shut out the hubbub long
enough to imagine what this river and its valley were like
before the town, the dam, and the lake. It isn't easy to do.
Isabella Bird wrote of the river "everywhere making music
through the still, long nights." The sound of the river is no
longer the same, nor, for that matter, are the nights.

Somewhere near the east end of the business district, I
stroll out to the main drag and amble back west, past art
galleries, wildlife photo galleries, coffee shops with or
without internet, cantinas, grills, mountain-themed
home décor and furniture shops, an outdoor gear store
with a climbing gym, a flyfishing store. The business
names emphasize locale: Trailridge Outfitters, Whiskey
Creek Mountain and Lodge Home Furnishings, Thirty

Below Leather, On the River Massage and Healing Arts, Rocky Mountain Stone Candles. A couple of real estate businesses stand side by side, each with plenty of property for sale—empty land priced at $119,900 and $214,900, houses between $329,000 and $989,000, a four-bedroom house for $1,190,000, a ranch for $4,975,000. Everything on the block targets conspicuous consumption, upscale recreation, vacation or investment property, luxury living. Clearly, this is no longer a valley for simple homesteaders. Elkhorn Avenue is not a street that makes you think anyone merely lives in Estes Park.

The next block wedges shops tightly together, leaving no spaces between one store and the next. Shops specialize in souvenirs, tee-shirts, bike rentals; in '60s hippiedom; in candles, outdoor clothing, fur & leather, gold, rocks, ore, toys, Japanese gifts; in the work of glass blowers and artists and artisans. A surprisingly good bookshop has a surprisingly good companion papeterie behind it. Within a dozen storefronts in the same small area, I pass two taffy shops, one snack shop, one fudge shop. At the corner of Elkhorn and Moraine Avenues a large cowboy-themed western wear store stands opposite an Indian goods store with kachinas painted on the windows. An old stone church has been subdivided into a collection of boutiques; near it is a Christmas store. I cross Elkhorn to the Mill Shops, where the river runs under a water wheel by a little park; the shops there cluster around an ethereally and altitudinally exotic theme: the Nepali Bazaar, Himalayan Imports and Adventures, Everest on Estes Spiritual Gifts of Karma, the Wapiti Bar and Grill, and Omnibus, specializing in jewelry and stained glass and metal mobiles.

I sit down near the river and watch people snacking and talking on their cellphones and chatting over bulging shopping bags. I can't quite grasp where I am, it seems so far removed from my expectations. My sense of Estes Park came from Isabella Bird and I was looking for some kind of glorious rustic retreat. I didn't know the area would be so developed and so crowded with tourists. It has a familiar feel—my wife and I visited Key West together once and revisited it for our daughter's wedding, a tourist town marketing a Margaritaville mentality; we ourselves honeymooned and later vacationed on Mackinac Island, which peddles the past with emphasis on historic structures, horses and bicycles, and the ambience of *Somewhere in Time*. Estes Park reminds me of each of them, though it is nowhere near as tawdry or as reckless as Key West, as kitschy and fudge-and-souvenir-ridden as Mackinac. But neither does it feel as site-specific as those other resort towns; in its boutiqueyness it seems like an upscale shopping district transplanted to an isolated western town, not so far removed from similar shopping districts we've happened upon in Denver.

I try to reassure myself that I haven't set out to find the Colorado of Isabella Bird's time but rather to roam the areas where she had been and find the Colorado that occupies those sites in my own time. This, I should feel confident, is precisely what I'm doing. But at the same time I can't help feeling that, except in longitude and latitude, I haven't arrived at any place I haven't been before. American commerce, perhaps in combination with American complacency, is the great leveler. Wherever you go in America you find yourself where you already were. Topography and climate vary, but not lifestyle or outlook or architecture or enterprise. I try not to wonder too long about whether my own enterprise is simply an exercise in futility.

Glumly, I head to the city library to do some local background research. It begins to rain as I enter the library, pours heavily while I work inside, and still drizzles when I leave. Under a gray sky I drive south on Fish Creek Road from around the area where the ranch was, expecting to travel vaguely near where Isabella Bird and Jim Nugent and others rode on their excursion to Longs Peak. The road winds through houses and fields and takes me out to the base of the Tahosa Valley where the rangeland spreads beneath the Twin Sisters and the Crags and the road dead-ends at the Chely Camp for teenagers. I cross over to Highway 7, perched on the side of the mountains south of town. It leads past Lily Lake—Isabella calls it "the Lake of the Lilies" and describes it with delight—and eventually reaches the turnoff toward Longs Peak, generally retracing Isabella's path. It's another steep, winding road, with sheer drop-offs and more vistas of the valley.

At the top of the hill I notice a sign for the Baldpate Inn, built in 1917, a couple of years after Rocky Mountain National Park opened practically across the road. In addition to rooms and cabins and a dining room, it houses an astonishing collection of keys, which hang everywhere in a museum room—the place was named after the mountain resort in Earl Derr Biggers's 1913 mystery *Seven Keys to Baldpate*. I turn off the highway and ease the car down the rough rocky dirt road. I take my time eating lunch, treat myself to pecan pie as a salve to frustration, chat with a waitress who has newly moved from California to Estes Park, watch a dozen or so hummingbirds hovering at a row of feeders outside the windows, and occasionally shift my gaze farther outward for a view of Estes Park from the top of the rise where Fish Creek Road used to go. The rain stops as I sit there by the window.

By the time I leave, I feel a little better about the day. Though it's cool, the sun has returned. The inn is the starting point for a hike down the Homer Rouse Trail, a short trek of a couple miles over what had been the main road from the south before Highway 7 replaced it. Now automobile travel on the dirt road ends at the far end of the Baldpate parking lot; only hikers, mountain bikers, and equestrians are allowed to follow the road down to the intersection near the turn-off for the Chely Camp.

With little forethought I launch myself into the hike, walking through stands of ponderosa pine and aspen, the trees closing off the view and giving me a sense of isolation. Only one mountain biker making the climb up toward the inn passes me along the route, and near the end of the trail I realize the path has been rerouted to avoid some private property and a solid house or two; otherwise I have the trail to myself for the hour or so it takes me to reach the Fish Creek Trailhead and return to the parking lot. Instead of going to my car, I find a place to sit on the spacious wooden deck below the inn, empty at the moment and still drying in the sun. I jot notes about my hike and the meal and feel fairly content about where I've been. I'm fully aware that I'm on a threshold here, not fully immersed in an inner world, but I feel a little closer to the area than I did walking the tourist district.

Perhaps it's a flatlander's sensibility. Never having been to the city of Estes Park, I'm familiar with it because its aspirations are those of resort towns wherever they may be located. But descending into, ascending out of, and gazing across the valley of Estes Park, I know I'm somewhere I've never been before, someplace of which I have no innate understanding. In that sense, I'm starting from the same place Isabella Bird did.

In a very short while I will return to Rocky Mountain National Park, to live in a comfortable cabin for two weeks as an artist-in-residence. The cabin was owned by the editor and author William Allen White, and that circumstance should help expand my horizons. Even as I explore terrain that may have been familiar to Isabella Bird, I would have to keep leaping the gulf between her time and mine; White will help me locate myself in the interval in between. More important, perhaps, this deeper immersion in terrain may teach me something about myself and this Colorado life to which I've committed myself.

ii

The routine of my day is breakfast at seven, then I go back and "do" my cabin and draw water from the lake, read a little, loaf a little, return to the big cabin and sweep it alternately with Mrs. Dewy, after which she reads aloud till dinner at twelve. Then I ride with Mr. Dewy, or by myself, or with Mrs. Dewy, who is learning to ride cavalier fashion in order to accompany her invalid husband, or go after cattle until supper at six. After that we all sit in the living-room, and I settle down to write to you, or mend my clothes, which are dropping to pieces. Some sit round the table playing at eucre, the strange hunters and prospectors lie on the floor smoking, and rifles are cleaned, bullets cast, fishing-flies made, fishing-tackle repaired, boots are waterproofed, part-songs are sung, and about half-past eight I cross the crisp grass to my cabin, always expecting to find something in it.

Isabella Bird, Letter VIII, October 3

I've been awake for an hour but I'm in no hurry to get out of bed. The scrabbling of a squirrel or chipmunk in the ceiling above me makes certain I don't go back to sleep. The cabin seems more of an apartment building than a single dwelling unit—I see none of my neighbors but suspect there are squirrels in the roof, mice in the walls, bats in the eaves, and perhaps a marmot under the floor. Sometimes I hear them in the night, even after I started using earplugs, and sometimes something or other thuds against the building, brushes along it, or steps onto the porch. Many of my wild neighbors are nocturnal but I also spot some of them in the daytime. I've seen a cottontail on the porch, a golden-mantled squirrel on the stone abutments along the stairs, a Colorado chipmunk on the railing, and mule deer browsing near the closed cabins behind mine. Previous temporary residents, artists of one kind or another like myself, were visited by bats, chipmunks, hummingbirds, and, once, memorably, a bear. The bear story is now routinely told as a cautionary tale about setting strong smelling garbage out on the screened-in back porch. If not for steady vigilance by the Park Service, the wildlife would make a tenement of this place in no time.

I kick off the covers and will myself to swing my legs off the bed and stand up. As is my habit first thing in the morning, I pull on sweatpants and pad through the front room, open the front door, and step out onto the porch to check the day. The sky was cloudy all night, after a long rainy afternoon and evening, and so the morning is not as chilly as other mornings have been. A few days ago the temperature dropped into the low thirties and ice was thick on my windshield when I got up. Today, as I glance down the slope at the car, parked near the road, the windows look clear. The sky is generally light before five and I can usually expect that, though the parklands before me will still be shaded, the sun will be already illuminating Longs Peak's eastern face by now. But, above the mountains to the west, more patches of blue sky and fewer clouds are showing and the day promises to clear somewhat, eventually.

Perhaps because of this morning's rain or because the tourist season is winding down, traffic is lighter than it has been. Usually, headlights coming down the switchback north on Bear Lake Road sweep past my window and flicker across the ceiling as early as four-thirty—hikers or fishermen hoping for an early start, perhaps—but today, even after sunrise, the vehicles seem mostly connected only to the road construction between Glacier Basin and Bear Lake or possibly to the morning shifts of the park rangers. I hear hummingbirds buzzing each other and magpies squabbling in the driveway. One magpie flies up to check me out on my steps, struts around the porch, and then ascends to the porch roof to pace heavily. A robin perches for a moment on the side porch railing, then sails off in the direction of thickets where I have seen goldfinches, sparrows, a green-tailed towhee, and a gray vireo. Otherwise, Moraine Park is quiet. In moments like these I often think about Isabella Bird's location a few miles and over a century away.

At Griff Evans's ranch Isabella Bird delighted in the cabin she was given, a little apart, up the slope near the lake. She notes in Letter VIII that it was "a very rough one. My door opens into a little room with a stone chimney, and that again into a small room with a hay bed, a chair with a tin basin on it, a shelf and some pegs. A small window looks on the lake, and the glories of the sunrises which I see from it are indescribable. Neither of my doors has a lock, and, to say the truth, neither will shut, as the wood has swelled." On her first night in the cabin, she heard a wolf howl and owls hoot as she was escorted from the main cabin and she claimed that she "was frightened—that is, afraid of being frightened, it was so eerie." After she fell asleep, she "was awoke by a heavy breathing, a noise something like sawing under the floor, and a pushing and upheaving, all very loud. . . . The noise went on for an hour fully, when, just as I thought the floor had been made sufficiently thin for all purposes of ingress, the sounds abruptly ceased." Eventually, she slept and the next day observed, "My hair was not, as it ought to have been, white in the morning!" The nocturnal noise came from a skunk living under the cabin; it seems disturbingly similar to the noise that occasionally wakes me in the middle of the night (probably the marmot that, the rangers claim, lives under the building) and sounds very much like something trying to gnaw through the foundation of the cabin.

Like Isabella Bird, I too am living for a limited amount of time in a park in the Rocky Mountains, in a cabin that belongs to someone else. I too am not far from the Big Thompson River, which flows through my valley as it did hers. Like her, I can see Longs Peak from my cabin and, like her, I monitor its moods. My cabin is on a slope below Eagle Cliff Mountain, on its west side, and faces southwest. Longs is directly in front of me, the first thing the sun hits in the morning. After Longs Peak turns on the day, the sun rapidly spreads across the other peaks and then, as it clears Eagle Cliff, brings daylight to Moraine Park. My view is so panoramic that I can see from Estes Cone, almost due south, past Mt. Meeker and Mt. Lady Washington near Longs Peak, to Hallett Peak and Flattop Mountain, to Stone's Peak due west, to the Mummy Range west northwest behind Deer Mountain, and to others to the north that I can't identify. This morning the distant falling rain obscures my vision of them, the curtain sometimes thicker and more impenetrable in one place than another and then thinner and more revealing in the same place a moment later. I can tell there is sunlight beyond the mountains to the southwest and in the north patches of light illuminate the sky beyond the mountains. Mt. Ypsilon emerges from the clouds and the growing brightness holds out the promise of the storm moving through eventually. I'm ready to start my day with a pot of coffee but keep looking over my shoulder as I move back inside.

The cabin I write this in is rustic by some standards—upright plank walls, weathered plank porch floor, wooden shingles on the roof, stone supports to the porch and its roof, a stone wall running along the southern and western sides of the porch, a log wall on the eastern end. The broad porch wraps around the building on two sides, but only the front porch is roofed and angled to keep the sun from entirely exposing it. Weathered rocking chairs and a small wooden table and chairs attest to quiet hours in the shade on the sunniest day. The western portion of the porch, the short end of the backwards *L*, is unroofed, giving more light to that end of the cabin, especially through the six large square panes of the window that makes up the central portion of that wall. In the afternoon the sunlight streaming in can heat the room, but the porch shades the front, south-facing portion of the house, and the cabin is cool most of the day.

That window and the cushioned bench that runs below it intimate how much more comfortable this cabin is than the one Isabella Bird had, which could easily fit into my large main front room with space to spare. This building is a National Historic Landmark and no one is allowed to use the stone fireplace on the east wall. When you consider the fireplace and add the walnut-stained wainscoting that extends from its mantle on either side to circle the room on the lower half of the walls, and the high china cabinet built diagonally across the northwest corner of the room, and a glassed-in bookcase and a roll-top desk on either side of the fireplace, and cathedral beams across the ceiling and hanging wagon-wheel-shaped light fixtures and electricity and running water, you realize that the cabin's rusticity has a certain elegance, not posh by any means but hardly backwoods minimal. Behind that large main room are a small bedroom with an adjacent indoor bathroom running off of it—the bathroom is dominated by a large, deep, old-fashioned clawfoot bathtub—and a kitchen with a refrigerator, stove, coffeemaker, and microwave. If I'm cold in the night and uncomfortable during the day, it's likely to be my fault rather than the fault of my surroundings. The level of comfort the cabin provides is merely an extension of the quality of life the original owners enjoyed, but, when I think about the simplicity of Isabella's cabin and the relative decorousness of mine, I feel rather effete and privileged. Nonetheless, like Isabella, I'm content to have a cabin all to myself, a comfortable base camp from which to explore the vast spaces of Rocky Mountain National Park.

* * *

> We had a hurricane of wind and hail last night; it was eleven before I could go to my cabin, and I only reached it with the help of two men. The moon was not up, and the sky overhead was black with clouds, when suddenly Long's Peak, which had been invisible, gleamed above the dark mountains, all glistening with new-fallen snow, on which the moon, as yet unrisen here, was shining. The evening before, after sunset, I saw another novel effect. My lake turned a brilliant orange in the twilight, and in its still mirror the mountains were reflected a deep rich blue. It is a world of wonders.

> Isabella Bird, Letter VIII, October 10

In the early days of cinema, the moving image was so mesmerizing that the most mundane and familiar occurrences seemed fascinating, electrifying, as they flickered on the screen in front of viewers. The stationary camera captured the motion of trains approaching a station, trolleys and horseless carriages and pedestrians crisscrossing a city street, the bustle of passersby in a park; the Lumière brothers' short films centered on such subjects as the departure of a ship from port, employees leaving a factory, strollers on the Champs d'Élysées, the Eiffel Tower. Such images held audiences spellbound. Andy Warhol may have been ironically commenting on—or trying to revive—that lost sense of wonder, our ability to marvel at the everyday, when he filmed the Empire State Building with a stationary camera for over eight hours.

Since I first settled in Colorado, I've been both fascinated by its sky and also perplexed by my inability to find a way to share it with anyone not standing next to me at the moment I behold it. I admire Albert Bierstadt's efforts to paint that sky—I'm very fond of his view of Longs Peak and Estes Park that now hangs in the Denver Public Library (and decorates a large number of dust jackets of Colorado books)—and at certain times have thought the sky looked just as he and Thomas Moran and Frederic Church and other Hudson River School painters depicted it. Yet I'm very aware that, to the degree their art was successful, it really only portrayed an instant, a static representation of a dynamic process. I sometimes take photographs in vain hopes that the camera will record for me in an image what I am unable to record in words, but even if I were a better photographer or an *en plein air* painter of appreciable talent, like so many of the artists I encounter in the park, I still wouldn't achieve the sense of the sky that so transfixes me. Perhaps the solution lies in going beyond the Lumières and Warhol and using some cinematic process like Cinerama or IMAX, the largest possible breadth and height to the recorded image, the largest possible screen on which to project it, the closest approximation possible in scale and scope to being beneath the sky in motion, truly overwhelmed by it.

When cold and rain deter me from hitting the hiking trails and confine me to the cabin, I find myself absorbed in the weather and its outward show. So it is today. I look out again at the mountains that have been rain-shrouded all morning. Longs Peak begins to clear, though there is still a bright white cloud, a flume of smoke, seeming to rise from somewhere near Chasm Lake at the base of the mountain's Diamond face. The high peaks begin to reveal themselves but it's still dark in the mountains at the west end of Moraine Park.

It's not simply the clouds and the changing color of the sky. Amazing things happen with light almost from minute to minute here. Looking off at the other end of Moraine Park earlier, I was struck by the way the various slopes coming down from either side of the valley behind the low ridge in the middle seemed like colored paper cutouts of mountains, but then the sunlight behind and above them lightened everything so that the slopes and the air between them were gleaming, glowing, and the wet rocks and crags visible through the darkness of the trees caught some of that light, and they gleamed too, lights in the darkness I could only fathom by examining them through fieldglasses. The play of light and shadow meta-morphoses subtly moment by moment.

Now Longs is dense with cloud and rain is falling but the sun is shining also, high above the park, and making the steady rainfall gleam as well. Rain falls between my gaze and the little pine down the hill, but at the same time sun-light falls through the window and brightens my floor as if the rain weren't there. Sometimes while hiking I have been simultaneously heated by direct sunlight and cooled by sprinkling rain. From minute to minute I'm often uncer-tain about the weather, even while I'm standing in the midst of it. At such moments I desperately long to be some sort of sponge of the senses, able to take it all in, fill myself up with it.

* * *

Isabella Bird adapted readily to her life in Estes Park. She found her "short and small" landlord, Griff Evans, con-genial. In her view he was "hospitable, careless, reckless, jolly, social, convivial, peppery, good natured, 'nobody's enemy but his own.'" She took delight in his "cheery laugh" and willingness to join the evening chorus on songs like "D'ye ken John Peel?" "Auld Lang Syne," and "John Brown." She enjoyed the interactions of the small community at the ranch: the socializing in the evenings, the secular songs on weekdays, the Sunday evening "sacred music and singing in parts" to the accompaniment of a harmonium, the conversations at any time focused on "the last grand aurora, the prospect of a snow-storm, track and sign of elk and grizzly, rumors of a bighorn herd near the lake, the canyons in which the Texan cattle were last seen, the merits of different rifles, the progress of two obvious love affairs, the probability of some one coming up from the Plains with letters, 'Mountain Jim's' latest mood or escapade, and the merits of his dog 'Ring' as compared with those of Evans's dog 'Plunk' . . . topics which are never abandoned as exhausted." She looked forward to her moments of solitude as well—"To be alone in the park from the afternoon till the last glory of the afterglow has faded, with no books but a Bible and Prayer-book, is truly delightful," and she appreciated the more direct communication with her Creator than was possible in a church filled with people conscious of Sunday fashions. She found herself surprisingly compatible with the sociable and sedentary activities on the ranch.

But she was particularly thrilled by her chances for outdoor activity, and perhaps especially appreciated Evans's willingness to acknowledge her horsewomanship by coming to her cabin early in the morning, "when Long's Peak is red, and the grass crackles with the hoar-frost," and "arous[ing] me with a cheery thump on my door" and an invitation to help drive in the cattle. Even after Isabella decided to take a tour through southern parts of the Front Range, "so at least as to be able to compare Estes Park with the better-known parts of Colorado," she claimed to have difficulty getting away because Evans continually called upon her to help with the cattle drives. She was flattered by his appreciation of her riding and herding talents. As she reported, "Two thousand head of half-wild Texan cattle are scattered in herds throughout the canyons, living on more or less suspicious terms with grizzly and brown bears, mountain lions, elk, mountain sheep, spotted deer, wolves, lynxes, wild cats, beavers, minks, skunks, chipmonks, eagles, rattlesnakes, and all the other two-legged, four-legged, vertebrate, and invertebrate inhabitants of this lonely and romantic region." Her catalog isn't always clear—rattlesnakes tend to be found at lower elevations and by wild cats, brown bears, and spotted deer she may mean bobcats, black bears, and white-tailed deer—but her observation that the cattle wandered freely among the local wildlife is well made. She noted that the cattle "show a tendency rather to the habits of wild than of domestic cattle" and that when they wandered up distant canyons "they incur a risk of being snowed up and starved, and it is necessary now and then to hunt them out and drive them down to the 'park.'"

On one occasion she and a party of four men, including Evans, and four "big, badly-trained dogs" set out after breakfast. "We were all mounted on Mexican saddles, rode, as the custom is, with light snaffle bridles, leather guards over our feet, and broad wooden stirrups, and each carried his lunch in a pouch slung on the lassoing horn of his saddle." She thought it one of "the most splendid" rides she ever took, nearly thirty miles and several hours long. They "started over the level at full gallops, leapt over trunks of trees, dashed madly down hillsides rugged with rocks or strewn with great stones, forded deep, rapid streams, saw lovely lakes and views of surpassing magnificence, startled a herd of elk with uncouth heads and in the chase . . . rode to the very base of Long's Peak." The breakneck pace and the thrills of instantaneous decisions made on the fly exhilarated her and she basked in Evans's praise of her abilities and her own sense of adventure. She was particularly proud of bringing "a herd of over a hundred out of a canyon by myself," driving them across a river, and surviving persistent attacks on her horse by "one specially vicious cow." She found herself depending on her cow pony on several occasions when cows rushed at her. By the time the cattle were all corralled the weather had turned cold and snow began to fall, and they "galloped the last mile and a half in four and a half minutes."

The park days of Isabella Bird kept her ranging across the valleys and into the canyons, continually breathing the autumn mountain air and feeling the days warm up and the nights cool down, and having her choice of energetic activity, charged social interaction, or peaceful solitude. They were days when she was fully alive in the moment and, for the most part, she reveled in them.

*   *   *

Estes Park, the town that fills the valley, refers to itself as the Gateway to Rocky Mountain National Park. To reach Moraine Park, where I temporarily reside, you have to pass through the "gateway" and out the western side, drive up to the Beaver Meadows entrance to the national park, and wind your way down Bear Lake Road a couple of miles. It's a ten- to fifteen-minute drive, depending on the density of traffic in the center of town and at the park entrance fee stations, from the sunken site of Griff Evans's ranch. Both Estes Park and Moraine Park are valleys linked by the Big Thompson River, which flows through both, and it's difficult to imagine the overdeveloped Estes valley as unpopulated and open as the Moraine meadows.

Two paved roads, the one to Bear Lake crossing below my cabin and, at nearly a right angle, the shorter one to Moraine Park Campground, skirt this two-mile by one-mile rectangle of meadow and riverbed on roughly its eastern and northern margins; a dirt road leading to inholder cabins—property still privately owned in the midst of public lands—disappears below the trees on the southern margin.

The broad floor of the valley is open. From the southwestern corner Cub Creek wanders out to join the Big Thompson, which begins farther off to the west, up near the Continental Divide, almost all the way across the national park. The Big Thompson flows down through Forest Canyon, all the while picking up tributaries, surges through a narrow channel and emerges at the west end of Moraine Park, then braids its way across the valley floor to its southeast corner, and plunges down to meet icy Glacier Creek and rush toward Estes Park.

Moraine Park would really be a fitting moniker for many of the valleys on the east side of Rocky Mountain National Park, which often were shaped by glaciers plowing their way down earlier river valleys. Moraines deposited by the Thompson Glacier, estimated to have been an ice mass at least 750 feet deep, form the boundaries of Moraine Park. The pragmatically named and thickly wooded South Lateral Moraine stretches the full length of Moraine Park and looms over the inholder cabins; a smaller, unnamed lateral moraine on the other side separates this park from Beaver Meadows farther north; the terminal moraine at my end of the park once created a lake of glacial meltwater that time and silt and plant decay filled in to form the savannah floor. Evidence of the glacial past is abundant, though it takes a geological cast of mind to notice it in the immediacy of the present moment.

Though Isabella Bird doesn't specifically indicate whether she ever rode into the valley we now designate as Moraine Park, it seems likely, given the lushness of grass along the Big Thompson and the freedom of cattle to range everywhere, that her wrangling days, if not her random rambles, brought her into the area. But it matters little where she might have actually roamed. I'm touring terrain and topography rather than historical and biographical sites, and my park days give me ample opportunity to take in the landscape at a leisurely, contemplative pace. If I'm emulating her at all, it's in reveling in my solitary moments in the park.

Today I intend to circle the South Lateral Moraine. I take the shuttle bus from the Moraine Park Museum near my cabin to Hollowell Park, the next valley south from Moraine Park, and get off at the Mill Creek Trailhead. It's a little before ten in the morning, a late start to the day, when I start hiking.

The tramp across the mostly flat, open meadow is hot and exposed. Hollowell Park seems, to my untrained eye, rampant with native grasses, unlike Moraine Park, where ranching and tourism introduced hardy and prolific invasive species. After a half-mile or so, the trail winds around toward the Bierstadt Moraine on the south side of Hollowell Park, away from the South Lateral Moraine that here is the northern margin. I climb a steep, broad, stepped path to a point where the trail meets Mill Creek. It's a narrow, gushing stream, much clogged with fallen timber but open in this spot where two channels round small mossy boulders and spread across a flat pebble-strewn shelf before gliding under fallen trees and over the lip. The creek rushes by close to where I stand. I pause here and close my eyes to listen to the rush of mountain water; behind my eyelids light still dances, dappled by the reflection of sunlight in the water near my feet. The sunlight finds its way easily through tall aspens, whose thin crowns are thirty or forty feet above the creek. For a few moments longer I try to make creekflow and forest breeze the entire focus of my consciousness.

I'm in no hurry to push on, but eventually I do. The trail rises steadily but easily, then forks in two directions, one leading toward Cub Lake, the direction I need to go, the other heading across a wooden bridge toward Mill Creek Basin and a campground there. I linger only a few moments on the bridge to listen to the creek again. I know that my path will lead away from it.

"In the brookleap of / afternoon, sunlight shapes itself / like a hand," Wayne Dodd wrote, in a poem I discovered in the cabin's artist-in-residence logbook. It was this poem, "Beside Mill Creek," that made me consider taking the Mill Creek Trail in the first place; that, and the chance to spend time listening to "the sound of mountain water" (in Wallace Stegner's phrase). To walk alongside the creek is to hear the endlessly variable voice of mountain water, the way it deepens or lightens, roars or gurgles, flows or foams, with changes in volume, speed, the shape of the creekbed, the nature of the banks that enclose it (or in spring disappear beneath it). "[T]he air your skin / ripples in is green / with duration," Dodd wrote. "You are how the earth remembers / itself, how it knows time / as sensation." The shapes and sounds of flowing, tumbling water have always fascinated me, and Mill Creek, however modest in scale, easily satisfies my longing.

At this point, a mostly flat stretch, the creek flows through tall shrubs, willow or alder birch. Looking up the trail toward Cub Lake, I notice considerably more aspen. Steep Mountain rises to the north, just in front of the South Lateral Moraine. The creek can still be heard as I walk on but disappears from sight under lush thickets; gradually, I angle away from it and its gurgle fades away. I hike toward the aspens through a field of purple thistles, taller than I, some as tall as sunflowers. The trail through the trees, at first rocky and rough, grows smooth as I cross another field toward a towering stand of aspens.

The aspen stand, the trees' lower bark blackened by the nibbling of elk, is dense and broad and the trail winds steeply up through them. Fir closes in with aspen, until the trail emerges at a more open level space where junipers thick with unripe berries are surrounded by a scattering of relatively young ponderosa pines. Then an open field, the clack of grasshoppers, wind rustling widespread aspen and a few tall ponderosas and me. I pass through a dry, gritty ponderosa parkland, then come onto a descent toward a grassy valley filled again with aspen and fir. The grasshoppers achieve the volume of the Mormon Tabernacle Choir. At the bottom of the slope I reach another fork and take the one that promises to lead to Cub Lake. All of this is new to me, and I try to avoid settling into the rhythm of the trail, the steady pace of the hike, in order to take in as much as I can as I pass through it.

Another long hot climb, the trail straight and gritty up through pines, the sun directly overhead a half-hour or more before noon. I stop and check my pack for trail snacks and liquid. I've brought an unfamiliar energy drink, vitamin water with a sweet orange flavor that my thirst makes acceptable. The whole grain and yogurt bar I decided to experiment with is as tough to chew as moldy logs and about as flavorful. I take only a bite or two, then put it away and eat a couple handfuls of trail mix.

A few minutes past noon. After a hot ascent, a crossing of a mostly flat ridge, a long, rocky, rubbly, screey descent, I find myself overlooking Cub Lake from its western end. I like having an overview of my destination, noting a ring of water lilies especially thick along the northern shore. A narrow open meadow stretches east away from the lake, and dark firs grow up the steep slopes surrounding the lake, especially on the South Lateral Moraine. A slope of that moraine shuts off the view of the meadows beyond the lake; the low ridge to the north that slopes back toward Windy Gulch separates this lake from the higher rocky walls of the Gorge of the Thompson Glacier, where the Big Thompson itself flows. In the far distance, through binoculars, I can see Moraine Park and the vicinity of my cabin. For the first time in the hike I observe other people moving below me. Their chatter drifts unintelligibly up to me on the overlook. The chickarees, vociferous red squirrels who have been complaining about my passage from time to time, are now more often silent.

It takes me another half-hour to descend to the shore of Cub Lake. Hikers lunch on the rocks at the bottom of the south-facing slope, under pines, looking across at huge firs thick on the north-facing slope. Greenwinged teal dabble in the reeds at the east end of the lake. I look for a place along the shore as distant as possible from other hikers and settle for a boulder close to the water, in earshot of two or three different parties. I divest myself of my daypack, try another bite of the yogurt bar, give up on it for good, and settle for a snack of trail mix and plain water. I'm somewhat surprised, but hardly disappointed, not to see more hikers—the Cub Lake Trail is an easy hike from the Moraine Park end, relatively short, readily accessible, the change in elevation slight; it's generally popular, one reason I avoided it so long—but it's a weekday and, in the middle of August, the tourist season is already starting to wind down, and the people relaxing on the rocks are widely spread out.

The remaining descent from Cub Lake, though not particularly arduous, is rocky and rough for most of the two miles to the trailhead. It circles the western ridge and piles of boulders and then opens into marshland and finally, with a short descent alive with flowers, exposes the whole of Moraine Park to view. I barely arrive at the trailhead before the shuttle appears and I ride back to the museum and cut across the slope to the cabin, tired and pleased with myself for the solitary circuit I have made around the South Lateral Moraine.

Late in the day, near sundown, after an afternoon of busyness, an early supper, and a long stretch of journaling, I find that the burble of Mill Creek is still on my mind and I long to hear it again. I drive myself to Hollowell Park, scurry up to the open spot where I'd sat earlier, and sit fending off mosquitoes as I tape-record many minutes of the sound of mountain water, the sound that will let me meditate my way back here, no matter how far away I am.

I haven't spent the day the way Isabella spent hers, but I have no difficulty amending her remark to fit my circumstance: to be alone in the park from the afternoon till the last glory of the afterglow has faded, with no companion but the sound of mountain water, is truly delightful.

*　*　*

"Such as it is, Estes Park is mine," Isabella Bird famously declared, in the October 2 section of Letter VIII, "mine by right of love, appropriation, and appreciation." She then provided a long list of attributes of the park she was "seizing." She'd been in the park for a week.

A Lady's Life in the Rocky Mountains is laced throughout with Isabella's enthusiastic appreciation of landscape. The very first letter opens with an admiring passage about Lake Tahoe: "I have found a dream of beauty at which one might look all one's life and sigh. Not lovable, like the Sandwich Islands, but beautiful in its own way! A strictly North American beauty—snow-splotched mountains, huge pines, redwoods, sugar pines, silver spruce; a crystalline atmosphere, waves of the richest colour; and a pine-hung lake which mirrors all beauty on its surface." The passage reminds readers (or intimates to those unfamiliar with her earlier book) how attached she became to her life in Hawaii; throughout the book, Hawaii is often invoked for comparison with certain locales and, in addition, the Alps, particularly the Matterhorn, surface for issues of scale and grandeur when she tries to take the measure of the Rockies and Longs Peak. In trying to express admiration and excitement over a locale, it's easy for a writer to gush with generalizations and to sentimentalize the settings, as so many of

Isabella's predecessors and contemporaries have been accused of doing.

But in Letter VIII, where we find her most effusive description of the park—and it's well to remember that the original letter to Henrietta was written after Bird's climb up Longs Peak, a summit even experienced climbers still hold in reverence—the length and the detail and the continual circling back to her theme ("But what is Estes Park?") suggests a determined wrestling with her feelings. She isn't merely recording experience here, but trying to determine all the elements that make the park so inspiring and fulfilling for her. What energizes Isabella's writing about locale in her Estes Park chapters grows out of what energizes *her* while she's there.

Since this is the case, I ought to acknowledge that I feel a fundamental sympathy with Isabella's perspective; her enthusiasms connect to my own innate proclivities—it's not likely that I would be following her path if she hadn't written so forcefully about Estes Park and if I weren't already in tune with her central passions. I'm also in sympathy with the "rights" by which she declares the valley to be hers, the rights of love, appropriation, and appreciation. I take them to identify, in order, emotional, experiential, and aesthetic responses to place, responses that are not really separate but tangled, each fostering and reinforcing the others. Experience instigates appreciation and both inspire love, which in turn enhances experience and appreciation recursively.

My stay in Rocky Mountain National Park corresponds to Isabella's stay in Estes, even if my solitude in the William Allen White cabin is not strictly equivalent to her socializing at the Evans ranch, and if the wilderness she rode through was literally unbounded while mine, for all its vastness, is preserved, restored, mapped and delineated, and frequently bustling. I spiral out from my center in Moraine Park to walk a portion of Black Canyon, on the north side of the park, an area I know she explored as well; to hike up Glacier Gorge beyond Black Lake; to climb to the top of Flattop Mountain and behold the terrain beyond the Continental Divide and the limitless openness of the top of the continent. I drive rough Fall River Road up to the Alpine Visitors' Center at the top of the park and return by way of smooth Trail Ridge Road, having taken in the tundra and risen in an afternoon through riparian, montane, subalpine, and alpine zones and then descended back through them again. My wife is with me on some of these excursions and together we also climb nearby Deer Mountain and, right behind the cabin, Eagle Cliff Mountain. On my own, in preparation for a Longs Peak climb that weather eventually forestalls during the residency, I walk up to Chasm Lake, below the Diamond face of Longs Peak and 2,500 feet lower than the summit.

I have little sense in these outings of covering ground Isabella would have covered; instead, I'm aware of space all around me, the prospect of continually encountering new terrain, the chance to move beyond my limits. Isabella's exuberance arose from wild rides across open range; mine arises from achieving ever higher altitude and pushing myself beyond my customary physical limits. Like Isabella, I'm continually thrilled to be where I am and I take delight in myself for who I seem to be while I'm here.

This is a kind of communion. If I can't occupy Isabella's space in time and place, I can certainly identify with the feelings she gives voice to. The sense of identification, of connection, with a place that enthralls you can make you confused about whether you possess the place or the place possesses you. But under these terms, such as they are, the Park is mine.

iii

Morning watch. Rewards of being slow off the mark. Usually by now I'd be off hiking one of the trails, but this morning I'm hunched over the cabin's heavy oak dining table, shifting through notes and reading and trying to catch up on journalkeeping. A sudden cacophony of coyotes, close to the cabin, startles me off the page. In one motion I drop my pen, scoop up my camera and binoculars, rise from my chair, and lunge toward the porch. I immediately spot five coyotes as I come through the door. They are twenty yards down the slope, yowling and yipping, heads raised to the sky, and stopping to regroup after emerging from a tangle of rocks, shrubs, and young trees. Their impromptu chorus pierces the clear morning air but lasts only a moment longer. They lapse into silence again as they descend in ragged formation, black patches bouncing at the tips of their tails. At the foot of the hill they divide around my parked car, file onto the paved road, pause casually, almost indifferently, for one lone passing vehicle, and then jog into the sparse growth of grass and shrubs on the valley floor.

On the porch, midway up the slope, I have a panoramic vantage point above Moraine Park. I watch the coyotes drift through the scrub, searching for ground squirrels plentiful in the dryer portions of the meadow. They gather again around a kill or a promising place where underground prey might emerge. The darker adult, the one with a distinctive white patch under his chin, soon strikes off on his own, and gradually the others wander away; the smallest one is the last to go, remaining at the spot and chewing on something, then lifting his leg, spraying a bush, and trotting off after the others. The coyotes range widely, two youngsters keeping close behind the light-colored adult, and the third pup following the darker one. The trio converges on a mound of dark green growth and stalk slowly through it while the pair strides briskly along the river. I admire their loping gait, their effortless canter across the field, their sharp attention to opportunity.

Is one of these adults the coyote I saw twice last week, the first days I was here? Beginning two weeks as an artist-in-residence, I'd driven up the private dirt drive circling behind the cabin, unpacked clothing, hiking gear, food-stuffs, books, and journals, and then driven my car back down to my designated parking space. Until I packed up again, for the rest of my stay I'd have to climb up the steep slope to the cabin rather than drive. In the moment I took to lean idly against the car, survey the open meadow stretching to the west and postpone the climb, the coyote appeared along the road. Cars were slowing near me because the drivers had spotted him. He was maybe thirty yards away from me. When the traffic paused, he crossed the road and began stalking something in the brush. He edged himself forward with deliberate, controlled steps, pounced, missed, whirled around for a second chance he didn't get, pawed at the ground briefly, then loped off into a trough behind a thicket.

By the time I'd climbed to the cabin the coyote had returned, slowing traffic again and veering toward the dirt drive beyond my car. The parking area across the way was nearly full and groups of tourists crowded along the path across the meadow to watch elk grazing in the high grass along the river. Perhaps the presence of all those humans persuaded him to retreat or perhaps he'd fed enough. Without a glance at people in cars doing bad coyote impressions to get his attention, he crossed the road again, slipped into the driveway, and slowly proceeded up the dirt road, finally disappearing into the underbrush.

I don't know if it was the same coyote or another—on those early sightings I paid little attention to details like coloring and markings—that appeared the next evening about the same time and caused another traffic jam. People were lining the trail to watch the coyote. He was hunting through the meadow parallel to the path, concentrating on ground squirrels and ignoring a line of shutterbugs keeping pace with him. He pounced unsuccessfully once and then soon afterwards caught a squirrel and shook it in his jaws. The bystanders, some of whom perhaps recorded the kill on film, kept photographing while he ate his dinner. I remember wondering: What's in this for the coyote? He behaves as if he's playing the part of a predator in a Natureland theme park. Is the Trickster aware that shuffling humans on gravel make more noise than stalking canines on grass and thus distract his prey for him? Coyote clearly knew that he had nothing to fear from the people, most of whom started milling forward toward the nearby elk even before he vanished into the thickets.

Perhaps the coyote I saw hunting flagrantly among tourists last week is one of the adults in the group I watch this morning—then foraging alone for food for the pups, now leading an early outing where the youngsters get to join in the hunt. Unlike a week ago, this morning I am the only witness to the coyotes' early hunt. I don't mind admitting that I like having them to myself. Soon both adults and one of the pups are across the river, their heads popping out of the tall grass, while two pups remain on the other side, gazing anxiously after them. Then, once the sun lights the major portion of the bottomland, all the coyotes dissolve into the deep grass and I can find no sign of them.

I think of this as a John Burroughs morning. Burroughs, who hung out in the woods in a more rustic cabin than mine, dubbed Slabsides, claimed to have "a half-defined suspicion" that, by "remain[ing] quiet and keep[ing] a sharp lookout," everything he wanted to see would eventually pass in front of him. Keeping close by my own cabin, the world comes to me. In the past several days I've seen cottontails, mule deer, magpies, a house wren, a green-tailed towhee, a Colorado chipmunk, a golden-mantled squirrel, all roaming by my windows, racing across my porch, or perching in the bushes nearby. Twice this morning, while I watch the coyotes, a hummingbird wings right in front of me and hovers; both times the chiming noise he makes in flight and his sudden appearance out of nowhere, like a feat of prestidigitation, surprise me. Like the coyotes' unexpected yowling earlier, the hummingbird's unexpected nearness makes me more alert to my surroundings, makes me feel rewarded simply for being here.

*   *   *

I have to admit that a large part of the appeal of this Rocky Mountain residency was the chance to stay in William Allen White's cabin. In his time, the first half of the twentieth century, he was a well-known figure—the owner/editor of the *Emporia (Kansas) Gazette*, a nationally published journalist, novelist, political commentator, biographer of presidents, and friend of the prominent and celebrated. In public libraries it's still fairly easy to find copies of *The Autobiography of William Allen White*, ironically left unedited and unfinished at his death and completed and published posthumously by his son, and *Forty Years on Main Street*, a good sampling of his editorials and articles, compiled by Russell H. Fitzgibbon and published in 1937. Though most of what an editorialist writes against deadline is only pertinent and timely for the day, White also wrote items in the vein of the familiar essay. His essayist's voice was warm, gracious, personable, and lively; his piece on turning sixty-five, for example, is one that ought to be more readily available than it is, perhaps sent out to ordinary citizens along with the notice of eligibility for Social Security.

White's best-known work is "Mary White," the essay/editorial he wrote on the death of his daughter at sixteen, from a head injury incurred while horseback riding. The essay opens with an irreverent, almost jocular tone, perhaps reminiscent of Mary's own spirit: "The Associated Press reports carrying the news of Mary White's death declared that it came as the result of a fall from a horse. How she would have hooted at that! She never fell from a horse in her life. Horses have fallen on her and with her— 'I'm always trying to hold 'em in my lap,' she used to say. But she was proud of few things, and one of them was that she could ride anything that had four legs and hair." In its specific detail and attitude the essay is a thorough eulogy, bringing to life Mary's energy and vitality, her independence and integrity, her sense of humor and social justice. The piece is properly sentimental and emotional but also memorably expressed. It concludes: "A rift in the clouds in a gray day threw a shaft of sunlight upon her coffin as her nervous, energetic little body sank to its last sleep. But the soul of her, the glowing, gorgeous, fervent soul of her, surely was flaming in eager joy upon some other dawn."

First published on May 17, 1921, the day after her funeral, and frequently reprinted over the years, the essay is beautiful and affecting, and it moves me each time I read it. It is a powerful evocation of Mary White's personality and a delicately balanced expression of her father's love and grief as well as of his ingrained decency. What touches me most about it, as both an essayist and as a parent, is how it puts into perspective the profoundest and most enduring feelings of a private individual against the considerable and temporary prominence of a public figure.

It's hard not to be mindful of the Whites' presence here. The spacious main room, roughly thirty feet by fifteen feet, dominates the cabin. Its vaulted and beamed ceiling, wainscoted walls, fireplace, built-in cabinets and bookcase, and rolltop desk all bespeak a taste for rustic comfort. The western wall is centered on a low bench with flat green cushions on top and storage units secreted within running below an enormous window, with a view of Moraine Park across the unroofed section of porch. Some of the furnishings in the cabin were originally owned by the Whites: the rolltop desk and swivel chair, the kitchen Hoosier (an ingenious early-twentieth-century storage unit), the wicker rockers on the porch where distinguished guests may have sat. These authentic biographical trappings make the experience of staying in the cabin not only an occasion for creative sanctuary but also a chance for historical connection.

It's also hard not to be aware of the family tragedy that clouded the last decades of their lives. In the White cabin, on top of the rolltop, is a small double picture frame with a five-by-seven-inch photo of Mary White on the left and a typed portion of her father's essay on the right. In the nearby Moraine Park Museum hangs a fabric and appliqué work by Susan Ragan, a past artist-in-residence, titled "Mary's World." It is a patchwork quilt into which have been inserted photos of Mary White and her family—her parents, William and Sallie, and her brother, Bill—as well as photos of the cabin and White at work at a log desk in his "office and retreat" above the main building. On one side of the quilt, handwritten text runs through three panels separated by triangular patterned conifer trees; the words are a condensed rephrasing of White's essay about Mary. Except for a gouache rendering of lichens, it is the only artwork in the museum that is not a landscape.

I understand why an artist would want to honor William Allen White, not merely for the use of the hall, as it were—for the legacy of this comfortable cabin—but also for the accomplishment of a piece of literary art that grows out of the deepest, most intimate human experience. Some portion of this is what we all (we "artists" in or out of residence) want to accomplish. As an essayist, I say to William White, Thanks for that example. And thanks for this place of temporary sanctuary, inspiration, and restoration. I hope what any of us accomplishes here honors that legacy.

As an essayist occupying a space that belonged to another essayist, I feel a certain bond with William White and I'm curious to know how deep it runs. My own presence in the cabin as an artist-in-residence is largely an effort to further my growth as an essayist of place. I like to think of myself as an *en plein air* writer, setting up my daybook or journal like a canvas or sketchpad on an easel and painting what I see with words. I'm here to write about what I discover here. White was a man with a social conscience and an editorial position; despite the occasional essays on personal events and experiences, writing about the politics of his community and his nation was his most urgent concern. Aside from brief mentions in his autobiography, he seems to have left no essays or letters or journal entries that describe his experiences here more fully, more intimately. I have only intuitions gleaned from my own experiences, along with some supposition and surmise inferred from items in his autobiography, to give me any feeling for what William White and I are sharing on this common ground.

The last photograph of White in Colorado was taken in the living room cabin in the summer of 1943, while he and his wife, Sallie, posed at either end of the window seat, Moraine Park partly visible in the space between them. A painter's enlarged reproduction of the photo hangs above White's rolltop desk. Each time I sit on the window seat, journal or daybook and pen in hand, binoculars on the window shelf, I am aware that I'm sitting where William Allen White sat, and I sometimes wonder, how much of what I see—and what I feel about what I see—echoes what White saw and felt?

*   *   *

Each morning, usually well before sunrise, I shuffle stiffly out of the bedroom and tread barefoot to the front door, to glance outside and gauge the mood of Moraine Park. Often, because the nights in the mountains are so much cooler than the days and the valley floor is moist from the meanders of the river or an evening rain the night before, I see horizontal cylinders of bright fog lying idly on the savannah. Usually, no matter what the weather, I step out onto the porch for a closer look, savoring a moment of solitude shared only with the morning. If the day promises to be clear and bright, I simply smile at my good fortune and go back inside to make my toast and coffee and plan a distant outing. But on a day when seemingly tangible rollers of fog lie baled and pulsing, I long to go down to the river and vanish into the fog where it conceals the savannah. Today I don't resist my longing but instead surrender eagerly to it.

I know just where to go, to a massive glacial erratic nearly my height that demands some agility to mount. I descend my hill, cross the paved road and the unpaved parking area and the wooden bridge, and stride along a narrow footpath through grasses heavy with dew. It's a mid-August morning but it's cold. Frost is clinging to the grasses and the flowers, ice pellets hard enough that, when I pause to touch them, my fingers' warmth, now rapidly decreasing, can't melt them. Soon I seat myself on this granite rock, my nose and hands cold, my pants legs and shoes wet, watching the fog drift low above Moraine Park. The sun already gilds the mountaintops, but has yet to climb high enough to light this valley. I turn around and see its glare just rising above the shoulder of Eagle Cliff Mountain behind and above the cabin. The mountains across the valley are still dark but the spaces between the near and the far mountains are filled with mist as the frost metamorphoses into fog and rises. I wait until the sun is full over Eagle Cliff, shining, without warmth, on me on my rock, then swivel away from the glare and discover my solitary shadow cast long on the grasses, extending from the larger, elongated shadow of the rock. In shadow we erratics have merged.

Ahead of me the fog is retreating, and the open space between it and me has broadened. The fog seems to be marching back up the valley, like a receding glacier. The sun lifts wisps of mist from the plants and they lose their frosty pallor and blush moist green. In the distance I hear the bugling of elk, a single call answered by a chorus. The fog in the distance is thinner and grayer than the white thickness that greeted my gaze an hour ago. Most of the park is in sunlight except under Eagle Cliff Mountain, and behind me, in shadow still, the plants are all gleaming with ice, waiting for the sun to relieve them. All the while the gurgling creek flows swiftly, shallowly across the glacial debris that forms this meadow, loose pebbly soil. It doesn't take long before only the faintest haze lingers in the air between me and the distant roche moutonnée and the western wall of Moraine Park beyond it. I puff out a little steamy breath to watch it float away toward the sun, which is just beginning to warm my cheek. No luck with my hands. Birds become active; sparrows flit low above the ground, dashing into shrubs and tall grass, and magpies glide over the ground, then land and strut.

It looks like another lovely morning in Moraine Park. By the time I slide off my rock and stroll along the river back to the bridge, more people have appeared in the area—a woman taking close-ups of plants, a fisherman or two, a solitary walker. I wonder how much of this morning transformation they came early enough to see. The day will be splendid, brilliant, ideal, again, but the glory of Moraine Park is its metamorphosis, its unheralded and inevitable shape-shifting, the changes in sky and shadow and light and texture that so often make each view from the cabin porch a new experience. How grand to have a stationary vantage point on a constantly changing landscape, the time to take in whatever I behold, the chance to be wakeful in the fog until it clears.

*   *   *

Moraine Park takes the second part of its name from the French word *parc* as applied to open valleys and meadow-lands among the mountains—Hollowell Park is just to the south of Moraine Park; North Park, Middle Park, and South Park are major basins separating the Front Range of the Rockies from ranges farther west—and also occurring, Anglicized, in the names of Colorado towns—nearby Estes Park, for example, and Allenspark and Winter Park. Moraine Park and Hollowell Park are located on the eastern side of Rocky Mountain National Park, in whose title the word *park* is meant to indicate a distinct, specially reserved area, in this case, a vast mountainous tract preserved by the federal government in 1915. The term *National Park* tells you nothing about geography; the term *Moraine Park* tells you everything about this location.

The first part of Moraine Park's name comes from its glacial origins, the moraines deposited to form its boundaries on three sides. The park is broad and flat between the slopes of the moraines and the distant granite walls of the glacial gorge.

Midway across Moraine Park to the west, erupting out of the grasses, is the roche moutonnée, the "sheep rock" outcropping in the middle of the meadow. The roche moutonnée (pronounced "roe-chay moo-toe-nay") intrigues me because it resisted the glacier's flow, all that force of ice, and made the glacier flow over and around it. It held its ground through millennia of the glacier's advance, its stasis, melting, and retreat, its lake's slow solidification. Once the roche moutonnée was an island in that lake and now it is an island of rock in a flat, grassy savannah, and though the trees have made little progress colonizing the meadow, the roche moutonnée has gathered enough soil to nurture them itself. The roche moutonnée is steadfast and solidly anchored and, over eighteen hundred centuries, a witness to the valley's ancient beginnings and long history, the unassuming, unprepossessing emblem of indefatigable time. William Allen White, who summered here with friends and family over a span of fifty-some years, and I, who will reside for two weeks in his cabin, alone except for a weekend when my wife joins me, are, by comparison, the merest transients, simply sprigs of river birch in the current of the Big Thompson.

The cabin perches part-way up the slope between the valley floor and the abrupt bluffs of Eagle Cliff Mountain. I look out on a circle of mountains. On a clear day I can identify almost all of them; on a rainy day the clouds sheer off their peaks, fill the lowlands between them with a screen of mist and fog. When there is rain in Moraine Park, the sunlight often still gleams beyond the mountains, or shines through the rain, making the raindrops crystalline and brilliant.

Here in the window seat, looking out at Moraine Park, my notebook perched unsteadily on my knee and a staticy transmission of classical music playing on the radio, I struggle to interpret and identify what I see. A few moments ago, across the valley, gray-white ragged tufts draped themselves along the medial ridge and in the gulches beside it, as if they could not decide whether to be clouds or fog. Rain-saturated air hung like gauze curtains between the cabin and that end of the valley, but there was enough light in the tufts to make them seem alive, arguing among themselves whether to lift off the landscape or let their watery mass sink further onto it. Yet, by the time I write so meager a description of the scene, the tufts elect to sink, to merge—with the exception of one dingy band of darker gray above the lowest white near the bottom of the South Lateral Moraine—almost seamlessly with the sky. Now the sky in the west, from south to north, is one almost uniform color, a thick, tightly woven cotton shroud of spectral white. I can still see the grassland and shiny stretches of meandering river, but there is no breeze, no sign of life, just a heavy, chilly stillness. This treetop-level sky seems to be creeping toward the cabin. Ragged, tattered wisps of cloud unravel from the bottom and hang down, and as the space beneath the sky becomes gauzier and more translucent I suspect it's being filled with a slowly advancing, almost lackadaisical rain.

The weather confines me to quarters but it gives me time to sit on the window seat and keep a sharp lookout on Moraine Park. I wonder how often William Allen White sat here and what he saw. Because I saw that photo of the Whites at the window before I ever came to the cabin, I first imagined, with some pleasure, that when I sat here I would see the same view he saw. In 1921, when his daughter Mary died and his son Bill went back to college, White was in his early fifties, with more than twenty years left to him. I suspect that, gazing out this window or out of the windows of his writing cabin higher up, he must have viewed the park with considerable melancholy, yet it's hard to know how well he was comforted by the scene that so often before had restored him.

*   *   *

To William Allen White, Moraine Park was a special place. He had vacationed here in 1889, with college chums from

Kansas, "camped in a cabin by the Big Thompson River in Moraine Park, a valley above Estes," as he put it in his auto-biography. He claimed it "was the most notable summer I had ever had," and wrote fondly of conversations with his chums and afternoons reading in "a hammock in the pine woods above the cabin." They visited the ghost town of Lulu City on the western side of the Continental Divide and twice that summer White climbed Longs Peak. "It is a hard, long climb," he wrote. "Of its 14,500 feet you go up 2,000 on all fours, creeping and climbing along crevices and cracks in almost perpendicular rocks. You come down on all fives until you strike a level 2,000 feet above timber-line. Then you walk a mile over huge boulders, jumping from one to another." The first time he reached the summit he thought he could see, to the south, "the smoke of Pueblo two hundred miles away" and, to the north, Wyoming. But he was unnerved by the descent: "When I started down that precipice I was frightened, literally scared numb and stiff, and Kellogg [who climbed it with him] had to coax me down." Nonetheless, he thought his experience in Moraine Park was the making of him: "If I ever grew up and became a man, it was in the summer of 1889, in Colorado, in a little log cabin filled with a dozen boys on the Big Thompson River."

Later, when he married Sallie Lindsay, they spent part of their honeymoon in Moraine Park, in May of 1893, accom-panied by Sallie's mother and frail teenaged brother, Milton. As White tells it, "We rented for five dollars for the season a log cabin on the banks of the Big Thompson River, far up in the canyon a mile and a half from any human habitation, in the heart of what became, many years later, Rocky Moun-tain National Park. We bedded on spruce boughs, cooked over an open fire, and Milton furnished the fish. He was a wonderful fisherman. We picked red raspberries and wild strawberries and had watercress unlimited for salads, bought fresh beef from the ranch house when they butchered, and fared sumptuously if roughly." It was an idyll of a different kind than his earlier stay.

For a time the Whites vacationed in Manitou Springs, near Colorado Springs, and returned to the Estes Park area in 1911, renting a cottage from a university professor from Kansas (the area had a concentration of Kansas academics and professional men). Most of the summers afterwards followed the pattern he established that year: "[We] set ourselves up on the side of a mountain, with the two children, their Grandma White and their Aunt Jessie Lindsay. I set up a tent a hundred feet up the hill, put my cot and a typewriter there, and every morning after breakfast went up to write. It was a summer of pure delight." Family life added to making the summer a "sheer joy": "In the evenings we gathered the children, seven and eleven, around the fireplace and read Dickens until Mary had to be lugged off dead asleep to bed, and Bill, who always wanted more, had to be dragged to his couch; then his mother and I sat up until all hours while she read aloud to me." The balance of strenuous work habits and familial interaction seems to be one White strove for, though it's most often his work that gets the emphasis in his autobiography.

The Whites eventually made the possibility of summers in Moraine Park more permanent. In the hectic election year of 1912, for "a few hundred dollars," they "bought a cabin on a hillside near Estes Park, Colorado. It was surrounded on three sides by snowcapped mountains that looked down into a valley, a peaceful green valley through which the Big Thompson River wound its way." Looking back on that summer, he said of the cabin that "it was to be for all our lives a haven and refuge" and "a place of peace to which we were to withdraw in summers for thirty years and more." Such remarks make his feeling for the place seem uncomplicated and unambiguous.

Yet elsewhere in his unedited autobiography he reveals something of the preoccupation with his work back home that was typical of him even in the midst of this "haven and refuge." He also writes of that same summer in the cabin, "I don't know how or when I squeezed in two weeks . . . But the fortnight filled the cisterns of my spiritual and physical energy, and I came back to Kansas full of a dozen maturing plans, mostly political." His attention was clearly divided.

And the pattern of his summers is soon clear. Though he treasured the cabin, "only eighteen by twenty-four, with a fireplace in a little living room, two bedrooms, and a kitchen," by the following summer he could report having "enlarged our cabin, building a fourteen-foot porch on three sides of it. We also built a log cabin one hundred feet up the hill, and two small bedroom cabins, so we were living like princes." The log cabin on the hill was White's Colorado office. "So for a couple of months I went up from the main cabin of our Colorado home to the log cabin on the hill and pecked away at my typewriter." As he did in the tent on the hillside, White created a private workspace for himself, complete with extra bedroom, behind the family vacation cabin. Such passages about his summers confirm the image of him in the "office and retreat" photo on Susan Ragan's quilt. It shows White in the writing cabin, in three-piece suit, white shirt, and tie, sitting at a long desk constructed of small sections of pine logs and topped with two thick planks. An overwhelming litter of paper is scattered across the desktop, on which also sits a heavy manual typewriter and a two-pronged candelabra with unlit candles. Only the crudeness of the desk construction reveals that he is not being pictured at work back in Emporia.

The events at the cabin he talks about in the autobiography tend to be more political than social or familial. He tells of William Jennings Bryan visiting—"came over to our cabin and sat on the porch for an hour"—and recalls Bryan's response to the terrain: "After a few casual, rather perfunctory remarks about our view of landscape around, he was not interested in it. That landscape was our pet child—it just had to be admired; but Bryan patted Longs Peak on the head and sent it away with the other snow-capped mountains, which amused me." Clarence Darrow visited soon after: "From time to time as he talked I caught his eye delighting in the scenery. Once or twice he cried out in joy at its beauty." In 1916, White and Charles Evans Hughes "went for a ride up Fall River and climbed a hundred feet or so among the rocks and sat down for a talk."

That "hundred feet or so" is the farthest White ventures out into nature in his autobiography, after his account of his climbs up Longs Peak in his college days, and he himself tells us that he never hunted or fished. For me, that's a somewhat problematic record of White's presence in the cabin and in the park. What did he really experience of Moraine Park or the larger national park that had absorbed it in 1915?

* * *

Early evening. I notice the elk working their way across the valley and the walkers and joggers and kibitzers arriving and spreading themselves along the trail. Somehow the distant throng of people and elk lures me off the porch. I stuff a camera, binoculars, bottled water, daybook, and pen into my day pack and stride off briskly for the Big Thompson footpath. Just beyond the parking area a large bull elk is rounding up stray cows that drifted away from the rest of the herd to the other side of the trail. The bull lumbers deliberately, with heavy footsteps, across the trail, and one man close to his projected path holds ground cautiously, hoping the bull will ignore him and provide an opportunity for a close photograph. Other people, including those traveling with the photographer, back off a ways, and everyone tries to appear nonchalant and harmless and to avoid startling or alarming the bull, though most are ready to snap a picture of the elk charging the man should it happen. Soon the cows trot back toward the river and the bull jogs after them with raised head and snorts of exasperation or annoyance. I see the tension go out of the photographer's body as he steps away from the place he posted himself.

For a few minutes I mill around with the scattered crowd watching the elk mill around, but I feel hemmed in by so many people and amble farther off down the trail, to see where it might lead me. At first I think I will head for the roche moutonnée but quickly realize it is on the far side of the river and not easily accessible. Ahead of me, in the grass farther upriver, another, smaller group of elk graze; beyond them shuffles another group of drifting observers. My path seems to lead me from one dense population to another. I pause for a moment, then leave the trail and clamber onto a low, broad outcropping of rock to ponder my next move.

I'm not alone on my perch for long; magpies and mountain bluebirds and even a green-tailed towhee soon show up in the rocks and grass nearby. I jot down some notes in my daybook about what I'm seeing, and when I look up I notice a young cow separating from the smaller, western group of elk and uncertainly making her way up the park toward the larger group. She advances a distance, then pauses and looks back, then stands as if deciding what to do, then advances again. When she nears the larger group, the bull marches over to meet her, then pointedly ignores her as she merges with the others. The western group then begins to move away from the river and further divides itself into two sections. One segment, composed of young bulls, heads across the hiking path and past the outcropping where I sit. From time to time they pause in their grazing and drifting and eye me warily. A second segment, all cows and calves, mostly stay closer to the river, occasionally glancing in my direction. To watch both groups I keep pivoting on my rock, my movement causing squeals from some of the cows but no panic, and then both groups are past me. I watch them for several more minutes, until the cows and calves are close to the main group by the river and the young bulls drift into low shrubs and trees nearer the road.

When I finally stand up, I realize the sun has nearly settled on the mountaintops. The distant mountains are already deep blue and blue light seems to fill the distance between the near and the far. And then shadows fall across the valley and move toward the distant slope where the cabin is. All at once it is markedly cooler in the meadow.

I trudge back up the trail, pleased to have been able to simply sit apart from other people in Moraine Park and observe for a moment the lives of elk and bluebirds and towhees. Back on the porch I watch the shadows deepen and the valley darken and cars slow for a last, lone buck still browsing on the north side of the valley after all the other elk have regrouped in the center. I make my supper in the back of the cabin and when I sit down to eat it the sky in the west is a deep brilliant blue and the elk are gone. I feel quietly content.

*   *   *

Autobiography is a chronological art, an act of recordkeeping with commentary, not, like memoir, an attempt to revivify a period of the past, make it possible for another person to live the moment too through reading. Autobiography eschews the intimate, the commonplace detail, the unexceptional private life; memoir embraces them. It's only in the aftermath of personal tragedy that William White pulls back the curtains of a window into their life in Moraine Park, as a memoirist would.

Describing the summer of 1920, White doesn't avoid inferences to his career—his writing and his connection to the prominent—but he subordinates them to the portrait of family life he wants—needs—to record.

> The summer in Estes Park was pure joy. The two children, Bill and Mary, and their mother and one of her sisters and, I think, my mother and Sallie's mother. It was a gala time by day. Up in a log cabin, one hundred feet above the living quarters, I hammered away at my typewriter, writing something, perhaps part of a book, perhaps a magazine article. But Bill was twenty and Mary sixteen, and they were forever going out to parties and dressing, and little dances were springing out of the cracks of the boards on the wide porches and in the living room. The phonograph was forever chirping its Gargantuan cricket song, either for dance or diversion, for I had brought some records out of the big box of classical records that had come from London. Friends were continually coming and going. We gave a tea for Jane Addams, I remember, and had faculty people from the neighboring valley crowding on the front porch, and Mary was there, lovely, being a child and stuffing herself with food in the kitchen but being quite a young lady on the porch serving our guests. And Bill was fishing and supplying the frying pan and tramping all over the hills, sometimes gone for a day or two camping. The Estes Park markets in the village were filled with fresh Colorado fruits and vegetables, and we rarely sat down to a meal without company. It was a gay, boisterous summer, the last we were ever to have as a united family.

That final ominous phrase more than justifies White's sudden shift from historian/autobiographer to memoirist. Because Mary's death will soon follow, his memory of this summer is perhaps more powerful and more important to him than other summers have been, and he needs to reflect about his children's lives here far more than he does any-where else in the book. His writing voice takes on an elegiac urgency.

White explains:

> That summer in Estes Park, where we had been going regularly for nearly a dozen years, and where Bill and Mary had grown from childhood into rather mature adolescence, we saw more of them and came to know them better than ever before. Bill had come to the park when he was eleven years old and loved overalls and wanted to go barefoot, which was impossible in the sand and pebbles and cactus of Colorado. Mary had come to the park when she was a five-year-old. We turned them loose then as children with the children of the academic people from Kansas University on the hillside and in the valley. We could locate Mary with our field glasses by the little red-ribbon topknot on her towhead, a mile away in the meadow by the brook that played through the grass. Bill, like all the Lindsay men, was an expert fisherman. Mary tried it and gave it up. He had patience. She was highly energized and could not slow down for fishing. As the summer passed, Bill began to climb mountains. Mary's heart was wedded to the burros. We had, at one time, three which she pick-eted and fed; and by the time she was a dozen years old, she was in overalls renting her burros out to tourists and cottagers. Bill, when he was sixteen, had climbed all the mountains there were, had gone all over the range, could guide parties, and did, to remote places, and knew all the fishing holes of the region.

He writes that in the park they read avidly, especially Dickens, and dressed "as all children wish to dress, like little ragamuffins" in overalls, galluses, and shirts.

At the end of that summer Bill would be going to Harvard, transferring from Kansas University, and all were aware that the family would, in White's phrase, "be badly battered. So Sallie and I cherished every happy day of it. Mary came home for meals after spending her mornings in the Y.M.C.A. grounds, half a mile away, and spouted a fountain of miscellaneous and generally useless information about that citadel of morality—the term was hers." White concludes: "That summer in the park, where we all huddled together in three little cabins around a living room cabin, was a fair and sunny one which we shall cherish through the years as our brightest memory of the family."

The following year Mary died and White, speaking to his community and Mary's, wrote of her life and death in that enduring editorial. The essay continued to be reprinted and anthologized for the remainder of White's life. In his unfinished autobiography he wrote, rather presciently, "Probably if anything I have written in these long, happy years that I have been earning my living by writing, if anything survives more than a decade beyond my life's span, it will be the thousand words or so that I hammered out on my typewriter that bright May morning under the shadow and in the agony of Mary's death." When he considers—tentatively, uncertainly—her mother and himself reuniting somewhere in the universe with Mary, he imagines, "just as she grinned and looked up at her mother that evening when we climbed the mountain in Colorado, she will grin:

"'Daddy and I have had an adventure!'

"It would be a gay and happy meeting."

Those were the final words he wrote about Colorado.

* * *

I gaze out the huge glass window, past porch pillars of glacial rock, at a broad, flat valley floor. At two lateral moraines along the sides of the valley, the southern one thick with firs, the northern well spaced with ponderosas. At the roche moutonnée in the middle distance, anomalously rising from the flat valley floor and sprouting trees. At a treed ridge headed by huge boulders beyond that. At gorges and mountains farther and farther in the distance. In spite of tourists and traffic passing along the periphery, the natural history of Moraine Park seems to have escaped the intrusions of cultural history.

Yet I know that's not the case. Above the futon on the interior living room wall, balanced on a grooved display shelf at the top of the wainscoting, a long, framed black and white photograph displays a panorama of Moraine Park in 1925. It seems to have been taken from some point on Eagle Cliff Mountain, behind the White cabin, off-scene somewhere below the bottom of the picture. I've climbed Eagle Cliff and photographed the park; I recognize the perspective in the picture. Comparing the photograph with the view from the cabin, I realize how much the cultural history has altered.

The Big Thompson River winds through the center of the picture, then as now, but, throughout the valley, buildings were scattered of which no trace now remains—a cluster directly across from the wooden bridge, a farm or ranch a little farther on, just where the river bends south, another cluster of buildings to the north, another house with outbuildings off to the west. The inholder dwellings along the South Lateral Moraine at this end of the park are still in place more than seventy-five years later, but the horse and hiker trail everyone uses these days follows pretty much the same track as a dirt road extending all the way across the park and looping towards the northwest corner. At the point in the picture that would be the intersection of the road that now leads to Moraine Park Campground (that road doesn't appear in the photo) and the road that arches around to the Cub Lake and Fern Lake trailheads, I notice a large cluster of buildings. It must be the location of the dude ranch J. D. Stead developed from the homestead, built in 1875, of the pioneer Abner Sprague; in the photo the Stead Ranch hasn't yet reached its full development— it later added a golf course and indoor swimming pool— but it has a commanding place in the park. All that is gone now, except perhaps for a secluded building I seem to detect directly back of the Stead place, more a dark blur than an image, that corresponds to an inholder structure still standing in that location. The perspective of the picture, which leaves out the terminal moraine at the east end of the park and the slope of Eagle Cliff Mountain, doesn't show buildings that I know were once there—a store, the Moraine Park post office, and the Moraine Lodge, which stood where the Moraine Park Museum now stands—nor any of the other cottages and cabins between the lodge and the White cabin. One of them, called the Scottage, still had occupants during my first week in the park.

This would have been the view the Whites had from the cabin in 1925, when Moraine Park was more populated, more commercial and more exclusive with its resorts and private retreats. Though the present plethora of recreational vehicles, trailers, and tents secreted in the forested campground and shared activities like fishing, hiking, birding, and elking may create certain kinds of transitory bonds, in William Allen White's day Moraine Park had a more intimate, more neighborly, more permanent sense of community. It wasn't permanent, though some inholder families still hang onto and pass on their cottages, instead of selling or donating them to Rocky Mountain National Park for conversion to such a use as the artist-in-residence program or, more often, for demolition. Most visitors don't realize that the wild mustard, the thistles, and the timothy grass are all invasive plants, brought in by ranchers and resort owners and tourists, which have crowded out the native species, that the elk were killed off and had to be reintroduced, that the coyotes were killed off and reintroduced themselves, that buildings which were once here have been so thoroughly obliterated only skilled historians can locate their sites. *Où est le parc d'antan? Où est la villégiature d'ete de Stead?* A great deal of Rocky Mountain National Park may be as wild as the day it (the Park if not the wilderness) was created, but little of it is completely untrammeled by man; the theme of the Park's work is restoration as well as preservation.

The sun is out, shining through the dripping pine just down the slope and the empty wine glass on my table, shining on me as I scribble in my journal and take in the view from my windowed wall. It's something to feel yourself sitting in another's place, connected across time. I know what I see from here and have overcome the delusion that I see what William White saw. And what did he see of what I've witnessed? Were the coyotes and elk as much in the open, so much a part of his landscape? I can't tell without his testimony and he's simply silent about the natural world. But I know he saw the circle of mountains, could remember as a young man climbing Longs Peak, the most awesome peak in his view, and I'm sure he must have seen those sunsets, those sunrises, those clouds, those fogs, the tireless shifting changes of light, must have heard the chiming flight of the hummingbirds, the *pew* of the bluebirds, the *queg* of the magpies. Moraine Park is still here, and the mountains beyond it and the sky above it and the river running through it. It's not so much the physical space and the historical moment but the fundamental elements we share across time. Those are what give us common ground.

Isabella Bird, in a photo taken in San Francisco around the end of
August 1873, between her Hawaii and Colorado travels and at the
beginning of her career as a travel writer. Courtesy Lyman Museum,
Hilo, Hawaii.

Helen Hunt Jackson, poet, novelist, travel writer, and Indian advocate, circa 1875, around the time she married William Sharpless Jackson and settled in Colorado Springs. Courtesy Helen Hunt Jackson Papers, Part 6, Ms 0353, Folder 9, Colorado College Special Collections.

Grace Greenwood (Sarah Jane Clarke Lippincott), circa 1870, journalist and poet, was one of the most popular lecturers and literary celebrities of her time. From "Representative Women," Boston: L. Prang & Co. Courtesy Library of Congress, Prints & Photographs Division, LC-USZ62-5535.

William Allen White, editor of *The Emporia (Kansas) Gazette*, on November 11, 1910, two years before he purchased the cabin in Moraine Park. Courtesy Library of Congress, Prints & Photographs Division, LC-DIG-ggbain-05296 (George Grantham Bain Collection).

The restored William Allen White Cabin in Rocky Mountain National Park houses artists-in-residence throughout the summer months. Photo by James Lindberg. Originally published in *Rocky Mountain Rustic: Historic Buildings of the Rocky Mountain National Park* by James Lindberg, Patricia Raney, and Janet Robertson, edited by John Gunn (Estes Park: Rocky Mountain Nature Association, 2004). Courtesy Rocky Mountain Nature Association.

The White Cabin, in the foreground, looks out on Moraine Park and a panorama of mountain summits along the Continental Divide, August 2004. Photo by the author.

The prolific photographer William Henry Jackson included Longs Peak in many of his Colorado photos; this view across a lake in Estes Park dates from around 1880. Copyright © Colorado Historical Society, William Henry Jackson Collection, CHS.J2062, Scan # 20202062. Courtesy Colorado Historical Society.

Hikers cross the Boulderfield on their way toward the summit of Longs Peak in the background, August 11, 2005. Photo by the author.

Colorado Mountain Club members are among the climbers ranged across the broad summit of Longs Peak, August 11, 2005. Photo by the author.

(*opposite page*) A group of hikers pose on a pile of rocks on the summit of Longs Peak in a picture in William Allen White's collection of photographs from his first climb, 1889. "On Longs Peak." RH MS 939.33. William Allen White Collection, Kansas Collection, RH MS 929, Kenneth Spencer Research Library, University of Kansas Libraries. Courtesy Kenneth Spencer Research Library, University of Kansas.

The Peak

The four hours' ride to the camping ground was one series of glories and surprises, of park and glade, of lake and stream, of mountain on mountain, all culminating in the riven top of Long's Peak, which grew grander and more ghastly as we rose to a height of 11,000 feet. The slanting sun added new beauty every hour,—black pines against a lemon sky, gray peaks reddening in the light, gorges of deep and infinite blue, floods of golden glory, an atmosphere of crystalline purity, a foreground constantly of the cotton-wood and aspen flaunting in red and gold, deepening the blue gloom of the pines, the trickle and murmur of streams fringed with icicles, the strange, weird sound of gusts moving through the pine-tops—sights and sounds, not of the lower earth, but of the storm-riven, beast-haunted, frozen upper altitudes. Nothing so wonderful and vast in scenery ever met my eyes; its individuality and beauty are altogether unrivalled.

Isabella Bird, "Long's Peak,"
Out West, December–January, 1873–74

The air is cool and damp a little before five in the morning and, though the sky is clear and the stars display their brilliance in such myriads as I've not witnessed for years, the trail is dark enough that we need the headlamps and flashlights the five of us wear or carry. From our rendezvous in Golden at 3 a.m. all the way through Boulder and Lyons and partly up the South St. Vrain Canyon, the rain persisted and the gloomy thought that this would prove to be nothing but a damp, dark drive to a slick, waterlogged trail hung thick in the air like the morning's moisture. But somewhere in the canyon the road became dry and beyond it stars became visible through the clouds; when we found the trailhead dry, we set out eagerly, briskly.

I am fourth in line, flashlight in hand, behind Dave, the leader of this Colorado Mountain Club hike, Steve, and Joe, and just ahead of Mark, who brings up the rear. His headlamp sways with the rhythm of his steps and the alternating movements of his walking poles, and I watch my shadow shift positions across the trail ahead of me. We seem to have plenty of light and occasionally I flash my beam into the woods on either side of the trail, wondering if any wildlife are watching us pass. None appears. I also try to shine the light on what appear to be piles of dark brown apples on the trail—fresh horse manure—so Mark will notice them as he follows me. The trail is broad and mostly flat and the upward slope gradual enough that it is easy for me to keep up even at a pace somewhat faster than I would have chosen for myself.

From the Longs Peak Ranger Station to the Summit is roughly eight miles and a gain in elevation of 4,855 feet. Common wisdom says that, in the summer, it's best to be off the summit before noon, when the thunderstorms roll in and lightning is a serious threat—hikers have been killed on the mountain by lightning. Common wisdom adds, as a corollary, that hikers should either camp overnight more than half-way up, at the Boulderfield, and ascend in the morning or do the hike by setting out in darkness, as early as 2 or 3 a.m., and reaching the summit by midmorning.

At around 9,900 feet, I hear the sound of mountain water rather than see our first encounter with cascading Alpine Brook. By the time we climb a series of tight switchbacks and, at 10,600 feet, cross the two short plank bridges where the brook plummets out of the darkness of the woods and rushes through the lush greenery of the steep slope below, we've turned off our lights and are hiking in pale predawn light. We pass treeline, through the *krummholz* and onto alpine terrain. By 6:10, as we near Chasm Junction, the sun illuminates the Diamond above Chasm Lake. On other mornings, from the cabin porch in Moraine Park, I've watched the sun start the day at the distant top of Longs Peak. Now I see the blazing mountaintop from less than a mile away and when I look off toward Moraine Park it's still in darkness, the cabin too small to see from this distance. Behind us, the sun has yet to clear the Twin Sisters, outlining their double peaks in golden brilliance while their western slopes remain darker than night.

At Chasm Junction we've come three and a half miles in an hour and a half. We press on toward the Boulderfield, another mile and a half away. The climb is persistent and the trail generally clear. At the Boulderfield we find a broad flat area abounding in jumbled slabs, spikes, and giant cobbles of rocks. A campground offers level tent sites surrounded by stone breakwalls piled to fend off often brutal mountain winds. We rendezvous and take lunch near the camping area.

By now I'm lagging behind the others and Dave is hanging back to keep an eye on me. He worries about dividing the party but the other three are very experienced on the trail and he can send them on ahead, expecting to rendezvous from time to time. They are relatively agile and surefooted; I'm tentative and cautious crossing the boulders. The Boulderfields are 5.9 miles from the trailhead, at 12,760 feet; we've risen 3,360 feet, roughly 640 feet per mile. This is the staging area for the climb up to the summit, about 1,500 feet and less than two miles away. Dave says to me, "The good news is, we've reached the Boulderfield. The bad news is, this is where the hike starts."

*   *   *

Most of the people who recognize the name Isabella Bird identify her as the woman who climbed Longs Peak and/or the woman involved somehow with Rocky Mountain Jim. Attitudes vary in regard to these aspects of her Colorado persona, but what strikes me is how little space they occupy in her book compared to how much emphasis they are given by readers. Because I'd known early on that I, too, would climb Longs Peak and thought it the most difficult of her excursions to repeat, I may have given it disproportionate emphasis myself. I needed to remind myself that her original goal had been to reach Estes Park, not to summit Longs Peak, and that the intent to climb came later in her plans.

Her first reference to Longs Peak comes in Letter V, datelined "Canyon, September," a "dateless day" because, in the Chalmers homestead, she's lost track of the calendar. Expecting Chalmers to take her to Estes Park, she thinks they "shall sleep tomorrow at the foot of Long's Peak." Later, wandering the canyon, her gaze rises to "the splintered, pinnacled, lonely, ghastly, imposing, double-peaked summit of Long's Peak, the Mont Blanc of Northern Colorado." She reports, a few pages afterwards, information she either later learned from her own experience or simply had been told by others prior to her outing in the canyon: "From the top of Long's Peak, within a short distance, twenty-two summits, each above 12,000 feet in height, are visible, and the Snowy Range, the backbone or 'divide' of the continent, is seen snaking distinctly through the wilderness of ranges, with its waters starting for either ocean." (The term "Snowy Range," which she uses so often, was a common one at the time referring to a stretch of snow-coated mountains from Mount Evans to the south to the Mummy Range north of Longs Peak.) When the party retreats back to the homestead, Isabella tells how, awake in the night, stargazing, she "thought of Long's Peak in its glorious solitude, and resolved that, come what might, I would reach Estes Park."

Longs Peak, previously unmentioned in her hopes, has become an emblematic figure for her, so that her first account of Estes Park, when she sees it from the ridge now called Park Hill, describes "sentinel mountains of fantastic shape and monstrous size, with Long's Peak rising above them in unapproachable grandeur" and points out how, in the sunlight, "Long's Peak was aflame." She closes that September 28 letter with reference to "this glorious upper world, with the mountain pines behind and the clear lake in front, in the 'blue hollow at the foot of Long's Peak.'"

The first the reader learns of her interest in climbing Longs Peak comes in the opening sentence of her next chapter, Letter VII, which is her account of the excursion. Referring to Longs as "the American Matterhorn" this time, rather than as the American Mont Blanc, she tells us that, after initially discouraging her, Evans thought the weather settled enough that it would be worth it to at least reach timberline. The only prior expedition she mentions is the first recorded ascent of the mountain by Major John Wesley Powell's party in 1868. In fact, as she must have known, little more than two weeks earlier, on September 13, the lecturer Anna E. Dickinson had ascended in the company of Ferdinand V. Hayden's geological survey team. Dickinson is often credited as having been the first woman to make the ascent. In fact, Addie M. Alexander of St. Louis seems to have reached the summit in August 1871; her companion, Henrietta Goss, may have also completed the climb, but other than their names nothing else is known about these two women. Isabella may have mentioned Dickinson's climb in her original letter to Henrietta, now lost, but the chapter in her book, whatever its indebtedness to that letter, draws very much on a shorter, more compact article about her ascent that she first published in the Colorado Springs magazine *Out West*, in its December 1873–January 1874 issue, an article completed before she left Colorado. It's unlikely that she was unaware of Dickinson's ascent; the lecturer's travels and performances received considerable attention in territorial newspapers in September 1873, and she had stayed at the ranch and met Evans and Rocky Mountain Jim. It may have been Dickinson's climb that put the idea of her own ascent into her thoughts.

Jim Nugent volunteered to guide Isabella up Longs Peak, accompanied by the two young men who had brought her from Longmont to Estes Park, Platt Rogers and Sylvester Downer. Isabella recounts gathering three days' worth of bread, fresh steaks, tea, sugar, and butter, camping blankets and a quilt, and borrowing a pair of hunting boots from Evans. In her article she merely identifies her guide as "Mr. Nugent, (Better known as 'Rocky Mountain Jim')" and claims "a better, kinder, more thoroughly competent, considerate, and cautious guide could not be found." In her book chapter she is more thorough in her description of him, calling him "a shocking figure" dressed in high boots, baggy deerhide trousers, "a leather shirt, with three or four ragged unbuttoned waistcoats over it," and "an old smashed wideawake," and carrying a knife and a revolver—"he was as awful-looking a ruffian as one could see." She says nothing about the appearance of the two young men.

The party rode south up the valley of Fish Creek from the ranch in Estes Park, passed Lily Lake, and continued along the Tahosa Valley to the base of Battle Mountain. Ernest Bernard, an editor of her Rocky Mountain book who has attempted to retrace her specific route, is certain that

Jim led them toward Pine Ridge along a creek drainage and then followed Alpine Brook and Larkspur Creek to an elevation of around 11,200 feet, where they camped in a grove of limber pine, spruce, and fir (now called Jim's Grove). They were in the *krummholz* and Isabella was much impressed with the setting: "The trees were in miniature, but so exquisitely arranged that one might ask what artist's hand had planted them, scattering them here, clumping them there, and training their slim spires towards heaven." In the book she talks at length about Ring, Jim's dog, and the scene around the campfire of Jim and the young men singing and Jim reciting a poem and telling Indian stories. The dog slept by her side and helped keep her warm. "I was anxious about the ascent, for gusts of ominous sound swept through the pines at intervals. . . . But, above all, it was exciting to lie there, with no better shelter than a bower of pines, on a mountain 11,000 feet high, in the very heart of the Rocky Range, under twelve degrees of frost, hearing sounds of wolves, with shivering stars looking through the fragrant canopy, with arrowy pines for bedposts, and for a night lamp the red flames of a camp-fire."

The following morning Isabella was summoned to see the sunrise: "We looked to where the Plains lay cold, in blue-grey, like a morning sea against a far horizon. Suddenly, as a dazzling streak at first, but enlarging rapidly into a dazzling sphere, the sun wheeled above the grey line, a light and glory as when it was first created." Jim took off his hat and declared that he believed there was a God, and Isabella claimed the desire to worship as if she were witnessing creation.

After breakfast, with Bird on horseback and the men walking, they made their way up to the Boulderfield, which no horse could cross. Bird found the borrowed man's boots too large for her to boulder-hop safely, but fortunately they found a pair of small overshoes under a rock.

Isabella surmised that they were left by the Hayden party—she mentions no one in particular among that group—and it is generally assumed that the shoes had been worn by Anna Dickinson, the only woman among them. James Pickering, in his book on Estes Park, remarks in a note that the women were luckily the same size, although it is recorded that when the Hayden party came down from the summit another group getting ready to ascend included several women. Certainly the idea that Isabella Bird was able to fit into Anna Dickinson's shoes to make the ascent has good deal more metaphorical and biographical resonance than if an anonymous woman had accidentally left them behind. If that party completed their ascent, and if Addie Alexander and possibly Henrietta Goss reached the summit earlier, the celebrity accorded Anna Dickinson and Isabella Bird for their ascents of Longs Peak seems somewhat less merited, though perhaps the accomplishment itself says something about their characters.

* * *

Though sunrise earlier tinted the east face of Longs Peak a ripe tomato red, by the time we finish a quick, restorative lunch in the Boulderfield, the sheer surface of the Diamond is gleaming gray. Dave points out the distant outline of the Keyhole against the sky, its south side looking like the profile of some gigantic primitive sculpted head, and we all start for it. I fall behind almost at once, cautious about the boulder hopping from flat rock surfaces to rounded or spiky rock edges over gaps and openings of painful possibility. Boulder hopping calls for balance and agility and step-by-step calls upon the hiker's capacity for instant judgment and spontaneous route redirection. These are not skills I've had much call to exercise since I was ten.

We approach the Keyhole across a disordered brown jumble of stone broken off the jagged stone ridge at skyline. I only recognize the existence of a man-made structure below the Keyhole as I close in on it. The stone shelter, composed from the very materials I stumble and clamber over, blends in perfectly with the rock wall it's set against, except for small, dark windows; often, indeed, the joints and fractures of the granite everywhere around us has a look of chiseled intention rather than natural happenstance. The shelter commemorates two people who died on the mountain and offers shelter to others who may be at risk. Reg Saner wrote of the building that its "stone shape vaguely resembles a skull, complete with eye-socket windows," and that it "perches right beside the Keyhole like an omen." In January 1925, Agnes Vaille, a thirty-five-year-old Coloradan with considerable mountaineering experience, attempted a winter ascent of the East Face in the company of an experienced Swiss climber named Walter Kiener. The cold and the exertion took its toll on her and she fell 150 feet. Kiener went for help but by the time the rescuers arrived Vaille was dead. Kiener himself lost his toes to frostbite and one of the rescue party, Herbert Sortland, disappeared after separating from the others; his body wasn't found for over a month. A plaque on the wall of the shelter commemorates Vaille and Sortland.

Curiously enough, the first recorded death on the mountain was that of a woman, Carrie Welton, who also died of exhaustion and hypothermia, in September 1884. The most recent accounting lists fifty-five deaths, most caused by falls from technical climbing routes but half a dozen or more on the popular Keyhole route. Dougald MacDonald, who provides a two-page chart in his book on the mountain, credits hypothermia, heart attack, and lightning for a number of other deaths. Two deaths have been attributed to suicide and one to gunshot (a climber carrying a loaded gun who accidentally shot himself and died from his wound on the mountain). Perhaps, given the phenomenal number of people who have successfully summitted Longs Peak—an estimated 140,000 people come to the trail each year, though less than 20,000 of those reach the peak—the percentage of deaths is statistically small, but nonetheless no one has told me about any other mountain as a friend did about Longs: "Always keep in mind that the mountain can kill you." It's a warning supported by plenty of evidence.

And even among people who haven't read about the fatalities, the terrain itself sends plenty of warnings about the potential for mishap. The thinness of the air at this altitude, the bumps and scrapes of the Boulderfield and the scramble past the Vaille shelter, the recognition of how much heart and lungs and legs have labored to reach this point—these things should alert anyone to the need for caution. And then, finally, there is the Keyhole.

Reg Saner opens his essay "Longs Peak Labor Day Weekend Parade" with a conversation about the Keyhole, where a couple from Cleveland have turned back. He tells us that "up to there it's a hike. . . . Then the Keyhole. You poke your head over its sharp ridge—*voila!* The bottom drops out. No warning. Just instant 'exposure,' the mountaineer's word for how far you can fall." Later, when he meets others who have given up their quest for the summit at the Keyhole, he refers to their trepidation as "openness overload."

When I first contacted Dave Turk about joining this group, he asked me whether I'd hiked that kind of distance, whether I'd been to that kind of altitude, and how I felt about exposure. I resisted the urge to make a smart-alecky answer to the third question and instead asked him what he meant. He meant, as Saner says, something rather specific to mountaineering, what the Colorado Mountain Club defines tersely as "risk of falling." I doubt that I told him I was acrophobic enough to sit below while my wife and daughter rode the giant Ferris wheel on Chicago's

Navy Pier, but whatever I said allayed his fears enough that he let me join the hike but not so much that, below the Keyhole, it doesn't occur to him to ask me about it again. The men he doesn't have to ask about exposure are waiting above, in the opening of the Keyhole.

"You know," he says, "it's an accomplishment to make it this far. If you don't think you want to deal with the exposure, I can let those guys go on their own—they're old hands at this—and I can hang back here with you. Actually I wouldn't mind scouting the North Face for awhile." Dave takes being the leader of the hike seriously; he doesn't want me going beyond my limits, endangering myself or others, and he knows he has to monitor the time and the weather and the trail conditions for all of us.

"I'm sorry to be slowing everyone down," I say, the second or third time—I'll repeat it again—that I apologize for my pace, "but I don't think I'll have a problem with the exposure. Thanks, though." One recurring thought has kept me company through all my anxious anticipation and bumbling progress—men and women in their seventies and children as young as five and six and thousands upon thousands of other people of ages in between have made the summit. As tedious as I find boulder hopping and tired as I am by the pace and the distance and the elevation we'd gained in about four hours, I see no reason to quit. Even if I'm the weakest link in *our* group, I'm no less capable than the average hiker who achieves it.

Perhaps because I've been on enough mountains in Colorado by now, to my surprise the view through the Keyhole *doesn't* intimidate me, though I appreciate how some people might feel "openness overload" when they contemplate the other side of the mountain. The Keyhole, at 13,150 feet, is 1,105 feet below the summit but 2,530 feet above Black Lake, which I recognize below me. The broad, open, gradually sloping comfort of the approach behind me, now bathed in sunlight, is replaced by the precipitous granite and talus slope in the shade and a vast panoramic space before me. I can identify Glacier Gorge below, recognize lakes within the gorge and formations like the Arrowhead and the Spearhead, and locate thirteeners like Chief's Head Mountain and McHenry's Peak, their summits a few hundred feet higher than where I stand. Other mountains stretch away beyond their shoulders. Openness indeed.

Earlier, Dave counted at least forty-four people who had signed in and left the trailhead before us that morning; more might well have spent the night at the Boulderfield or the lower Battle Mountain group site to get a leg up on the climb to the summit. When I look off at the Ledges, a considerable stretch of exposure, I see plenty of foot traffic ahead of us. Dave tells me to concentrate on my immediate vicinity, to use my hands to steady myself and to plant my feet surely, and to ignore the trail ahead and the space alongside of us. I pay attention to his movements as I follow him across the ledge and find the exposure nowhere near as unnerving as I worried it would be. Alone on an empty mountainside I would have been reluctant but, seeing throngs ahead of me and no especially ominous locations, I am neither casual nor especially concerned, though I would admit the situation focuses my concentration.

*   *   *

Passing through the "Notch," we looked along the nearly inaccessible side of the Peak, composed of boulders and *débris* of all shapes and sizes, through which appeared broad, smooth ribs of reddish-colored granite, looking as if they upheld the towering rock mass above.

Isabella Bird

At the Keyhole, which she mistook for the Notch, a formation on the other side of the mountain, Isabella Bird gazed at the panoramic view west of Longs Peak. She describes it at length, in admiring and effusive language, but ends on a sudden, ominous reversal of tone: "Never-to-be-forgotten glories they were, burnt in upon my memory by six succeeding hours of terror."

The standard nontechnical route from the Keyhole to the summit is usually divided into four sections. The section now called the Ledges follows a (very) roughly horizontal path across the west side, and then is succeeded by the Trough, a rough scree- and loose-rock-filled couloir, usually to some extent snow-filled, that runs vertically down the mountainside. At the top of the Trough a somewhat tricky bit of clambering through a corridor of rock leads to the Narrows, another mostly horizontal stretch that culminates in the Homestretch, a steep climb over slabs of rough, clear granite to the summit. More perilous and more arduous routes have been discovered over the years by climbers in search of life-threatening challenges, but for the multitude of dayhikers who reach the summit—or who turn back, unnerved and chagrined at the exposure revealed to them—the Keyhole route is challenging and arduous enough.

Climbing at the end of September on a mountain that, as many people have told me, "makes its own weather," the Bird party discovered an icy surface on the Ledges. When Isabella offered to stay behind, her young companions, Platt Rogers and S. S. Downer, eagerly continued across the usual route, pleased to be free of the encumbrance of a woman, but Jim Nugent insisted on leading Isabella downward to a point where they would intersect the Trough and then climb up to meet the two men. Jim's way was less risky but considerably more strenuous. Isabella complained of "fatigue, giddiness, and pain from bruised ankles, and arms half pulled out of their sockets," and claimed, "I should never have gone halfway had not 'Jim,' *nolens volens,* dragged me along with a patience and skill, and withal a determination that I should ascend the Peak, which never failed." Her path, under Jim's guidance, was more demanding than most hikers face today, but her summary of it accurately captures physical demands with which most can identify: "Slipping, faltering, gasping from the exhausting toil in the rarefied air, with throbbing hearts and panting lungs, we reached the top of the gorge."

Eventually, reunited with Rogers and Downer, they continued on through the Narrows to the Homestretch. At the final stage, she wrote that it made her "perfectly sick and dizzy to look at . . . a smooth, cracked face or wall of pink granite, as nearly perpendicular as anything could well be up which it was possible to climb." Her description of the final leg of the climb is still accurate: "*Scaling,* not climbing, is the correct term for this last ascent." It took them an hour. "The only foothold was in narrow cracks or on minute projections on the granite. To get a toe in these cracks, or here and there on a scarcely obvious projection, while crawling on hands and knees, all the while tortured with thirst and gasping and struggling for breath, this was the climb; but [she adds with relief] at last the Peak was won."

*   *   *

The Peak is a nearly level surface, paved with irregular blocks of granite, and without vegetation of any kind, except a little gray lichen. The outline is nearly a parallelogram—east and west—widening a little toward the western extremity, and five or six acres in extent. On the eastern end are some large boulders, giving it an apparent altitude of ten or fifteen feet above the remainder of the surface. Along the northern edge, and especially at the northwest corner, the surface rounds off considerably, though the general appearance is almost that of a perfect level.

William N. Byers, "The Powell Expedition"

The Trough is a steep slope with loose rock and scree and, this season, for the first time in years, free of snow. But the rain from the night before and the meltwater from ice below the stones make portions of it mushy or slick. On Dave's advice, I move slowly, making certain the ground beneath one foot is firm before trusting it and giving up the solid hold of my other foot. The pace is determined by the need to continually test your footing. The others have gone on above, to wait at the Narrows, but Dave hangs back and cautions me to let my heart rate slow down and not let it rise above my pace. The thinner atmosphere is apparent with every breath and I feel the exertion of the climb in my lungs and my pulse. I slow down continually, trying not to over-tax myself. By this point, I know, simple endurance and steady forward motion are all that can get me to the top.

At the top of the Trough the passage onto the Narrows requires full-fledged free-hand climbing—what Isabella refers to as "scaling"—by clambering onto one high ledge and then hauling yourself up a narrow slot to slip through. Then it's easy to reach the Homestretch, another steep climb. Joe would later say that the Homestretch should be considered a technical climb, regardless of snow or ice, because it involves not merely scrambling but real physical climbing—here we are not simply hiking. We search for handholds and footholds to pull ourselves up the rectangles of fractures on the open granite. Off to our right where the slope plummets away are straight enormous palisades and above them downward sloping strata that give us a good idea what we're climbing, a cross section of the rock beneath us. Dave tells me to be secure at three points before moving a hand or foot; now I'm counting on firm hand-holds as well as firm footing and again my progress is slow. People coming down the Homestretch tend to slide on their backsides, facing the descent, and Dave warns a few of them that they're getting too far away from the wall, too close to places where, if they can't stop themselves, the momentum will make them plunge rapidly over the rocks.

The ascent is essentially a slow line of people following one another to the top, watching where the people ahead put their hands and feet, what kind of effort their upward progress requires, how far they are from the summit. In time, though I pay attention chiefly to the rocks I cling to, I realize that people are hauling themselves through a narrow cleft at the end of the Homestretch and sense rather than see Dave's feet disappear above me. Someone encourages me that I am nearly there, and suddenly I am.

Nothing much prepared me for this broad flat surface with slabs of stone all across it and people everywhere, not crowded but still well populated. I cross to the others, who have been to the top awhile and already look relaxed and rested. Dave points me to the true peak, a large rock rising above the surface, where a brass circle marks the highest point. People pose on it, exchanging cameras and jokes about the ascent, and I wait my turn to sit on it. One of the teenagers who followed me up agrees to take my picture, and I drag myself up on the rock, burnishing with the seat of my pants—as countless others have before me—the U.S. Geological Survey disk marking 14,255 feet above sea level. Though I can see where others are signing the register of peak baggers, I haven't the energy to wait my turn again, but simply return to the group, grab a sandwich, a water bottle, and my camera, and go off to look at the view from the edge.

From the center of the summit, long and wide and as level as a field of boulders and stone slabs can be, it's difficult to see into the distance because the rest of the world is lower, out of sight, for 360 degrees around you. At the edge I identify the Ship's Prow, the arête jutting out between Longs and neighboring Mount Meeker, and the icy gully known as Lamb's Slide. With a map and a compass I might identify other mountains but now they all seem merely indistinguishable masses of rock punctuated by snowfields and ice troughs. It isn't the view below or far off that stuns me but the sight of clouds rising from below us and peering over the rim, as if they too labored to climb this high. The billowy clouds are lower, hanging above and between the surrounding mountains, and above us are thinner, wispier clouds, smearing the clear blue sky with light smudges of white and gray.

I notice the group watching me. Dave waves me over. He's watched the clouds all along and now, a little after eleven, they have built up enough that he is concerned about the descent. The sky amazes me, but in August thunderstorms and lightning can emerge quickly in the afternoon. Too soon to suit me, we elect to go down. The last to reach the summit, I've had the least amount of time to recuperate from the climb, but I understand their desire to get off the summit by noon and acquiesce to their judgment. Since I know this is very likely the only time I will ever be on Longs Peak, I slip on my daypack with equal portions of weariness and regret.

* * *

The way down is tougher than the way up. As William Allen White observed, you go up Longs Peak on all fours; you come down on all fives. The fifth point is your rear end and your arms and shoulders and legs and sense of balance get a workout. Somewhere on the Homestretch Dave tells me I look exhausted and reminds me to have three firm points of contact before reaching for another. I *am* exhausted, scrape my hands at one point and then step on a loose rock and shove another into my knee. Sharp pain immobilizes me momentarily but I shake it off. My descent is very slow by my companions' lights, though not necessarily by those of other untrained climbers on the route, and I realize my reaction time is often off.

Some stretches are more difficult than others, like the climb down at the Narrows, where the difficulty has made traffic congest, or on the treacherous loose scree, but I take Dave's advice and treat it all as potentially dangerous. Descending from the Keyhole and crossing the Boulderfield are agony. My knees hurt and I don't trust my legs or my sense of balance. Once I fall backwards and hear a crack as a point of rock jabs into my rib cage. I wait a moment, to see if I've broken a rib, and rise when I realize I haven't. I creep across the rocks. Clouds settle in around the peak, and once we hear thunder not far off; it rains intermittently as we descend toward treeline. By the final stretch through the forest to the trailhead everyone else is already waiting for me outside the ranger station as I walk the last half-mile or more alone. It's after 3 o'clock. We've been on the trail for eleven hours.

Isabella Bird, too, found the descent difficult. The four of them "accomplished the descent through 1,500 feet of ice and snow, with many falls and bruises, but no worse mishap," and then parted company again, Rogers and Downer heading over the Ledges and Bird and Nugent following "what he thought the safer route," a long descent and then a strenuous climb up to the Keyhole. Their route was far more physically demanding than the route the young men had taken; she noted that "the ascent was tremendous . . . and the steepness fearful." She clambered and crawled and often needed Jim to pull her or lift her. They reached the Keyhole around six p.m., having spent the day since early morning ascending and descending the final mile of the climb, with neither food nor water the whole time. Isabella needed help to cross the Boulderfield, had to be carried to and lifted upon her horse, and later, back at camp, had to be lifted off. Jim wrapped her in blankets and helped her lay down. It was, she wrote, "a humiliating termination of a great exploit."

In the night she woke to find that "the moon was high shining through the silvery branches, whitening the bald Peak above, and glittering on the great abyss of snow behind, and pine logs were blazing like a bonfire in the cold still air." Sitting by the campfire, she found her surroundings "weird and gloriously beautiful." By noon the following day, back at Evans's ranch, her spirits and her energy had revived enough that she could declare, "A more successful ascent of the Peak was never made, and I would not now exchange my memories of its perfect beauty and extraordinary sublimity for any other experience of mountaineering in any part of the world."

As eager as I am to be out of my hiking shoes and as tired as I am at the end of my adventure, I don't have to be carried or coddled. We stop at a bar and grill in Lyons, and I feel obliged to reassure the group that, however apprehensive my appearance and my pace may have made them, I feel better, less wiped out and exhausted, than I have on some lesser outings. As of this day, the Longs Peak hike is the longest I've ever taken (at sixteen miles), the greatest elevation gain I've made (at 4,855 feet), and the highest altitude I've achieved. Dave, who's climbed it so often he's lost count, and the others, who have routinely done longer, harder, and riskier climbs, all assure me that it's an accomplishment, something I can be proud of.

I'm certainly pleased, but because I'm in good health and because thousands of other, similarly average people have achieved the summit as well, I don't feel especially remarkable or extraordinary. But driving home through the gathering dark, I try to sort out my feelings about reaching the summit and ponder how they compare to Isabella Bird's.

In the article she published in *Out West*, her account of the descent was compact and brief: "We placed our names, with the date of ascent, in a tin within a cairn, and afterwards accomplished the slippery and perilous descent in safety, remaining that night at the camping ground owing to fatigue, and reaching Evans' delightful ranch, in Estes Park, at noon the following day." Her sentence about the success of the ascent and her refusal to exchange memories is identical to that in her book but seems more organic to the focus of the article, which is more narrowly on the ascent. In both publications her expression of what it meant to be on Longs Peak is essentially the same:

> From the summit were seen in unrivalled combination all the views which had rejoiced our eyes during the ascent. It was something at last to stand upon the storm-rent crown of this lonely sentinel of the Rocky Range, on one of the mightiest of the vertebrë of the backbone of the North American continent, and to see the waters start for both oceans. Uplifted above love and hate and storms of passion, calm amidst the eternal silences, fanned by zephyrs and bathed in living blue, peace rested for that one bright day on the Peak, as if it were some region
> *"Where falls not rain, or hail, or any snow,*
> *Or ever wind blows loudly."*

She and her three companions were alone on the peak that day; I and my four companions were merely one small group among dozens, and it was harder for us to make the comparison of that well-populated summit to the peaceful isle of Avalon (the subject of the poetic passage from Tennyson's "Idylls of the King" that she quotes). Distracted by the exertion of the ascent, it's easy to give the feat you've accomplished more attention than the destination you've attained.

But if you step outside your exhaustion and pain and stand apart from your exhilaration with yourself, you find that Isabella was right—it *is* something, at last, to rest upon this storm-rent crown and recognize how distant and irrelevant the affairs of mankind are from this perspective. There was ever in Isabella Bird a need to retreat, to escape from a crowded and complicated world into an ever simpler and ever more serene world. On Longs she reached the limits of retreat from the world; Avalon is, after all, the remote, isolated resting place of King Arthur and it is telling that it's the location she alludes to when describing the summit of Longs Peak. Though I don't think of Longs as Avalon, I share the instinct to retreat from a world too often too much with me and I welcome the times when I feel I have reached the far boundary of retreat.

Perhaps then the descent is all the more taxing because, in addition to repeating physically the exertion of the ascent, it is also a departure from a serenity and grandeur and peace that *must* be temporary, given the summit's excitable nature and uninhabitable altitude. The mountains have a scale of time and space that diminishes the world we return to—we can almost feel it compress and dwindle as we approach it, re-enter it, adjust our breathing to the density and constricting closeness of its scope. Descent, return, feels very much like exile. We can only hope that the sense of accomplishment, of arrival, will be stronger, will linger longer in our unconscious, than the sense of loss that follows it.

The Tour
Southern Circuit

i

Miss Isabella T. Bird, a Scotch lady, and a noted traveler in new and strange countries, is in Denver. She has recently traveled extensively in Australia, New Zealand, the Sandwich Islands, and California. For a month past she has been in and about Estes Park, having ascended Long's Peak September 30. She travels almost altogether on horseback, and has laid out a pretty good winter's work in Colorado.

Rocky Mountain News, October 23, 1873

October 27, 2004. Today I retrace the southern loop of what Isabella Bird termed her "tour" to parts of the territory that others recommended she visit. Her circuit began in Denver, struck south to Colorado Springs, then generally west and northwest up to the Continental Divide, and finally northeast along the Denver Stage Road, ending where it started. Though she mentioned her tour as early as October 3, she spent a few weeks more in Estes Park, herding cattle and waiting out wintry weather. On October 20, 1873, she mounted a "bay Indian pony, 'Birdie,' a little beauty, with legs of iron, fast, enduring, gentle, and wise," and, in the company of a young French Canadian also leaving the ranch, set off for Longmont. The following day she rode alone across the plains to Denver. Bird had been in Colorado nearly six weeks before she finally saw Denver, which she dismissed scornfully as "the great braggart city" and "the metropolis of the Territories."

It will take me about ten hours to cover the ground—though hardly the experience—of her travels over a period of seventeen days. When she left Denver on October 22, she was, after all, riding alone through the snow, depending on the hospitality of friends, acquaintances, and strangers. I travel by Toyota Corolla, my day unremittingly sunny, cool, and dry, my only challenge trying to be both pilot and navigator on busy roads. She had selected the destinations for her tour on the advice of friends like Rose Kingsley and acquaintances like Alexander Hunt and William Byers; I'd selected my destinations because of her narrative and accounts by other writers of her era like Rose Kingsley, Grace Greenwood, and Helen Hunt Jackson.

My wife and I leave home early, so that she can catch a bus into Denver from the Westminster Park and Ride. Behind us on the Boulder Turnpike, the full moon is bright and clear in a cloudless dark blue sky. Soon after I leave the bus stop, the sky grows light, a pale, pale blue to set against the dark clouds emerging in the West, where night lingers. I skirt the west side of Denver, watchful of the thickening commuter traffic, thankful not to be among the throngs massing toward the city.

Isabella Bird rode out of Denver and south across snowy plains, generally following the track of the Denver and Rio Grande Railroad, a narrow-gauge rail line whose proportions she thought "quaint," resembling "toy cars." In the October 23 entry of Letter IX, she tells us how her "very cheerful ride" on "a lovely Indian summer day" took her over the plains into "the rolling country along the base of the mountains"; she saw "settlers' houses about every half-mile" and "passed and met wagons frequently." We can't be certain of her route but she says she rode twenty miles the first day. Since snowy weather made her abandon the idea of going up into Platte Canyon and since she was often in sight of the railroad, it's likely that her trail followed the course of the South Platte River from the heart of Denver, near the confluence of the South Platte and Cherry Creek, to somewhere beyond modern Littleton.

Nowadays the route passes a couple of nondescript parks and golf courses and a good deal of business and industrial real estate. The South Platte River is often invisible. Having tried to follow the river through the city before, I don't bother trying to duplicate Isabella's route from the center of the city this morning. Rose Kingsley observed as early as 1871 that Denver "looks just as if it had been dropped out of the clouds accidentally, by someone who meant to carry it further on, but got tired and let it fall anywhere." In a sense my feeling about Denver agrees with that view—it seems to me, a flatlander from the Great Lakes, as if Denver had been transplanted ahead of me from almost anywhere else I've been.

It's hard for the modern traveler to imagine the sparsely settled country and frequent passage of wagons Isabella Bird described. Colorado 470, the road I drive, is a super highway arching along the rolling country west of the city; east of the highway cluster dense growths of subdivision and development. I take the expressway in hopes of avoiding the congestion of Denver traffic, but it's not entirely escapable. Just as I exit the highway for Wadsworth Boulevard, the street running along the west side of the Chatfield Reservoir, I notice traffic slowing to a halt at the next exit down the expressway, where exits and entrances merge and lines of vehicles intersect. Wadsworth is less crowded, but the flow of traffic is swift and thick. I glance often at the rough outcroppings of the Dakota Hogback and the barren foothills farther west. Both look grim in the morning light. The sun hasn't yet cleared the eastern horizon high enough to illuminate the ground here, but the clouds are a radiant pink and the day gives the promise of brightening. A flock of geese fly rapidly across the reservoir.

At the parking lot of the Corps of Engineers Visitor Center, I have a panoramic view of the reservoir, around which a state park has developed. Isabella Bird's friend Rose Kingsley, taking the train to Colorado Springs nearly two years before Isabella passed through, found "the land on either side of Plum Creek taken up by settlers, and fenced off into ranches for sheep, cattle, and agriculture." Grace Greenwood, who rode through only a few months before Kingsley, on "a modest little excursion to Platte Cañon and the famous Red Rocks in its vicinity" recorded in her August 13 entry, noted, "It was harvest time, though the grain was, for the most part, cut and bound in great bounteous sheaves; they were gathering it into barns, or stacking it in mighty piles,—mountains of gold." She commended the "beautiful farms along the Platte and Plumb Creek," which she claimed had produced "thirty and forty bushels of wheat to the acre, and the fairest, plumpest, sweetest grain I have even seen." She also thought the livestock grazing on the "wild, open pasture . . . was looking very finely."

Isabella Bird stayed the first night of her tour at lodging she identified as the Van Warmer Ranch in her private letters but left unnamed in her published version; I'm uncertain of its exact location but it must have been near the confluence of the South Platte River and Plum Creek, both of which flow north and both of which now have to pass through Chatfield Reservoir. She described the ranch as having "a large frame house, with large barns and a generally prosperous look." "You must understand," she explained, "that in Colorado travel, unless on the main road and in the larger settlements, there are neither hotels nor taverns, and that it is the custom for the settlers to receive travelers, charging them at the usual hotel rate for accommodations. It is a very satisfactory arrangement." Bird had been given a letter of introduction by the former Colorado territorial governor, Alexander Hunt, which was supposed to ease her entrance into such houses, but it had little effect on her first stop. The man of the place, who opened the door "look[ing] repellant," was someone "unwilling to receive people in this way." Luckily, his wife accepted her.

Her account of the Van Warmer ranch is a good example of how she modified her letters to Henrietta for publication. For example, the explanation of frontier lodging practices above was written for the book and does not appear in the letters. Throughout her published versions, she omits or alters names of many people she meets, unless they have significant roles in her experiences or in public life; instead of identifying the Van Warmer ranch in the book, she gives the location as "Great Platte Canyon"; the Barker Ranch, her second stop, is not named in the book either but labeled "Ranch, Plum Creek" in the dateline. The revisions build in some confusion for the reader, because when she refers to "Ranch" in the book she seems to mean the site of the first night's stay, yet that segment is clearly written at the Barker Ranch, her second night's stay; in her correspondence it's much clearer in which locations she's writing the letters.

Other differences emerge in comparison, some mildly stylistic, others more substantive. At the conclusion of the Van Warmer account in the book, she merely states, "I soon found there was a screw loose in the house, and was glad to leave early in the morning, although it was obvious that a storm was coming on." I'm always startled by that phrase, "there was a screw loose," which I had thought to be modern American slang. The phrase is also in her letter to her sister where she writes, "I soon saw that there was a screw loose in the house and that the man was a perfect brute and this lady [Mrs. Hutton, another guest] told me that he was nearly killing his wife with cruelty." She adds that Mrs. Hutton "was leaving because of the domestic troubles and I left just after breakfast, giving up the Platte cañon because of the weather." Her revisions remind us that she was often more circumspect in her published versions than she was in her original letters, which makes the moments of tart commentary in the book all the more striking and yet not always as grounded in rationale as the letters are.

I scan the scene before me, wondering idly what the lay of the land had been when Isabella Bird and, before her, Rose Kingsley and Grace Greenwood, had passed through. It's cool in the morning air above Chatfield Reservoir, but the sun is already high and brilliantly white, the deep cobalt blue sky I started out under now lightened to azure and blue-white, with only the merest wisps of cloud overhead. The waters reflect the sky, lighten the brown grasses stretching into the distance, and dim the yellow of the aspens along the shoreline. Haze fades the view of the western foothills. Somewhere under the impounded waters of the South Platte River, very likely, is the site of the Van Warmer ranch. To the north, Isabella Bird's trail to this location has been obliterated not only by time but also by urban sprawl. As I return to my car I am reminded that my on-site observations often will be merely notations on what has replaced the past, confirmations of what has vanished beyond recall. In the mountains I seemed to be in touch with something enduring, something that touched others before me. As I drive through the plains along the Front Range, I can compare notes with writers from the past, but I'd better be ready to connect on my own terms.

*   *   *

I cannot describe my feelings on this ride, produced by the utter loneliness, the silence and dumbness of all things, the snow falling quietly without wind, the obliterated mountains, the darkness, the intense cold, and the unusual and appalling aspect of nature. All life was in a shroud, all work and travel suspended. There was not a foot-mark or wheel-mark. . . .

When the snow darkness began to deepen towards evening, the track became quite illegible, and when I found myself at this romantically situated cabin, I was thankful to find that they could give me shelter.

Isabella Bird, Letter IX, October 24

Bird's departure from the Van Warmer Ranch, in spite of the weather, introduced her to the tough traveling she would experience throughout much of her southern circuit. After the first four miles that day, she took shelter in a cabin where eleven other people had also taken refuge, and she stayed there for a couple of hours until the weather lightened. She set off again, forded a frozen creek on which the ice broke under her and Birdie's weight, and was unnerved enough that she only traveled a few miles farther, to the Barker place, which had been recommended to her. It was located somewhere along Plum Creek. By her reckoning, the Barker ranch was only twenty-six miles south of Denver and only about eight miles south of the Van Warmer place. Here she spent her second night.

The scene there, with bustling snow-covered men and dogs and farm animals huddling around the buildings, reminded her of John Greenleaf Whittier's poem "Snowbound, A Winter Idyll." It reads, in very small part:

Shut in from all the world without,
We sat the clean-winged hearth about,
Content to let the north-wind roar
In baffled rage at pane and door,

> While the red logs before us beat
> The frost-line back with tropic heat; . . .
> What matter how the night behaved?
> What matter how the north-wind raved?
> Blow high, blow low, not all its snow
> Could quench our hearth-fire's ruddy glow. (Lines 155–
>   60, 175–78)

Bird observed in her letters that the scene was "very tolerable" and, despite a man who railed against English people and their manners, she spent "a pleasant and diverting evening." She also noted, however, that she had no sheets and that the cold was "so awesome" that she "pulled the rag carpet from the floor to put over [her] bed."

I drive south on U.S. 85. The road is busy, crowded, thick with cars, and lined with businesses. I recognize again the difference between my form of travel and Isabella's. She and Birdie moved at a slow, steady pace and, except on those occasions like her second day, when snow balling up on the mare's feet made it necessary for Isabella to get down and either remove the snow or walk along ahead of the horse, Birdie was in charge of forward momentum. Most of the time Bird was free to look around, absorb the scenery with the cold, and ponder her impressions as she rode. I have no such opportunity with my pace determined by the flow of traffic. I am happy to get off 85 north of Sedalia and find a quiet road paralleling it.

Though I have no idea where the Barker Ranch might have been, I can see Plum Creek flowing at the foot of the slope parallel to the road, and the valley is open enough to farming and ranching, whatever the density of the businesses along the road, that I have some slight sense of how such a ranch might be situated. It occurs to me that it's the open ranchlands of Colorado, rather than the everchanging cities or the changeless mountains, that are still most in touch with the Colorado of the nineteenth century, a territory then just beginning to develop.

Highway monotony frees your mind for reflection, but driving a speeding car doesn't give you much opportunity for observation. The main highways are way too busy for you to do much more than pay attention to the road, and you have to keep up with the flow of traffic or you're in trouble or they're in trouble and you can't concentrate on any part of the world passing you by. Today, even on the two-lane, traffic keeps me focused on my driving. The solid double stripes running down the center of the road prevent—or at least discourage—easy passing by someone coming up behind me and I feel impelled to go at a rapid pace. Moreover, the road has almost no real shoulders, which makes politely pulling over difficult. Often I whiz past something that catches my eye, and then I have to debate whether to look for a place to turn in, turn around, and come back.

I notice a weathered plank barn and the valley beyond it and the distant foothills. To study it further, I pull into a driveway and wait for the heavy clubcab truck speeding behind me to thunder past so I can back out onto the road. Farther down the driveway, a rancher steps out of a pickup truck to close a steel gate; he eyes me suspiciously and I try to smile my most innocuous town dude smile. I go back up the road, pass the object of my attention again, find another driveway to turn around in, and then park carefully by a recessed row of mailboxes. The complications of this kind of observation make me reluctant to repeat it very often, however much I'd like to stop and study any number of specific sites I'm passing.

Surveying the plank barn and the valley beyond it is one of my few moments of concentrated gazing on the road. The barn is tall and long, its large, sharply slanted roof descending from a central ventilating cupola and marked by two hay hoods that look like sharp wings extending from the ridge at either end. Below the high steep upper roof, a row of glassless windows hang in a low wall; a lower, shorter, more gently sloping roof covers an extension built out from the side of the barn, where horse stalls are lined up behind open windowed doors. The extensions running beyond the north end of the barn look like truncated arms reaching out toward a dingy white silo just ahead of it.

The morning sun, higher now, illuminates the entire valley. Grassy fields surround the barn, part-way down the slope, and, across the valley, a couple of horses graze; they have a very large pasture all to themselves. (Grace Greenwood commented about the area, "Little attention is paid to horticulture, but horsiculture is not neglected. I have seen many fine-blooded animals in harness and under the saddle.") The slope above the horses is thickly covered in scrub brush, and on the ridge top sit a farmhouse and out-buildings.

The distant farm has a rather late-twentieth-century look, but the nearer red and black barn seems in scale and style and degree of weathering to date back to early days of ranching along Plum Creek. When Isabella Bird rode through the valley, it was thick with snow, but Grace Greenwood observed it in milder weather. She wrote, "This prairie farming country is a singularly silent land. We heard no whetting of scythes, no tinkling of bells, little lowing of cattle even, or crowing or cackling of barn-yard fowls that day. There being so few trees along our way, we heard no birds; indeed, we missed nearly all the usual pleasant rural sounds, though occasionally we heard a mule bray, a teamster swear at his oxen, and at noon farm-hands and railroad-men called to their dinner by a joyful shout of 'Grub-pile!'" Despite the heavy pickup trucks on the road, I can't help but think that the valley isn't that different from what it was. Ranchland shouldn't be as susceptible to transformation as cities are.

Isabella Bird claimed in the October 28 section of Letter X that, as she continued south, she followed an untrodden track, breaking her trail through the snow, and eventually left the road to seek shelter at the Perry Ranch. I've plotted my route down Perry Park Road, Colorado Highway 105, from Sedalia, a quieter road than either U.S. 85 or Interstate 25, possibly simulating Isabella's trail. I pass a ranch being converted into a housing development, its homesites already mapped on a large sign where the entrance to the ranch had been. The suburbs of Denver are on the march. But then I pass the Allis Ranch, a gigantic spread sprawling all over the valley, and know at once that the only thing that keeps all of this from becoming outlying districts for Denver is the dogged survival of such ranches. All the way south to Palmer Lake, signs identify such persistent places: Sandstone Ranch. Haystack Ranch. Coyote Ridge. Crystal Way. Double J. Thunder Valley. Ranches lining Perry Park Road make the landscape seem peaceful, bucolic, pastoral. Magpies glide across the highway before me, and horses graze everywhere I look.

The 1869 Hayden Geological Survey named the area where the Perry Ranch was later located Pleasant Park, and it was Perry's ranch that renamed it. William Henry Jackson photographed Pleasant Park around 1871–1872, while it was still unsettled terrain. His photograph gives a wide view of the park, a broad expanse of relatively flat grassland encircled in the distance by high rock formations of eroded sandstone and shale. The exposed rock ridges and hills shelter the park on three sides. In the foreground a member of the survey team lounging in the grasses gives not only an awareness of scale but also a visual sense that this is, in fact, a pleasant park.

The man for whom the park was later renamed, John Dietz Perry, was a millionaire industrialist and president of the Kansas Pacific Railroad. He acquired property around the West Plum Creek area and established his ranch in Pleasant Park, in a gorge below a 300-foot-high ridge called Nanichant Rock. Perry's home base remained St. Louis, Missouri, but his family spent their summers at the ranch and Perry's son Charles managed it year round. In its early days, it was the kind of destination that seemed obvious for people like former Governor Hunt and *Rocky Mountain News* editor Byers, who had provided Isabella with letters of introduction to the prominent citizens of Colorado.

Perry himself was not at the ranch when Isabella Bird arrived, but his daughter, "a very bright-looking, elegantly dressed girl," proved to be a willing and charming hostess. Bird was provided "stewed venison and various luxuries on the table, which was tasteful and refined," and she found the daughter's company very enjoyable. In her book she briefly mentions that, on her return from her after-dinner ride, "I passed into a region of vivacious descriptions of Egypt, Palestine, Asia Minor, Turkey, Russia, and other countries, in which Miss Perry had travelled with her family for three years"; in her letter recounting the same conversation she credits her hostess with being "most intelligent in her descriptions." In neither does she provide the first name of the daughter, whose further identity is unknown.

In the evening a "gentleman cousin" took Isabella riding to see Pleasant Park, "which takes rank among the finest scenery of Colorado." They "entered it by a narrow pass guarded by two buttes, or isolated upright masses of rock, bright red, and about 300 feet in height." She thought "the narrow canyons which came down on the park gloomily magnificent" and took note of "a quantity of 'monumental' rocks, from 50 to 300 feet in height, bright vermilion, green, buff, orange, and sometimes all combined, their gay tinting a contrast to the disastrous-looking snow and the sombre pines."

Determined to see "Pleasant Park" for myself, I turn off onto a road through Perry Park Gateway, a natural resources preservation area along West Plum Creek. It is chiefly notable as wetlands habitat for the Preble's Meadow jumping mouse. The mouse, an endangered species, three inches long with a six-inch tail, can launch itself a foot and a half into the air, change directions in mid-jump, and leap up to a distance of three feet. It also swims, and the wetlands with their moisture and long grasses are ideal habitat. The jumping mouse is difficult to see in the best circumstances—access to the wildlife area is restricted—and neither Isabella, traveling in deep snow, nor I, driving, spot it.

On Red Rock Drive, I ascend a ridge and head down the other side, passing through an area of spacious houses, nicely placed among plentiful ponderosas that proliferate here. The community seems oriented toward preserving the trees despite the housing. I begin a long descent into another open park, with red rocks and white rocks on my right, almost certainly the formations pictured by Jackson in the USGS photograph. Perry Park is like any other mountain park, a basin surrounded by mountains that opens up to view as you top a pass between bluffs. In this case it's a pretty park, pleasant still because not yet overdeveloped. Pike National Forest abuts the west side of the community and puts limits on its growth in that direction. Rock formations around the basin resemble the shapes of those in Red Rocks and Roxborough State Parks, to the north, and Garden of the Gods, south near Colorado Springs. At one time they drew visitors to the area, and some of the formations were identified with fanciful names—Castle Ridge, the Vale of Cashmere, the Walls of Jericho, Hay Stacks—the kind of geological Rorschach test that such places inspire.

At the bottom of the valley I take a turn that leads toward the country club and find myself in the setting where the

Perry Park ranchhouse had been. The road parallels Bear Creek, the stream where Bird and her companion broke through the ice while crossing, through the gap between Castle Ridge and Nanichant Rock. After Perry sold his property to the Red Stone Town, Land, and Mining Company in 1888, the new owners dammed the creek and formed Lake Wauconda, the centerpiece in a proposed village of the same name. That sudden flat expanse of blue water is startling when you first encounter it, especially with bright green fairways surrounding it. The lake is now the focal point of the golf course, with the clubhouse situated above it, and a rocky ridge closing off the eastern view. The Perry Park Country Club is a private eighteen-hole course, which, according to its website, bans denim and requires collared shirts and spikeless shoes (the site says nothing about garish polyester pants or loud floral patterns on shirts). I park in the paved lot near the lake and step out to look around me.

Lake Wauconda glows placidly with the reflection of the sky. Across from me, beyond a fairway and near two comma-shaped bunkers of sand, stands what is now called Sentinel Rock, formerly known as Washington Monument, a massive, upright, weathered sand-colored rock formation. Similar shapes protrude above the distant trees and at the tops of ridges. The country club is not the sprawling bulldozed and sculpted artificial terrain you might expect, the kind I was so familiar with in the East, though I know it has been thoroughly landscaped. In a book on Douglas County, where Perry Park is located, one page displays both a photograph of Perry Park Ranch, the buildings spread across the edge of a broad open field with a high bluff behind the main building, and a second photograph of golf course and road construction that shows a considerably scarred terrain. I doubt that there's a native stem of grass anywhere on the grounds, but rather than being located in the open parklands the course somehow works its way through the terrain as if its greens, fairways, and sandtraps were regional curiosities amid sandstone outcroppings and circling mountains. The natural rock formations, the forested hills, and the sky dominate the view, and make it difficult to reconcile manicured greens and artificial lake with these surroundings.

In the opposite direction from the country club I see abrupt heights, tree covered and jagged, and feel a sense of enclosure. Only an outburst of brilliant yellow aspen glowing in the sun interrupts the solid dark green mass of firs on the heights. It takes me a moment to realize that a sumptuous and costly house looms above me as well, tucked into the trees. Nantichant Rock, the ridge that helps form the canyon where Perry built his house, is named for the echo of a figure in an Indian legend. A few of the roads leading away from the country club are named Echo Valley and Echo Gap, and clusters of townhouses on those roads are named Echo Hills and Echo Village. I have a feeling about the community that it was fabricated with a kind of singular and single-minded vision.

Leaving the lot, I spot eight deer in the high grass across the road, just below a glorious house with a gigantic deck set up high on the side of the bluff. Yet another house perches above that, right on the top of the ridge. I noticed neither of them before. I stop the car to watch the deer for a moment, but a golfer racing down the boulevard in a golf cart spooks them. They don't bolt very far, however, and soon continue grazing fairly close to the road. The interchange between golfer and ruminant suggests how little attention the wildlife in these parts pay to the domestic life around them. I suppose the deer in Perry Park, like the elk in Estes Park, are simply part of the ambience—just another group of neighbors you notice in passing but no longer stop to gape at.

The high foothills close in this little valley, make it feel secluded, tucked away. Especially if the floor of the park were open the way it is now—and it's mostly open now because of ranching and the towering bluffs on the north side of the park—I can see why someone would think this to be a pleasant park. I wonder how the Perrys would feel about the way the land has been both preserved and developed—Perry himself had once hoped to establish a resort in the park—and I have the feeling that they would feel very much at home.

* * *

The rest of the day's ride was awful enough. The snow was thirteen inches deep, and grew deeper as I ascended in silence and loneliness, but just as the sun sank behind a snowy peak I reached the top of the Divide, 7,975 feet above the sea level. There, in unspeakable solitude, lay a frozen lake. Owls hooted among the pines, the trail was obscure, the country was not settled, the mercury was 9° below zero, my feet had lost all sensation, and one of them was frozen to the wooden stirrup. I found that owing to the depth of the snow I had only ridden fifteen miles in eight and a half hours, and must look about for a place to sleep in. The eastern sky was unlike anything I ever saw before. It had been chrysoprase, then it turned to aquamarine, and that to the bright full green of an emerald. Unless I am color-blind, this is true. Then suddenly the whole changed, and flushed with the pure, bright, rose color of the afterglow.

Isabella Bird, Letter X, October 28

Palmer Lake, both lake and town, is located on the divide between the watersheds of the South Platte and the Arkansas Rivers, the two major eastward-bound rivers of Colorado. The divide, usually called the Palmer Divide but sometimes the Monument Divide, is, in a sense, also a divide between what I think of as principally Isabella Bird's territory—everything to the north—and what I think of as terrain she shares with her female contemporaries. Isabella's approach came on a wintry late October day, and winter weather would dog her through her southern loop, restricting what she was able to take in and what she was able to respond to. Others, like Rose Kingsley in late 1871 and early 1872, Grace Greenwood in autumn of 1871, spring and autumn of 1872, and, with Eliza Greatorex, September 1873, and Helen Hunt Jackson from November 1873 on, traveled in better weather and viewed the landscape without snow cover. For example, Rose Kingsley, traveling by train from Denver, took note of "the Pineries, a great source of wealth all along the Rocky Mountains," and later spotted "a large steam-mill in full work." She claimed that, going up the north side of the divide, "the grade was very steep, seventy-five feet to the mile," and wrote that it "was the highest point of ground [she] had ever been on, being 7,554 feet above the sea." Helen Hunt, who took up residence in Colorado Springs, could admire the seasonal attractions of the divide: "On its very summit lies a lake, whose shores in June are like garden-beds of flowers, and in October are blazing with the colors of rubies and carnelians." Isabella Bird, adding 400 feet to Kingsley's elevation (the highest point on the Palmer Divide is Monument Hill, at 7,332 feet, about 100 feet higher than Palmer Lake), saw only a frozen lake. What we see, when we see it, and who we are determine our reaction to—and interpretation of—where we are.

Isabella Bird left the Perry Ranch on "a pristine morning," under a cloudless sky, windless, ice-bound, silent and cold, hearing only "the crunch of snow under Birdie's feet." It took her all day to ride the dozen or so miles to the divide. She noticed only its isolation and frigidity but was singularly impressed by the shifting colors of the eastern sky. I travel in the middle of the morning, rather than late in the afternoon, and the sky is uniformly bright blue instead of metamorphosing into an array of colors. In the sunlight the car is starting to take on warmth beyond what the heater gives off.

Entering Palmer Lake, the road arcs around a large depression in the ground. It takes me a moment to notice a few large pools and puddles scattered throughout the depression and an absence of the scruffy grasses one might expect in such an open field. When I see the gazebo positioned to look down on the depression, I comprehend that I'm looking at Palmer Lake, for which the town was named. I stop at a convenience store on the highway and ask the kid behind the counter if the depression is Palmer Lake, and whether it's been hard hit by the continuing drought. He nods and tells me, "My daddy say he don't know how it will ever come back." Palmer Lake fills only from runoff and snowmelt, and there's been little of that in the region.

I drive to the far side of the lake, through a large empty parking lot, and leave the car to walk out on a short pier with a protective chain across the end. I guess the chain is there to keep people from falling into the lake, but there's only dry ground beneath it. A few mallards lunch in the deepest pool but the lake bottom is for the most part parched and broken in the sun, just dry, cracked earth, empty and lifeless. I see another pointless pier in the distance. Two signs near where I stand read as unintentionally ironic. "No Swimming. No Boating," one says. Not to worry. The second one explains with pride how the restoration of the lake had been completed in November 1999 and credits the Sport Fish Restoration Act and the Colorado Division of Wildlife with making it possible. It is a point of pride that the drought seems to have taken away.

On the other side of the lake, the town seems fairly prosperous and well established. Houses spread through the hills, a library isn't far off the highway, one building still displays a sign for Kaiser-Frazer, the long-defunct auto company, and a surprising variety of restaurants line the main drag. To the west are the foothills and to the east buttes rise above the plains. Palmer Lake looks like a well-established little community, and I hope it doesn't depend much on the actual lake, considerably less of an attraction now than when Isabella Bird found it frozen in an unbroken field of snow.

When I drive back around the lake, I pass again a sign I barely noticed earlier, a big slab of red stone with an open window in it and black letters reading, "Almost Paradise. Palmer Lake. 1889." Irony abounds in the signs at Palmer Lake. In between Isabella's passage and mine, cycles of aspiration have gone unfulfilled or have been altered by circumstance throughout the Front Range, as here at Palmer Lake, as at Perry Park. It's hard for a transient to determine whether what he sees now is achieving the aspirations of current inhabitants.

* * *

Following Interstate 25 south to Colorado Springs, I am soon drawn into the maw of an untidy, overgrown city, hell-bent on expansion, among whose speeding denizens I'm as indistinguishable as a single cell in a bloodstream. Given my earlier experience with cities on the plains, I'm not surprised by this urban turmoil, but I'd been reading early accounts of the community and imagining it in terms of when the 1870s began.

Like Greeley's Union Colony, Colorado Springs grew out of the Fountain Colony, a planned community instigated by General William Jackson Palmer—the Palmer of Palmer Lake, which was a watering stop for his engines—who owned the Denver & Rio Grande Railway and wanted to create an elegant resort on the scale of Newport or Saratoga in the East. In 1871 Colorado Springs was launched and Maurice Kingsley arrived as assistant treasurer of the Fountain

Colony. His sister Rose accompanied him. Her account in *South by West* is a true frontier portrait.

In November 1871, Rose Kingsley wrote, "You may imagine Colorado Springs, as I did, to be a sequestered valley, with bubbling fountains, green grass, and shady trees: but not a bit of it." Instead, she found "a level elevated plateau of greenish-brown, without a single tree or plant larger than a Spanish bayonet (Yucca) two feet high" where streets were laid out but unfinished, houses scattered and usually under construction, and tents abounding. The Denver and Rio Grande office housed railway and colony business as well as the "post-office, doctor's shop, and general lounge for the whole town." The Kingsleys lived next door, in a sixteen-foot by twelve-foot wooden shanty with an attached tent for a "sitting-room by day and [Maurice's] bedroom at night." Already significant points of local interest were established—the mansion General Palmer was building in Glen Eyrie, the park known as the Garden of the Gods, the hot springs at Manitou with its temporary inn, and the trail up Pike's Peak, where a "half-way house" let tourists ascend in stages over two days.

Grace Greenwood toured the area in July 1872, arriving by train, staying at "a good hotel, . . . sleeping deliciously under the shadow of Pike's Peak and a couple of blankets," and on the following day visiting "the most attractive points in the vicinity"—Glen Eyrie, Garden of the Gods, Manitou Springs. The area was developing quickly. A year later, having toured the region again with "a great caravan of pilgrims," she wrote her introduction to Greatorex's *Summer Etchings in Colorado* (datelined September 26, 1873) while she looked out "the windows of the principal hotel of *Manitou*, the most fashionable and delightful watering place of Colorado."

Two months later (around the time Isabella Bird rode through), Helen Hunt arrived in Colorado Springs. She later wrote, "I shall never forget my sudden sense of hopeless disappointment at the moment when I first looked on the town." She claimed to have arrived, "ill, disheartened," in search of a healthful climate. "There stretched before me, to the east, a bleak, bare, unrelieved, desolate plain. There rose behind me, to the west, a dark range of mountains, snow-topped, rocky-walled, stern, cruel, relentless. Between lay the town—small, straight, new, treeless." The view first made her despair, but she grew to love the area. She described wide, well laid-out streets, an abundance of young cottonwood trees, and all manner of establishments: "bakeries, laundries, livery stables, billiard halls, restaurants, mills, shops, hotels, and churches," concluding that "the town is far better provided than the average New England town of the same population."

Greenwood and Hunt (who married William Sharpless Jackson in 1875) wrote about the Colorado Springs area after establishing some familiarity with it; Isabella Bird was simply a transient, no doubt still under the influence of her Estes Park idyll and certainly affected by the arduousness of her wintry travels from Denver. Feeling conspicuous as she approached "the bleak-looking scattered houses of the ambitious watering place of Colorado Springs," she dismounted, put on a long skirt over her riding outfit, and "rode sidewise" into town. On reflection, however, she thought "the settlement scarcely looked like a place where any deference to prejudices was necessary. A queer embryo-looking place it is, out on the bare Plains." Its "utter treelessness" made it particularly unattractive to her. As period photographs show, the cluster of buildings seemed surrounded simply by miles and miles of empty dirt.

Isabella's brief stay in Colorado Springs, partly to give Birdie "the Sabbath she was entitled to," gave her an opportunity to socialize. She was welcomed by an English couple whom Rose Kingsley knew, J. E. Liller and his wife. Liller had been hired by Palmer to serve as editor of *Out West*, the magazine in which, a few months after her visit, Isabella first published the article about her ascent of Longs Peak that she later revised as a chapter in *A Lady's Life in the Rocky Mountains*. She was also visited by other friends of the "much remembered and beloved" Rose Kingsley and shown the sights of the tourist circuit.

The first stop was Palmer's estate in Glen Eyrie. When Rose Kingsley first visited, the Palmers were still at work on what was meant to be "a most charming large house" but living "in a sort of picnic way in small rooms in the loft above the stable"; Grace Greenwood, a year later, found the building to be "an elegant country-house" located in "a lovely, romantic spot"; Eliza Greatorex, visiting shortly before Isabella, sketched the buildings with massive boulders towering over and around them. Isabella thought of the place as a "baronial mansion," its "fine hall filled with buffalo, elk, and deer heads, skins of wild animals, stuffed birds, bear robes, and numerous Indian and other weapons and trophies." Period photos show a solid and spacious frame house.

The Lillers also took Isabella to the Garden of the Gods, an area of impressive, stark red sandstone formations. Grace Greenwood described it as "a wild, singular, natural park, the gateway of which is formed by two stupendous rocks, marvelously architectural and cathedral-like in character. They always look solemn and worshipful, and there is certainly no hollow mockery of religion about them." Isabella, the clergyman's daughter, was less appreciative. She thought the name fantastic and the locale one "in which, were I a divinity, I certainly would not choose to dwell." She commented disapprovingly, "Many places in this neighborhood are also vulgarized by grotesque names." No doubt she was thinking of the formation then known as "Seal Making Love to a Nun." Rose Kingsley was circumspect in her description, claiming only that it showed "a red sandstone nun, with a white cowl over her head, looking at a seal who stood on his tail, and made faces at her." Once a suggestive name has been given to such a structure, it merely invites the viewer to see that shape rather than another.

Isabella parted from the Lillers after the Garden of the Gods and rode on alone into "the Great Gorge of the Manitou." She referred to it as "chill and solemn," but Helen Hunt Jackson described it as "a little fairy canyon, full of rocks and fir-trees, and the creek, and effervescing medicine springs." Isabella elected to stay overnight at one of the hotels of Manitou Springs—undoubtedly the one Grace Greenwood stayed in two months earlier—"to have a last taste of luxury," an indulgence she seldom needed to grant herself. It was, she said, "only the fourth" [in her letters she says only the third] "night in Colorado that I have slept on anything better than hay or straw." There she saw relatively few people rather than the hundreds that thronged the place in the summer.

One aspect of Isabella Bird's personality that differentiated her from her writing contemporaries in Colorado was her disinterest in resort tourism and her disinclination to use its resources. She was inclined to look for locations reminiscent of Estes Park while they were inclined to make brief, preferably well-accoutered excursions outward from a comfortable base. It's significant that Greenwood and Hunt Jackson both chose the "most fashionable and delightful watering-place in Colorado" as the site of their cottages—Greenwood's was "a dainty cottage, in a clematis tangle," according to Jackson—and Isabella couldn't wait to get away from it.

Greenwood, in her introduction to Greatorex's book, used her reading of John C. Frémont's account of his explorations of the area thirty years earlier to highlight "[h]ow changed, and yet unchanged, the lovely valley of the fountain and its grand surroundings." She finds positive aspects in the replacement of deer, buffalo, grizzlies, soldiers, and Indians by locomotives, artists, photographers, and "jolly camper[s]." In place of wilderness, returning explorers from the past "would see hotels, cottages, bath-houses, summer-houses, bowling-alleys. They would see stage-coaches, ambulances, busses and barouches, horsemen and horsewomen dashing hither and thither." She contrasts the "inspiring war-whoop," now "silenced forever," with "the Italian *bravura*," the war-dance and the scalp-dance with the "Boston Dip" and the "New York Glide." On the tour with that "caravan" she "found beauty indescribable—grandeur unimaginable—delight incommunicable, everywhere; but no where the expected wildness, savageness and desolation." The statement likely is meant to reassure the reader, for Greenwood concluded, "The world is storming the Rocky Mountains. . . . They are not only a grand store-house of storms, and a treasure-house of incalculable wealth, but, what is better, they are to become, with their wonderful parks, their lakes, rivers, gorges, woods, and waterfalls, the great pleasure-ground of the world." This, it strikes me, is a particularly American, especially nineteenth-century American, way of viewing both landscape and change.

Helen Hunt Jackson responded to the setting in far more aesthetic ways, perhaps because, by the time she wrote about it, she had begun to dwell in it. The plains, the mountains, the sky, the weather, all provoked her admiration. She writes breathlessly of "days when the whole plain looked like a soft floor of gray mist, its mounds and hills like mounds and hills of vapor, slow curling and rounding; when it looked like a floor of beaten gold, even, solid, shining; or like a tapestry, woven in bands of brown and yellow,—a magic tapestry, too, for the bands are ever shifting, deepening, paling, advancing, receding, vanishing and coming again, as the clouds come or go, deepen or pale, in the skies above; or, if it be winter, like a trackless, illimitable, frozen ocean, with here and there dark icebergs looming up." Isabella Bird might have appreciated that last bit of description. Jackson was equally fervent about her view of the mountains and felt that "the whole rounded horizon is thus full of beauty and grandeur." Somewhat more profoundly than Greenwood, Jackson took inspiration in the transformations made in this setting: "Most earnestly I believe, also, that there is to be born of these plains and mountains, all along the great central plateaus of our continent, the very best life, physical and mental, of the coming centuries."

I'm well aware of the changes the intervening years have wrought on the "most attractive points in the vicinity." The Glen Eyrie estate was expanded and renovated into castle proportions, and eventually converted into a fairly posh conference center and bed and breakfast inn; meticulously restored and maintained by a Christian organization, it offers tours displaying the glories of Palmer's 1904 renovation, which obliterated the original structure. At the Garden of the Gods the formations have been renamed, given less imaginative, more circumspect and prim, monikers—Cathedral Spires, Three Graces, Pulpit Rock, Steamboat Rock, Balanced Rock, White Rock, Gray Rock; the most suggestive names now are tame: Siamese Twins, Toad and Toadstools, and Kissing Camels. Paths, drives, picnic areas, and viewing points are well maintained around the perimeters, interior paths are dense with piñon pine and juniper and scatterings of Douglas fir and ponderosa pine, and, though often overrun with tourists on the one hand and fitness buffs on the other, it is possible to spend a secluded moment or two of reflection at the base of some of the formations, thinking about the geological forces that shaped them, the evidence of eons of alluvial deposition and subsequent erosion. Manitou Springs is still a tourist center; nine of Manitou's twenty-six springs still function—there were seven when Isabella Bird was there—and the Cliff House, an elegant old hotel, originally opened in 1873, is still in business. The downtown boasts a National Historic District designation and, rather than the "water cure," tourists now come for the Victorian architecture of the later nineteenth century, or for the shops, all designated as either "quaint" or "charming."

"The great pleasure-ground of the world." "The very best life, physical and mental, of the coming centuries." Would Greenwood and Hunt feel their optimism rewarded if they returned to visit this region so dear to them? Would Bird's fears for what development might do to the territory seem even more prophetic? These are rhetorical questions from a man in thrall to horsepower, hurtling over pavement, for the first time this day aware that he has been swearing at others in similarly moving vehicles. Taking the back roads, I was, despite my speed, calmed by the openness of the ranchland and the space between the foothills and the buttes, felt—like Helen Hunt Jackson—attuned to the vastness. I've lost most of that calm by coming into Colorado Springs, have quickly gotten city-tense.

Being in the mountains has altered the pace and rhythm of my life, expanded and settled my outlook. If I feel the loss of the mountains—I who really live on the plains—what must the change in location have felt like for Isabella Bird? I feel more in sync with her emotions as I leave Colorado Springs. Like her, I'm eager to get away from industriously expanding civic and commercial centers. I've come as far south in Colorado as she traveled and now I'm ready to follow her trail west as far as it goes.

ii

All the time I was in sight of the Fountain River, brighter than any stream, because it tumbles over rose-red granite, rocky or disintegrated, a truly fair stream, cutting and forcing its way through hard rocks, under arches of alabaster ice, through fringes of crystalline ice, thumping with a hollow sound in cavernous recesses cold and dark, or leaping in foam from heights with rush and swish; always bright and riotous, never pausing in still pools to rest, dashing through gates of rock, pine-hung, pine-bridged, pine-buried; twinkling and laughing in the sunshine, or frowning in "dowie dens" in the blue pine gloom.

Isabella Bird, Letter X, October 31

Isabella Bird set out from Manitou on October 30, 1873, intent on completing her southern circuit. Following a wagon road up toward Ute Pass, she found the canyon narrow "with barely room for the torrent and the wagon road which has been blasted out of its steep sides." The closeness of the canyon, the cold massiveness of the mountains, and the roar of the river current near the road intimidated her. She crossed onto "a sunlit upland park" and soon found herself traveling for several miles "through a forest, which I always dislike when alone, from the fear of being frightened by something which may appear from behind a tree." In her letter to her sister her next sentence read, "That forest is full of bears and pumas," but for the book she replaced it with one that, in the letter, had immediately preceded it: "I saw a beautiful white fox, several skunks, some chipmonks and gray squirrels, owls, crows, and crested bluejays." In the book, then, she undercuts her fearfulness with a list of harmless creatures she actually saw rather than justify it by mentioning dangerous creatures she didn't see.

She was looking for Bergens Park, a specific location recommended to her by Rose Kingsley, who must have extolled its beauty. Isabella thought it reminiscent of "some dismal Highland strath": "It is long and featureless, and its immediate surroundings are mean." Bergens Park was occupied by Mr. Thornton, "an English gentlemen, who has a worthy married Englishman as his manager." Thornton expected to develop a resort on the site; Bird preferred such locations to go undeveloped: "I thought of the blue hollow lying solitary at the foot of Long's Peak, and rejoiced that I had 'happened into it.'"

Isabella Bird described the Bergens Park cabin as typical of the way "every man must begin life here." It was "long, low, mud roofed, and very dark," "full of raw meat, fowls, and gear," and "all very rough, dark, and comfortless." At one end of the cabin were a cookstove, table, benches, and stools, at the other a living area for the manager, his wife, and three children; a sheet partitioned the two sections and both sections were cluttered throughout with clusters of foodstuffs and gear. In addition to the family and Bird, their meal was shared with ten hired men while seven dogs and three cats rested by the fire. The setting quickly acclimated her once more to the rigors of finding lodging on the road.

As it happened, Bird was following in the snowy footsteps of Grace Greenwood, Eliza Greatorex, and their touring party. The circumstances of their travels were far more comfortable than Bird's, and Greatorex's impressions of Bergens (or Bergun's, as she spelled it) Park were more positive. In *Summer Etchings in Colorado*, she wrote of being in a camp, "with Park lands stretching around us so far and broad that all sense of locality is lost," and "with leisure for sketching and for enjoying the most 'realizing sense' of true ranche life." For her that meant eating well outdoors at a table topped with a tablecloth and fresh flowers, gazing off at livestock, "broad slopes of green pasture, . . . skies of purest blue, and mountains—mountains, all around."

She thought of the "ranche" as "a noble estate" and admired its "fine vegetable garden, neatly fenced around," and "the ranchero's particular pride and care, the dairy."

Greatorex and Greenwood help fill in the missing elements of Isabella Bird's route, but the conditions under which they traveled, generally pampered and looked after, in routinely warm and pleasant weather, and the circumstances of her travels, alone on horseback through snow, account for much of the difference in the tone of their writings. When Greatorex and her full party left Bergens Park and "started in full procession for *real camp life*" (my emphasis), she tells us that "baggage-wagons had been sent to the Platte River, forty miles away, but we camping people filled five 'ambulances,' as the wagons used for camping are called." In contrast to Bird's ride on Birdie, Greatorex could claim that the "long morning and afternoon rides were full of novelty and enjoyment; some of us on horseback, with all sorts of devices for saddles and riding-habits, made marks for the jests and merriment of the rest"—a jolly and sociable bunch apparently. The difference may be that between the tourist and the traveler, as Greatorex makes clear by pointing out how "often the wildest fun was silenced suddenly as some overpowering beauty of view opened before us, and the sunsets were of a glory beyond the power of words to describe." I don't recall ever running into the word *fun* in Isabella Bird's correspondence or published writings about the Rocky Mountains.

The narrow wagon road toward Ute Pass has been replaced by wide, well-paved U.S. 24. The swift highway takes me in no time from the junction in Colorado City to Manitou Springs, from where Bird departed. Immediately west of Colorado Springs, the rough, rugged country begins—canyons, arroyos, gulches, bluffs, mesas, rock outcroppings and intriguing geological formations abound everywhere I look. It's a different world than the high plains have made me familiar with; I've left the plains behind. Colorado Springs' elevation is 6,012 feet and in the twelve miles west to Woodland Park, over the Ute Pass Trail up Fountain Creek Canyon, I climb to 8,465 feet, a notable change in elevation.

Woodland Park didn't exist in 1873, but the broad, open plateau it spreads across seems a natural site for settlement. A turn-off there, up Highway 67, leads to the Manitou Park area of the Pike National Forest, where Bergens Park was located, but I have no inclination to detour. The road through Manitou Park leads into narrower terrain north of the valley and devolves into winding roads hugging low creeks flowing toward the South Platte River. The evidence of Bergens Park is gone now. Isabella Bird said she left the wagon road and "went up a long ascent in deep snow." My maps don't show the exact location of Thornton's place, but I know from having driven through Manitou Park that the valley is broad enough and long enough to be an inviting site for a ranch and a long haul in deep snow on horseback. It's another inner world, not as constricting as a canyon, not as exposed as the plains, but somehow comforting in its combination of space within limits.

Most of the area is now part of the Pike National Forest, and the Rampart Range walls off Manitou Park from the foothills and plains to the east. I am, as Isabella was, getting behind the Front Range and once again feeling a sense of discovery about Colorado.

Isabella Bird seldom quavers in her travels, but after she departed Thornton's late in the morning of October 31, delayed again by the need to give the packed snow time to soften and grow less slippery, the rigors of traveling alone on horseback through a rugged wintry landscape seemed to unnerve her. It may partly have been because this situation followed a period of five days of social activity, but it was also because her trail was taking her west into the mountains—that is, into more remote and less settled regions. Acquaintances shared with her the story of thirty people being lost on Ute Pass—likely the party containing Greenwood and Greatorex; the artist mentions such a mishap—and that gave her more reason to be unsettled by her route and by her circumstances as a foreign woman traveling entirely alone. Moreover, because of the weather, the road she was traveling was simply in worse shape than anticipated by those back in Denver who helped her plan her route. My circuit, though also taken, like Bird's, at the end of October, is driven on a dry, mostly sunny day, before this year's snowy season has really begun. It's not surprising to me, knowing her circumstances, that each night Isabella seems entirely relieved to discover whatever outpost she happens upon.

I pass the town of Divide, elevation over 9,000 feet, but otherwise indistinguishable from Woodland Park or Anywhere-else, America, and cross Ute Pass. Not far away I notice an area of open ranchland being converted—though I see no forest nearby—into "Sherwood Forest Estates." A street sign reads "Robin Hood Road." My own neighborhood in Lafayette, similarly once open range, is platted with streets named for characters out of King Arthur and Robin Hood legends, and elsewhere in town another development uses names from Greek history and mythology. The place names give no sense that any cultural or natural history particular to that place occurred in any of these locations. This area too is going the way of development but not quite as explosively as areas closer to Colorado Springs or Denver.

I soon come upon a dirt road where a large sign reads "Twin Rock"—a ranch where Isabella stayed was near here—and shows a painting of an upright mass of boulders. Not far from the turn-off, boulders on a ridge look as if they might be those on the sign, but I really can't be certain. The terrain I start through on the highway now has a number of similar outcroppings of greater and lesser mass, rocks piled up in odd formations, one on top of another.

I know this area a little bit from having hiked the other side of it. Sue and I once spent a day in the area taking in Florissant Fossil Beds National Monument. The petrified remnants of a redwood forest are accessible on a loop from park headquarters. On a stretch of that trail, the park attempts to illustrate the enormity of geologic time with signposts marking milestones in the earth's history on a scale where two inches equals a million years. Signs for "today" and for the "beginning of mankind" are side by side, but you have to walk a very long way to get to the period when those stumps were living trees and, by the time you get to the sign identifying when algae, fungi, and bacteria began to flourish, you can't see the sign for "today" back around the bend. Earlier on the loop, we saw a similar vertical scale showing how far below the present surface the shale that had preserved the fossils had gone, how much had been deposited above it. Those exhibits put into perspective the flourishing and subsequent fossilization of that forest and some of its inhabitants (paleontologists have identified one of the fossil insects as a tsetse fly, a species extinct on this continent and usually found in Africa) as well as the relatively brief time span of human history. It's a fascinating walk, particularly since you stroll in the setting of typical Colorado grassland, dry, thick with brown grasses, hot in the summer sun and fully exposed. The forest that was here 34 to 35 million years ago was lush, varied, verdant, and the fossil remains include utterly extinct species, preserved under thick layers of volcanic ash. Unfortunately, there was a time when visitors simply picked up fossils or chipped off portions of sequoia stumps, and there's no telling how much scientific evidence has been irretrievably lost from the site. But what's there is still enough to make a thoughtful visitor reflect upon the vastness of the earth's history.

More recent history is also on display in the monument. The Florissant Valley's first settler, Reverend David Long, arrived in 1873, the same year Isabella Bird and other women writers were passing by on the Ute Trail. The open spaces of the broad park are at least suggestive of the way the area might have looked then. At the north end of the national monument are the restored remnants of the Hornbek homestead, the house of a ranch run by Adeline Hornbek and her four children, as well as outbuildings from other ranches that have been moved from their original sites to a single location. The Hornbek place was homesteaded in 1878, in the early days of settlement. Looking outward from the perimeter fencing, it isn't difficult to sense "the solace of open spaces," in Gretel Ehrlich's memorable phrase.

The homestead is surrounded in part by a sizable ground squirrel village. The day we were there a gray-backed coyote prowled the meadow hoping for a ground squirrel meal. When he was some distance from where we stood, we realized that many ground squirrels had emerged from their burrows in the space between the coyote and us, all looking in his direction. The dance of life and death between coyote and ground squirrel has been going on for a very long time, well before the advent of homesteaders and ranchers and solitary travelers like Isabella Bird and hikers like us. Though there had been ranching here, the land was open and clear and the housing beyond the park's boundaries for the most part unobtrusive. I had the impression I was seeing the Florissant Valley the way it was before the white man came, the way it had been for millennia.

It was those exposed, weathering petrified tree stumps that made me think about the natural history that lies beneath the surface, all the buried environments or ecologies or habitats that have preceded the one we walked through. That's what Florissant Fossil Beds National Monument has to offer, the sense of perspective that's easy to overlook in all the other environments we'd been hiking through. If two inches equal one million years, what infinitesimal fraction of those two inches equals the history of Colorado, territory and state, compared to the incredibly long history of the land we parcel out under the name of Colorado?

* * *

That afternoon I rode through lawnlike upland parks, with the great snow mass of Pike's Peak behind, and in front mountains bathed in rich atmospheric coloring of blue and violet, all very fine, but threatening to become monotonous, when the wagon road turned abruptly to the left, and crossed a broad, swift, mountain river, the headwaters of the Platte.

Isabella Bird, Letter X, November 6

After a night in a cabin near Twin Rock, Isabella Bird spent two nights in more comfortable surroundings at the ranch of Colonel and Mrs. Kittridge, a dozen miles north of the wagon road. She found the Kittridges' cabin "very small and lonely" and thought "the life seemed a hard grind for an educated and refined woman" like Mrs. Kittridge. She noted that the people there could tell time by the distant peaks—"We had been in the evening shadows for half an hour before those peaks ceased to be transparent gold."

A few months earlier, in their "ambulances," Eliza Greatorex and her party lost their way, became separated from the others, and apparently by accident found Colonel Kittridge's place. She writes: "A true Western welcome was given to us, and preparations for affording us shelter for the night were quickly made." They were fed and provided places to sleep, the women in the cabin, the men in barn and hayloft; "all got through the night comfortably."

Greatorex found the situation less daunting than Bird did and the artist's account of the following morning has the air of a lark that fortuitously allows her to celebrate the pioneer spirit of the family that has sheltered them. Again well-fed at breakfast—"We had to go in companies to the table, but that was no hindrance to our glee"—she sketched, admired the scenery and appreciated the cabin's décor: "split log walls, hung with some pictures; a clock, antique and ponderous, making its appearance there an utterly unsolvable enigma; a great tub of water; a sewing-machine; and a guitar!" While Greatorex drew her holding her baby, Mrs. Kittridge "spoke much of their life, its enjoyments as well as hardships." Greatorex accepts without question the notion that winter visitors and eastern magazines and journals "made the weary months pass pleasantly." She tends to note tragedy and hardship when they are overwhelmingly obvious, not when they might be lurking below the surface. For many reasons Isabella Bird was more attuned to isolation and deprivation.

Isabella left Kittridge's on Monday morning, retraced the track to Twin Rock, and continued west on the wagon road. She wrote, "[E]very mile I have traveled since leaving Colorado Springs has taken me further and further into the mountains." Despite her solitary travel she continually met people on the road and, when she stopped for the night at the Link ranch, just across the South Platte River, she was joined by a German woman she had "met at Manitou" and three "gentlemen" traveling with her: "We were as sociable as people could be." Mr. Link and other men disagreed about the best route for her to take the next day, but she had already decided not to follow the wagon road into

South Park—her preference for less traveled paths and recurrent relief when she left populated areas was a constant subtext of her narrative.

The South Park–Colorado Springs wagon road was built on the trail taken for generations by native tribes. Along the north side of Florissant Canyon it is still possible to discern traces of the Ute war trail. First the wagon road, then the railroad, then U.S. 24 all followed Ute trailblazing. The highway speeds me across flat bottomland, mostly open range and few houses, and then suddenly across the South Platte River to Tappan Gulch Road. I briefly get out of the car to look out across the pasture through which the river meanders.

The South Platte is one of the major rivers of Colorado, flowing all the way from the Continental Divide near Leadville through Denver and then through the northeast corner of the state into Nebraska, where it joins the North Platte and eventually the Missouri. This is as close to its headwaters as Isabella Bird got, as close as I will get this trip, though both of us will also trace much of the bed of Tarryall Creek, one of its nearby tributaries. The river here is modest and clear, low running and almost lazy, drifting through a flat brown autumn landscape. The water gleams silvery, reflecting the brightness of a sky lit with long white clouds. Low ridges and mountains, green with conifers, circle the valley to the south and east.

Tarryall Road, also called 77 Road, quickly passes the convergence of Tarryall Creek and the South Platte River and follows Tarryall Creek upstream, through Tappan Gulch. The creek flows northwest to southeast, with the Tarryall Mountains paralleling it on the north side and the Puma Hills running along to the south.

On Tarryall Road, I soon discover, the recreation of the National Forest is interspersed with ranching and real estate. I quickly pass the turn-off for the Stage Stop Campground and, as the valley opens up, notice low, pointed peaks in the distance, rocky, either sparsely wooded or almost barren. The road is lined with trees, a hint of how well irrigated the valley usually is, and the valley floor is open and grassy. Where the valley opens I often see pastures, Hereford grazing in some, horses or black angus in others; toward the end of the road bison ruminate hard by a rancher's fence.

The valley walls are often high and rocky, and frequently the road twists toward a narrow passage between one wall of the valley and an outcropping of stone in the center, then emerges into open space, long rounded meadows of grasses through which the Tarryall Creek runs. Soon the rocks take on more weathered and distorted shapes, seem more and more isolated from the valley walls, piled and jumbled and seemingly dropped or clustered at random. The walls tighten on the road, then expand and rush away from it, then tighten up again as the road meanders along the south side of the valley.

Isabella Bird encountered no one as she passed up the trail along Tarryall Creek, but despite the National Forest designation to the area, I find considerable signs of life, past and present: a cluster of old buildings, weathered and collapsing, the remains of the town of Tarryall; Tarryall Estates, "a Covenant Controlled Community"; a series of ranches. Topping a rise gives me an impressive view of what Isabella would call the Snowy Range in the far distance and austere and craggy areas in the near and middle distance.

I soon approach Tarryall Reservoir, where jagged boulders top the ridges on either side and a curved grey concrete dam hangs between two steep walls. Signs warn me that the reservoir is presently closed to fishermen. Attractive little shelters are sprinkled all around the reservoir, picnic places with tables, and the campground is on the southern side of the lake. At the south end water accumulates against the dam, but the drought seems to have had an effect on the reservoir overall. The stubby stone jetties on the north end project out into emergent grassland rather than lake water; as at Palmer Lake, it has been awhile since water has been abundant here.

The land opens up more and more, and a kind of yellowy hue spreads over the terrain. The grass, not tall but vividly yellow, perhaps its autumn color, makes the hills yellow and because trees are so sparse and there seems to be little vegetation other than the grass, I feel as if I'm looking at the landscape with a jaundiced eye. I come around a bend and see an abandoned saltbox plank house, and instead of wondering if it had been Mrs. Link's, only think of how it seems to bespeak defeat.

At a Y-intersection, rather than continue on the paved road, I take the much rougher dirt road, the one perhaps less traveled by, where a sign warns about livestock on the road. There I realize, as Isabella did, that I have already crossed over into South Park.

*   *   *

At last we got through, and I beheld, with some sadness, the goal of my journey, "The Great Divide," the snowy range, and between me and it South Park, a rolling prairie seventy-five miles long and over 10,000 feet high, treeless, bounded by mountains, and so rich in sun-cured hay that one might fancy that all the herds of Colorado could find pasture there. . . . I came down upon it from regions of ice and snow; and as the snow which had fallen on it had all disappeared by evaporation and drifting, it looked to me quite lowland and livable, though lonely and indescribably mournful, "a silent sea," suggestive of "the muffled oar." I cantered across the narrow end of it, delighted to have got through the snow . . .

Isabella Bird, Letter XI, November 6

Helen Hunt, approaching South Park from the east, described it thus: "The scene seemed almost unreal. From our very feet to the distant western wall, forty miles away, stretched the soft, smooth, olive-gray surface of the valley, with belts and bars and flickering spaces of dark shadow and yellow sunlight playing over it." She noted, "There was no sound, no sight, no trace of human life. The silence, the sense of space in these Rocky Mountains solitudes cannot be expressed; neither can the peculiar atmospheric beauty be described."

After close canyons and narrow valleys, the scene in South Park stretching across to the mountains in the distance inspires deep breaths and slow exhalation. I'm surrounded by a vast reach of open space, passing a reservoir, herds of horses, herds of cattle, no sign of tree growth, all open territory. Although it looks dry as I drive through, it probably gets much more rain than, say, the east side of the Rampart Range and, because I see nothing but open grass, it does seem as if it were expressly designed for grazing.

Having left the wagon road that most people, including Helen Hunt, took to get to South Park, Isabella eventually lost the trail and had to flounder on horseback through deep snow; "once we went down in a drift the surface of which was rippled like sea sand, Birdie up to her back, and I up to my shoulders." It was an exhausting, frustrating struggle but eventually she reached open, snow-free ground. She tells in the book that she "cantered"—in her letters she says "galloped"—across the narrow end of South Park to the Denver Stage Road where she "supposed all difficulties to be at end."

The Denver Stage Road is now, largely, U.S. 285 and stretches roughly 330 miles from Monte Vista in southern Colorado to Denver, running for a long way down the west side of South Park. Coming off a long steady upward incline and a patch of dirt road, I find the relatively flat, rolling paved road, with its promise of intermittent towns and speedy transit, a relief to me too, though my passage through the Tarryall Valley was pleasant and easy. But then, I'm traveling under a blue sky only now filling with billowy clouds coming east from above snowy mountains, and the ground and the air are dry, and the car is a little too warm in the persistent sun. I too like South Park, like the realization that I've come beyond the Front Range for the first time in my Colorado travels, that the mountains I'm heading towards will be virtually new mountains to me.

Isabella Bird follows her expression of relief at reaching the Denver Stage Road with a single paragraph over a page long about her encounter with a man who "joined me and rode with me, got me a fresh horse, and accompanied me for ten miles." She tells of them crossing South Park and "ascending the Continental Divide by what I think is termed the Breckenridge Pass, on a fairly good wagon road." It was actually the Boreas Pass, over which a road led to the mining town of Breckenridge on the other side. After they "reached the crest of the Divide, and saw snow-born streams starting within a quarter of a mile from each other, one for the Colorado and the Pacific, the other for the Platte and the Atlantic," they separate and she returns the way they came. Stopping at a cabin where they had eaten earlier, she learns that her traveling companion was the fearsome Indian killer Comanche Bill. Isabella retrieves Birdie again and, having ridden fifty miles that day, rides six more miles to a likely stopping point. She writes (in the book), "The road ascended to a height of 11,000 feet, and from thence I looked my last at the lonely, uplifted prairie sea. 'Denver stage road!' The worst, rudest, dismallest, darkest road I have yet traveled on, . . ."

I find this a curious story.

Here's what raises my curiosity: the Comanche Bill and Boreas Pass passages in the book don't appear in any form in the original letter she sent to her sister. The *Letters to Henrietta* editor, Kay Chubbuck, reprints the ending of one paragraph and the beginning of the next paragraph this way:

> No snow on it I galloped across the narrow end of it delighted to be out of the snow and when I struck the "Denver Stage Road" I supposed all difficulties were at an end. Not so. They only began.
>
> The "Denver Stage Road." The worst rudest dismallest darkest road I have yet travelled. A winding ravine the Platte canon pine darkened walled in on both sides by mountains 13000 feet high.

The second paragraph opens as if she's scornfully repeating the phrase in quotes for emphasis. Chubbuck gives no indication of elisions in the text at this point, so this must have been the way the letter continued. Odd that Bird wouldn't have mentioned this encounter with Comanche Bill or the expedition up the Boreas (Breckenridge) Pass in the letter.

Earlier in the book (the corresponding letter is apparently lost, so we don't have an original text to compare against this passage) Isabella spoke disparagingly of the kinds of characters who frequent Denver's saloons: "The Denver men go to spend the savings of months of hard work in the maddest dissipation, and there such characters as 'Comanche Bill,' 'Buffalo Bill,' 'Wild Bill,' and 'Mountain Jim,' go on the spree, and find the kind of notoriety they seek." If these remarks were in the original letter in some form, they suggest that she had heard of Comanche Bill before she met him (though the passage may have been added years later in the revision of the letters). The particular names also suggest that her list of examples may only be representative of a character type she thinks she is identifying rather than specific individuals—is she referring to Buffalo Bill Cody, then a scout and only beginning his career as a showman, or Wild Bill Hickok, a lawman a few years away from a notorious death? I've found no firm identification of Comanche Bill, who might have been an Indian fighter and outlaw named William Mankin. The only one of the four names Isabella Bird had actual experience with was Rocky Mountain Jim Nugent, who was frequently characterized as a man fearful to behold when he went off on a tear. So we recognize part of her remarks to be grounded in personal associations and the remainder to be grounded in generalization, but the later meeting with Comanche Bill in person is difficult to corroborate, even in the evidence of her own writing.

I don't claim that the incident didn't happen—Bird elsewhere expands on what she wrote in the letters and also deletes or changes items that were more gossipy or disparaging, remarks acceptable to one's sister but not advisable in a published article or book. Certainly we find examples in her later letters where she confides to her sister personal experiences with Jim Nugent that she chooses to leave out of the book. Her book also has a number of glitches and inconsistencies in it created by the gap between the time the original letters were written and the time they were revised for publication. I can think of no other instance where readers have any reason to think she's making anything up out of whole cloth. Certainly she could have made more of the anecdote if she'd merely wanted to liven up her narrative. For all these reasons, I'm inclined to set aside my skepticism and accept the story as one of those anomalies that can take place in a long travel narrative.

Though she didn't mention it in her letter to Henrietta, in the book Isabella tells us she rode up to Breckenridge (or Boreas) Pass to achieve the Continental Divide. I feel I can do no less, since it gives each of us an attained goal as well as a place to start our return.

When I was routing the southern loop, I fretted about the possibility of the pass being closed by snow. Some roads around the state had already closed for the season, and other high passes had been closed intermittently. I didn't know what effect the weather was having near South Park, or whether I could get into it, cross it, and climb to the pass. But though the distant ranges are white—and are now less distant than they were—South Park is dry and clear. I zip along south on 285 and soon turn west again into the town of Como.

No town was here when Isabella Bird rode through and in the interval between her visit and mine the town began, flourished, and faded. It grew from ranchland into a community of six thousand people serving coal miners and the Denver, South Park, and Pacific Railroad. One source claims that it had "two Chinese laundries, three hotels, a red light district, and innumerable saloons—as many as eight in one block." It was a tough, lawless town, noted for brawls, saloon fights, and killings. It started as a tent city in 1879, its glory days lasted less than two decades, and it was devastated by fire in 1909, when most of the railroad holdings were destroyed. I've seen before-and-after photos; the town has shrunk by ninety percent or more. It was simply grassland when Isabella Bird rode through.

Como has a frontier feel to it. It's a disheveled cluster of weather-beaten buildings, little houses, and a business district mostly composed of a single building housing the Como Mercantile—general store, gift shop—and the Post Office. My camera quit on me before I reached Tarryall Reservoir, so I step into the mercantile and ask the woman alone in the crowded quiet interior if the store carries batteries. She shakes her head slightly rather than answers. Is there somewhere else I could try? "Hardware store." Where is it? "Fairplay." Is that far? "Ten miles." She nods toward the south. I thank her and ask if the road over the Boreas Pass is open. "Yes." I thank her again and leave.

The rough dirt road to Boreas Pass arcs out of town and heads up the watershed of the North Tarryall Creek, quickly entering grassy countryside churned up by mine tailings. It doesn't promise swift progress over the eleven miles to Boreas Pass. The aspen, thick along the lower level of the mountain, shows signs of elk browsing. When I leave the flatlands at the junction for the pass, a sign warns that a one-mile stretch of road ahead is steep and narrow. Damn tootin'. The steepness isn't the problem; it's the narrowness and the sheer drop-off on the passenger side of the car. It might be only a mile but it seems longer as, in spite of the threat of oncoming traffic difficult to predict around sharp curves, I steer down the center of the road, closer to the rocky mountainside and a roadbed strewn with fallen rocks roughly the size and shape of urban telephone books. Happily, no other cars appear. I'm rising quickly and, if I can look with more than the merest edge of my peripheral vision, I'll be able to see across the northern portion of South Park to the back of the Front Range. But I don't take my eyes off the road—I'm afraid that I'll quail at the exposure and acrophobia will overwhelm me. When I reach a widening in the road at the Davis Overlook, a place where the cliff edge is well anchored with aspen, I slide to a halt on the rubble and get out to take in the view. It's one I would have been sorry to miss.

I look down onto South Park, little Como already way in the distance, mostly open range surrounding it, and then the Front Range far off to the east. This is the first time in Colorado that I've looked toward the east and seen mountains instead of plains in the distance. Despite the drop-off, the view enthralls me. I feel as if I'm looking back in time.

I ascend slowly through a series of switchbacks, a rough road but no longer so rubble strewn and its shoulder no longer precipitous. At Windy Point another open bluff gives me an elevated view of North Tarryall Creek Canyon; far below, the creek winds through dense stands of dark firs.

Past Windy Point, the road opens up towards a broad, sharp valley, its slopes steep but widely spaced. Snow clumps in the shaded spots, and ice coats the water along the side of the road, but the terrain is open and gorgeous and unpopulated. I think, This is what this kind of place looked like before people; how pristine and undeveloped the mountains seem, how free, except for the road, from the hand of man. I haven't even completed that thought before I spot a railroad car ahead of me and a cabin on the other side of the road. They remind me that the road I'm on had first been a stagecoach route, when Isabella was on it, and later the track of the railroad most of the way over the pass and down to Breckenridge. The railroad is now gone and I suspect the road is little used—there are faster, easier ways to get to Breckenridge.

Before I know it, I am over the pass and headed down the other side on a roadbed much rougher than the one I've come up on. I realize I've gone too far, stop, turn around, and retreat to the top of the pass. The buildings and the railroad car there all serve as a museum, now closed for the season, commemorating the history of the Boreas Pass. Mount Boreas (13,082 ft.) is immediately to the east, Mount Baldy (13,679) to the north, and across the gulf of the North Tarryall Canyon is Mount Silverheels (13,822), a sharply shaped peak with snow clinging thickly to its precipitous face. Other mountains stretch off into the distance, but I feel as if I am truly in the Snowy Range. I've reached the point on the Great Divide that Isabella Bird reported reaching. Turning back, I see a spectacular view off down the canyon that I've been following, towards South Park and the mountains beyond it—an enormous and wonderful panorama. I've gone through this before, climbing a mountain and seeing a splendid view from one switchback, then a more stunning view from another switchback higher up, and then a still more glorious view a little farther on, each vista by the change in angle and elevation somehow not the same vista, each as breathtaking as if observed totally unexpectedly.

I surprise myself by suddenly feeling, for the first time in the day's travel, that I've finally gotten somewhere, reached some point that validates the journey and, instead of inviting me on, lets me know it's all right to turn back.

* * *

"Denver stage road!" The worst, rudest, dismallest, darkest road I have yet travelled on, nothing but a winding ravine, the Platte canyon, pine-crowded and pine-darkened, walled in on both sides for six miles by pine-skirted mountains 12,000 feet high! Along this abyss for fifty miles there are said to be only five houses, and were it not for miners going down, and freight wagons going up, the solitude would be awful. As it was, I did not see a creature.

Isabella Bird, Letter XI, November 6

Once I'm down from Boreas Pass and through Como and heading for Denver on 285, the pace of my travels alters abruptly. It's good highway, swift, well-maintained, not overcrowded until near Denver. It seems to merit little of Isabella's scorn for it as the Denver Stage Road, but it also makes little impression on me as I race along it. In no time at all, I am up and over Kenosha Pass, heading toward a passage through the mountains of the Front Range.

Isabella Bird left South Park about 4 o'clock in the afternoon. Traveling in the dark over an icy track through creaking trees in narrow North Platte Canyon disturbed her. The place in Hall's Gulch where she sought a night's lodging turned out to be a bar and an intoxicated man greeted her at the door. She slept in a roofless shed, "on a shake-down, with the stars winking overhead through the roof, and the mercury showing 30° of frost"; she claims she placed a revolver under her pillow, "resolving to keep awake all night," but fell asleep immediately, slept soundly until morning, and woke reproachful of her fears.

The next night she lodged twenty-two miles away in Deer Valley, "in a beautiful place like a Dutch farm" with "abundance of clean food and a clean, cold little bedroom to [her]self." Her third night was spent about forty miles farther on with a family in a grocery store; she left early, before anyone else was up. She rode down Turkey Creek Canyon "and over the gray-brown plains to Denver. Not a tree or shrub was to be seen, everything was rioting in summer heat and drought, while behind lay the last grand canyon of the mountains, dark with pines and cool with snow."

In the speed and openness of the modern highway that superseded the Denver Stage Road, it takes me little time to get from South Park to Denver. Once again the pace of traffic carries me along, particularly as I get closer to the metropolis, and the rhythm of the road makes me oblivious to much of what I pass. I see—or at least register—no sign of Hall's Gulch or Webster or Deer Valley. The road turns away from the track of the Platte and joins a separate river canyon, somewhat broader than northern canyons I am familiar with. The nearer to Denver, the more the canyon is crowded with residences, strip malls, businesses; the nearer to Denver, the hazier the sky becomes, the less distinct the mountains appear to the eye.

Soon I'm out of the foothills, passing the turn-off to Morrison and Red Rocks State Park, merging with northbound traffic on 470, taking U.S. 6 west to intersect near Golden with Colorado 93, and following that north to

Boulder. I'm unsure how long it takes me to go from Como to Lafayette but I reach home a little after five o'clock. I've covered Isabella Bird's southern loop in less than half a day, even though I started from north of the city rather than, as she did, at its center. Of course, I had considerably more horsepower.

If I were more inclined to be a purist in my research, I would attempt to emulate Isabella's conditions of travel—hire a horse and wait until the snows come on; I would be the kind of writer who faithfully follows in the footsteps of his subject, like those who travel to Canterbury like Chaucer, to the Hebrides like Johnson and Boswell, to the Pacific like Lewis and Clark. I have no doubt that I would have a better sense of Isabella Bird's experience that way, be better able to say: "This is what *she* went through." Without contest, I concede to her the prize for pluck and perseverance, for resolve and resilience. I admire her for all that. By comparison, I'm rather wussy and don't intend to be otherwise. But then, I haven't been hoping to replicate her experiences.

So, where has all this forward motion carried me? I now have a sense of the scope, the sweep, of Bird's travels in Colorado, but more important, my exploratory excursion in the path of Isabella Bird's grand adventure has given me a rich sense of the terrain. I've reached a different Colorado than the one I'm familiar with from my wandering along the Front Range. This land between the mountains is an inner world on a different scale than Estes; it's nowhere near as confined, as pent-up or circumscribed. Unlike the landscape along what at least one local weathercaster likes to call "the urban corridor," where everything has expanded and swollen, behind the Front Range I find a Colorado that has collapsed or dwindled or shriveled, retreated back into itself after attempting bold stances of occupation and exploitation. It's not so much that this part of Colorado has stepped back in time; it's more that it's stopped moving forward, perhaps stepped out of the flow of time. My own southern circuit has brought me around to a realization that's been lying below the surface of all my ramblings here—that this seems to be the kind of place where I'm most comfortable in Colorado.

The Tour
Mining District

i

Golden City by daylight showed its meanness and belied its name. It is ungraded, with here and there a piece of wooden sidewalk, supported on posts, up to which you ascend by planks. Brick, pine, and log houses are huddled together, every other house is a saloon, and hardly a woman is to be seen.... Golden City rang with oaths and curses, especially at the depôt. Americans are given over to the most atrocious swearing, and the blasphemous use of our Saviour's name is peculiarly revolting.

Isabella Bird, Letter XII, November 16

Despite over two weeks of almost constant traveling, Isabella Bird didn't give herself or Birdie much time to recuperate once she returned to Denver. After a single day, she claimed that the city was "too much of the 'wearying world' either for [her] health or taste." At four o'clock on a Monday afternoon, November 10, "the sun still hot," she departed for Golden, pleased to be out riding alone again. The sun had set by the time she "groped [her] way into this dark, unlighted mining town" and found accommodations for herself and her horse. This was her first stop on the brief northern loop of her tour, which would take her through the territory's central mining district. From very early on, these had been obligatory sites for visiting writers hoping to report on Colorado to their eastern readers. Bayard Taylor, Samuel Bowles, Grace Greenwood, Helen Hunt Jackson—all toured the mining district.

For me the circuit, newly familiar from recent reading of these writers, will be a day trip. I leave Lafayette early, cross over the Boulder Turnpike, and then head west on Colorado 128. It's 8:30 in the morning and the expressway and the roads leading up to the entrance ramps are crowded with commuters on their way to work. This is the part of Colorado living I usually plan ahead in order to avoid—the frantic pace and the tight congestion of all those cars (most vehicles have only one occupant, leaving the High Occupancy Vehicle lane for carpools nearly empty) and the tension, annoyance, and occasional rage they produce; even without a research mission, I would likely have chosen this route. I drive toward the Front Range, gazing at the foothills, the Flatirons, the summits of the Continental Divide, and distant Longs Peak, gigantic and snow-covered. On the passenger seat lies a printout of my itinerary, reminding me what sights to look for and which roads to take, and under it the paraphernalia of recordkeeping: tape recorder, daybook, camera, maps.

Once past the expressway and the Interlochen area, with its massive golf course, housing, industrial park, and sprawling Flatirons shopping area, I pass through mostly wide-open space, the nearly empty rolling terrain that I love about the plains where I live. The only structure of note is an installation for renewable energy through wind technology—in such terrain it seems well sited. Earlier that morning, at our apartment complex, I heard a robin singing, and now, just as I turn south toward Golden onto Colorado 93, I hear a meadowlark. It's only the third day of

spring and, with bird song and the heat of the sun pene-
trating the windows of my car, I feel eager to meet the day.

Of course, as I am aware, much of the reason all this grassland is so empty is the former presence and subsequent
removal of the Rocky Flats nuclear weapons plant. The site
is obscurely marked as a blank gray square on two of my
maps and innocuously labeled "Rocky Flats Plant" on one
and on another identified as "Rocky Flats Environmental
Technology Site." The actual sign at its entrance identifies it
as the "Rocky Flats Closure Project." Curiously enough, the
maps that would give me the closest rendering of the site's
location both choose to cover that space with blocks of text,
as if there were nothing there in the first place that the text
would be covering up. "Covering up" is exactly the phrase
often voiced when local environmentalists discuss the
clean-up of the plant site, where plutonium triggers for
nuclear weapons were manufactured and where the full
extent of the contamination has never been determined. As
I pass by, I gaze west toward the foothills rather than east
toward the clean-up site. It's a deliberate act of avoidance on
my part, one I may not be able to continue if I'm living along
the Front Range when that particular ground becomes the
foundation of housing developments.

A few minutes later, I begin to descend toward Golden;
the long outcropping of the Dakota Hogback comes into
view, humped up and sticking out of the ground like the
exposed spines on the back of a deeply buried Stegosaurus.
I note the fenced-off remains of a mine shaft at its base and
the signs of quarrying and trails across it. This is one of
those spots I like for how diverse the terrain is—in the
midst of all this rolling grassland something anomalous
like this crops up.

I sometimes think that, on the route that I'm taking, it's
possible to get a sense of what it must have been like for
someone like Isabella Bird to ride over unsettled, undevel-

oped prairie, heading from Longmont to Denver or crossing from Denver to Golden or Boulder, and how, alone on horseback, it would be easy for such a rider to lose her way. I recall the English writer Harriet Martineau being troubled by the prairies of Illinois and remarking, "when I saw a settler's child tripping out of home-bounds, I had a feeling that it would never get back again. It looked like putting out into Lake Michigan in a canoe." She meant that the child would immediately drop out of sight of the homestead and she wondered how it would know where anything was once it did that. As on an ocean—the reference to the prairie as a "sea of grass" was a common one, then as now—it's harder to get your bearings in a trough than on a crest and harder still when no direction seems to offer landmarks. At least on the Colorado plains it was possible, when you topped a ridge or a mesa, to catch sight of the mountains and know which way was west. I admit that my sense of open space today is somewhat illusory, sustained in part by keeping an eye on the mountains and averting my gaze from ever-expanding residential growth. Some acts of avoidance are habitual with me now.

Golden is situated in a valley between North Table Mountain and South Table Mountain on the east and Lookout Mountain and Mount Galbraith on the west. Either set of mountains is divided by the bed of Clear Creek, which flows east down from the Continental Divide past Georgetown and Idaho Springs through Clear Creek Canyon, at whose mouth Golden sprawls, and beyond to Denver and the South Platte River. Golden has only so far it can grow before reaching mountains and so has trended north and south, along Foothills Parkway (Colorado 93). The encircling mountains give the city a sense of enclosed limits which developers are doing their best to belie.

The mountains around Golden also give the city a distinctive landscape, the way Boulder has the Flatirons as a constant backdrop; all the rest of the suburban sprawl heading out along the Front Range is across the plains, following the contours of the rolling hills. Here the mountains rise above the city on every side and impose upon the near horizon. The Table Mountains, their summits as much as 800 feet above Clear Creek, have sedimentary rocks at their base and are topped with columns of volcanic basalt distinctly visible from a great distance. On the west side of South Table Mountain an imposing point called Castle Rock overlooks the city, like some natural fortress. I'd like to live where mountains are the first thing I see in the morning, where they look over my shoulder throughout the day, loom over me at night. I think the presence of mountains might keep me and my neighbors humble. I can't tell in passing how much humility Golden has.

When Isabella Bird saw Golden, she felt it was a mean sight in daylight, with nothing radiant about it. The wooden sidewalks above dirt streets and the preponderance of dingy saloons in the business district were a contrast to a day she found to be, "as usual, glorious." Golden had grown from a trading center for the mining concerns up Clear Creek Canyon, especially in Central City and Black Hawk, into a community that once rivaled Denver in prestige and influence; it was the territorial capital from 1862 until 1867, before the capital was moved to Denver. Bayard Taylor, visiting in 1866, foresaw a brilliant future for Golden. He declared, "The quiet of Golden City will not endure much longer; and the day may not be far off when the smokes from its tall chimneys, rising up behind Table Mountain, will be seen at Denver."

In William Henry Jackson's black and white photograph of Golden taken from Lookout Mountain around 1885, the twin mesas of Table Mountain on either side of the frame and the broad, muddy channel of Clear Creek running up the center from the bottom dominate the image. The plains, visible in the distance between the mesas, seem almost empty, except for a large building in far-off Denver. Close enough to Taylor's prediction nearly twenty years earlier, two smokestacks belch white billows near the center of the picture, and the treeless landscape is dotted with buildings up either side of the Clear Creek Valley.

In a parallel color photograph by John Fielder, taken over a hundred years later from the identical vantage point, the mining enterprises, long defunct, have been replaced by the Coors Brewing megalith, an enormous conglomeration of buildings straddling Clear Creek and the valley between the mesas. Now the dominant feature of the vista, it sits like a gigantic plug against the eastward opening between North and South Table Mountains. Buildings fill in the valley. On the distant plains it is possible to find one towering building in Denver, but the metropolis with all its suburbs and outlying communities completely fills the space so empty in the earlier photograph—nowhere does there appear an unused piece of land, and the mountains, which seemed so limiting in Jackson's photo, seem more like defenses against that encroaching development on the plains.

I descend into Golden's business district on Washington Street, the slope leading down to the channel of Clear Creek, into the sweet smell of hops wafting from the Coors Brewery, and then up through a downtown marked with an arching sign across the wide street: "Welcome to Golden. Where the West Lives." (Originally the sign read "Where the West Remains," which may have seemed too funereal a slogan, especially with Buffalo Bill Cody's remains famously buried on Lookout Mountain, overlooking the city.) The main street maintains a western theme, particularly in the well-covered walks and wooden storefronts and preserved buildings. Dark metal statues—Colorado generally seems to go in for Remingtonesque statuary of people or animals—play upon the western motif; in one place a cowboy carrying a saddle, in another a little boy mounting a horse, and at the entrance to the downtown area Buffalo Bill himself, hatless, with a child on his shoulders. The Table Mountain Inn has an adobe pueblo exterior and the Foss General Store looks from the outside like a building that might be found in any Old West town. The Foss, which over its rear entrance has the slogan: "Where the West Shops," is one of my favorite browsing spots, crammed with oddities and novelties and thematic items, pottery, dishes, and western clothing; Indian blankets and cowboy lamps and lampshades; old gas station pumps redesigned as entertainment consoles and old car halves redesigned as furniture; souvenirs and knick-knacks and a collection of Colorado wines. It's a quirky, amusing spot even for indifferent consumers like my wife and me, and it reminds me, if I need reminding, that in "the Old West" issues of historic preservation and touristic exploitation go hand in hand.

Some historic buildings can be found west of the main street and I'm curious about what was standing when Isabella Bird was here. The first place I stroll by is the Astor House, a white stone three-story rectangle originally constructed in 1867 to house legislators when Golden was still the territorial capital; by 1873 it was a boarding house known as the Boston House. Isabella Bird doesn't tell us where she spent the night—she says only that she "had a very nice little bedroom" and that the landlady told her she had "never had a lady sleep in her house before"—but the Boston House is a likely candidate. Today it's a museum and gift shop. I note how simple and plain the exterior is and how much it seems of a different era compared to the later buildings of the business district.

I've been inside the Astor House and toured the nice but sparsely furnished little bedrooms, done up in the style of the turn of the twentieth century. Sue and I were there to

attend a Victorian tea at which a local storyteller imper-
sonated Isabella Bird. The others attending, a mix of teenaged girls and older women, mothers and grandmothers
with daughters, nieces, and/or granddaughters, seemed
quite comfortable with the setting, though a little disconcerted to find a lone man among them for tea.

I was a little disconcerted myself, though only partly
because of my gender. It seemed prudent not to mention
that I'd read a lot about Isabella Bird and was writing about
her time in Colorado or that I was there mostly in hopes
that the actress would somehow channel her. Since I
wasn't there for social or entertainment reasons and wasn't
going to reveal that my interest related to my work, I wondered if I appeared to be just a dimly pleasant retiree accompanying his lively wife out of duty or boredom. When the
performance started I dismissed these uncomfortable spec-
ulations to concentrate on the characterization.

The presentation was heavily indebted to Evelyn Kaye's
book, *Amazing Traveler Isabella Bird*. I was surprised that she
read at length from Platt Rogers's retelling of the climb up
Longs Peak, as if Isabella hadn't given an accurate account,
and that she emphasized Isabella's "comic trait of exagger-
ation," which undercut Isabella's credibility as a witness to
her own experiences. But it was intriguing to me to watch
someone impersonate Isabella Bird, especially since she
appeared to me more like the Isabella I imagine wandering
Colorado in 1873 than the one usually pictured on her
books and biographies. Instead of the bride in black from
her 1881 wedding to Dr. John Bishop or the matronly
writer of later years shown at her writing desk, she presented a solid, mature, simply dressed Victorian woman
(though without a British accent). She modified Isabella's
text liberally to recount the climb up Longs Peak and the
involvement with Rocky Mountain Jim Nugent, with
heavy emphasis on a possible romance and no mention of

his death. It occurred to me that, whoever I or others might think I was, I was not the right audience for the performance. The entertainment was well received by the rest of the company enjoying their Victorian tea.

On my own northern loop, I drift away from the Astor House and spend time in leisurely confirmation that the past has vanished. The Colorado School of Mines dates back to 1870 in one incarnation, but the site shifted over the years, the oldest building now was one built in 1894, and the oldest college in Colorado doesn't exist in its original form. But in the 12th Street Historic District, an area of half a dozen blocks dominated by houses constructed in the early days of Golden's history, seventeen houses still stood that were there when Isabella Bird visited, ten of them built that very year, one as long ago as 1866. Some have been much renovated since and some have been somewhat restored to their original appearance by stripping away additions and improvements. In the main, the earliest houses are small and compact and solid. This stretch of flatland not far above Clear Creek is where the city first established itself. A block north, closer to the creek, is the Clear Creek History Park, which collected a number of old buildings from Golden Gate Canyon, not far to the west of Golden, to stand in for the pioneer structures of early Golden, long ago demolished. The buildings, which include a log cabin, a blacksmith's shop, a barn, and a schoolhouse, are staffed in the summer by costumed historical re-enactors, so that visitors can somehow get a feel for the early 1870s. Of course, with walkers, bikers, skateboarders, and rollerbladers streaming down the paved paths on either side of Clear Creek, engaging in an enthusiasm for exercise entirely alien to hardworking settlers, it's likely difficult to get very lost in the past.

The inclination to preserve the past and the need to live in the present are often simultaneous but contradictory urges. Mere preservation doesn't guarantee connection with the past, though it may at least provoke momentary acknowledgment, and living in the present often keeps you from predicting how people in the future will view your moment as part of their past. On the way back to the car, I pass a small building with a sign for the Golden City Brewing Company that boasts it is the second largest brewery in Golden, an ironic smirk at the massive Coors Brewery facilities, begun on a similarly small scale by Adolph Coors in 1873. Since she observed that, in Golden, "every other house is a saloon," maybe Isabella Bird also smelled the hops as she passed through. A tourist like me can't be certain whether this is the primary constant that runs through Golden's history.

ii

Golden City stands at the mouth of Toughcuss, otherwise Clear Creek Canyon, which many people think the grandest scenery in the mountains, as it twists and turns marvellously, and its stupendous sides are nearly perpendicular, while farther progress is to all appearance continually blocked by great masses of rock and piles of snow-covered mountains. Unfortunately, its sides have been almost entirely denuded of timber, mining operations consuming any quantity of it.

Isabella Bird, Letter XII, November 16

Clear Creek Canyon is a very rugged canyon. When Isabella Bird traveled through it, the canyon already had been altered to provide space for a railroad. She wrote, "The narrow-gauge, steep-grade railroad, which runs up the canyon for the convenience of the rich mining districts of Georgetown, Black Hawk, and Central City, is a curiosity of engineering. The track has partly been blasted out of the sides of the canyon, and has partly been 'built' by making a bed of stones in the creek itself, and laying the track across them." Eventually, "the canyon widened sufficiently for a road, all stones, holes, and sidings." The railroad was as yet unfinished, and after a two-hour ride in a baggage car—the passenger cars were not available after "the season" had ended—Bird and a few other passengers were transferred to a large "Concord coach" and seated behind the driver; "the huge thing bounced and swung upon the straps on which it was hung so as to recall the worst horrors of New Zealand staging." The coach took her the rest of the way to Idaho Springs. By the time that, several years later, Helen Hunt Jackson came up the canyon, the railroad was complete. She observed, rather cheerily, "Wherever water can come down, a narrow-gauge railroad can go up. Side by side, on equal terms, asking no favors, it will make foothold for itself on the precipices, and follow the stream, leap for leap, grade to grade, coming out triumphant, abreast, at top of the mountain. This was the way we mounted to Central City, through Clear Creek Canyon."

Bird was not alone in noting the effect of mining on the landscape—other writers decried the loss of timber in the canyons and the ways that mining built up tailings of discarded ore and stripped rocky surfaces of soil and flora, creating a barren moonscape on which grimy houses and buildings were deposited—but she also shared an appreciation of the canyon's "twists and turns" and "nearly perpendicular" walls: "The singular grandeur cannot be described. It is a mere gash cut by the torrent, twisted, walled, chasmed, weather-stained with the most brilliant coloring, generally dark with shadow, but its utter desolation occasionally revealed by a beam of intense sunshine. A few stunted pines and cedars, spared because of their inaccessibility, hung here and there out of the rifts. Sometimes the walls of the abyss seemed to meet overhead, and then widening out, the rocks assumed fantastic forms, all grandeur, sublimity, and almost terror." Helen Hunt Jackson, herself as much an admirer of canyons as of mountains, was similarly impressed during her passage through the place: "The walls of the canyon are rocky, precipitous, and in places over one thousand feet high. It seems little more than a rift in the mountain, and we could easily fancy it closing behind us as we passed on. Fir-trees and aspens made a mosaic of dark and light green, like shaded malachite, on the sides. Wild roses and spiräas and blue-bells grew on the edge of the creek and far up in the clefts of the rocks."

Today the narrow-gauge railroad is gone and well-paved U.S. Highway 6 winds smoothly and quickly uphill, mostly along the bed of Clear Creek but occasionally through long tunnels that cut across the sharpest meanders and through the most vertiginous cliffs. The canyon's walls rise hundreds of precipitous feet above the road, often at the narrowest places leaning toward one another and overhanging the roadbed. The angle of repose of the rocks can be disturbing to drivers who glance away from the curves, since it seems as if tons of stone could easily slide down on them. I feel an ominous awareness whenever I pass beneath overhanging walls. (And that sensation will amplify for me in late June 2005 when, about a week after I drive up the canyon, some 1,400 tons of rock will collapse onto the highway, damaging a couple of trucks and slightly injuring one of the drivers. It will be a close call. A driver of one truck will notice the rocks giving way and warn the driver of a truck coming from the other direction so that both will be trapped by debris but neither will end up under it. It will take three months, until mid-September, after the road has been cleared and the walls are stabilized by removing even more rock—40,000 cubic yards total—before the road will be opened to regular traffic again.)

After a dozen miles the road intersects with Colorado 119 at the confluence of Clear Creek and North Clear Creek: U.S. 6 veers off across Clear Creek, past defunct Tunnel No. 4 and through two more tunnels before it merges with Interstate 70 near Idaho Springs and continues on toward Georgetown; Colorado 119 begins the Peak-to-Peak Highway that runs up along North Clear Creek into Black Hawk and Central City and becomes a well-known scenic byway along the Front Range all the way to Estes Park. The traffic around me divides, some veering toward Idaho Springs, the rest of us running straight ahead toward Black Hawk. The North Clear Creek Canyon is more open, the terrain more relaxed and less perpendicular. Occasionally, I notice houses on the tops of the canyon walls but encounter almost no housing anywhere within the canyon. Though Isabella Bird never took this road, many of her writing contemporaries did, and I follow in their wake.

Samuel Bowles came to the area five years before Isabella did and then observed that, with the combination of mining, milling, and recent heavy floods, the north canyon was "terribly torn to pieces, and look[ed] rough and ragged." Grace Greenwood, touring in 1871, found the road up Clear Creek Canyon blocked, and took a more roundabout route, coming out near the confluence of the two creeks. She had been admiring the scenery but wrote: "At the point where the road enters Clear Creek Cañon all beauty ends, for gulch-mining begins." Her reaction to what she saw was fierce. "It were, I fear, impossible to give one who has seen nothing of the kind an idea of the fearful transformation which this process works in a clear, beautiful mountain stream; of the violence and cruelty and remorselessness of its course; how it heads it off, and backs it up, and commits highway robbery upon it,—'Your gold or your life!'—how it twists it and tortures it, and dams it (no profanity intended), and ruffles and roils it by panning and sluicing and shaft-sinking, till its own pure mother-fountain up among the eternal snows wouldn't know it." With a combination of sympathy and disapproval, she observed the sluices—"narrow wooden channels with riffles in the bottom, up against which lurks the detective quicksilver, to arrest and hold the runaway particles of gold in the swift water"—and the miners manning them: "Men are kept at work carting gravel, or wheeling it in barrows, for these sluices. In some places they stood knee-deep in water, dipping up the precious mud. A more slavish business could not be imagined."

Helen Hunt Jackson, who visited the area half a dozen years later, also found the appearance of the canyon distressing. She wrote, "As we neared Central City, the hills on either side grew barer, stonier, higher; and along the creek we began to see the dreary traces of that dreariest of all things on the earth's surface, gulch mining: long stretches of pebble beds torn up, rent, piled, bare, desolate; here and there a few pallid weeds struggling to crowd their way down and up between the stones and live in the arid sand. They only made the devastation look ghastlier." Like a number of travelers who had developed an aesthetic for landscape, she mused about the destruction, "Is there not a significance in this thing, that men find no way of getting gold from the earth's depths, without so marring, blighting all the fair, green beauty of its surface?"

Around a century and a quarter later, though a great deal has changed in the cities I'm driving toward, the nearer I come to Black Hawk, the better idea I have of what caused their reactions. The trees are sometimes thick again on the slopes of the canyon but close to the creek bed in gray-brown ridges or in huge barren piles of yellow tailings poking through the trees are permanent reminders of the first glory days of the mining district. It's not hard to imagine what the canyon walls were like when they were stripped entirely of foliage.

In many of the places I've been along the Front Range, the land has either been set aside for conservation, as in the national and state parks, or left open for ranching, as in the valleys and plains, or it's been covered up by businesses and housing, streets and parking lots, as in the urban corridor. Mining, however, turns the landscape inside out, strews the unprofitable portion of its excavations onto massive fields and slopes of debris, and builds memorials to its short-sighted industriousness out of the rubble of ravaged terrain. The early writers I've been guided by felt the need to report on Colorado's promise, which from its earliest days was centered on mineral wealth in gold and silver. Those days are long past. If it were not for my dogged determination to see with my own eyes what my predecessors beheld, it might have been a very long time before I found myself in North Clear Creek Canyon, heading into the mining district.

*   *   *

To say literally how "it feels" to drive in the streets of this gulch, or the gulches of these streets, called respectively Black Hawk and Central City, would be to commit unpardonable exaggerations. Why the towns do not slide down hill any night, in one great avalanche of houses, stamping mills, smelting works, piles of slag, ore, mules, bowlders, and citizens, I do not know. To the unaccustomed eye, every thing and everybody seems to have been miraculously arrested in the process of toppling down.

Helen Hunt Jackson, *Bits of Travel at Home*

Early travel writers touring the mining district displayed little—or little genuine—enthusiasm for Blackhawk and

Central City. Bayard Taylor spoke positively of mining prospects in 1866 but complained that Central City "is the most outrageously expensive place in Colorado. You pay more and get less for the money than in any other part of the world." He quickly grew weary of "these bald, clumsy shaped, pock-marked mountains; this one long, windy, dusty street, with its perpetual menace of fire; and this never-ending production of 'specimens' and offer of 'feet,'" and declared he would "joyfully say good-by to-morrow morning." Samuel Bowles, two years later, thought "Black Hawk and Central City may be good places to get gold in, but there can be no genuine homes there." Here, he found, "all beauty is sacrificed to use . . . the mere use of washing out gold." He too seemed eager to move on.

Grace Greenwood tended to be a little more upbeat. She visited the mining district in its heyday, when the smelting works of Black Hawk were in full force, charcoal burning under the ore to "desulphurize" it day and night. She found the environment hellish. "There is something fearfully suggestive in that dark hollow, with its never-quenched fires, and those columns of yellow, suffocating smoke; and I did not doubt the story told of a drunken man, who, having wandered in here and fallen asleep, awoke in the sulphurous atmosphere to gasp out, 'In ___ at last!'" Approaching through North Clear Creek Canyon, Greenwood noted how the gulches were "all torn and tunneled and riddled, almost tumbled into chaos by miners and panners and crushers and smelters." The struggle between the forces of mining and of civilization in the valley created in her "a profound, almost a tragic interest," and she found the rigors of the work and the living conditions an indication of heroic efforts on the parts of workers and their families. "Narrow and dingy as is this mining town, its people are making a brave effort to give it a look of comfort, in pleasant private dwellings, neat churches and fine school-buildings, perched up against the mountain-side, where it would seem no building larger than a miner's hut could find lodgement." She noted the lack of trees and shrubbery, "or even a flower, except it be in some parlor window;" but was encouraged by the sight of "a very pretty conservatory, attached to a neat cottage. It was something strangely cheering, yet touching, in the universal dreariness. It was like a stray leaf out of 'Paradise Lost.'"

Greenwood found Central City to be "a wonderfully busy and interesting place." She was struck by the "swift, ceaseless currents of travel and traffic,—carriages, stages, loaded carts and wagons, trains of packed mules, miners in their rough, but picturesque garb; mounted drovers, eager-eyed speculators, sleepy-eyed Mexicans, sullen Indians, curious squaws, sunburned, lounging tourists." And she was encouraged by the presence of families, "merry children and bright-faced, handsomely dressed ladies," and by evidence that "people think of something beside mines," despite the signs of an obsession with gold where "hundreds of men . . . lie down to prospect in dreams, and rise up to pan or dig" and where people "mine in their cellars and wells and back yards, and a careful housekeeper examines her teakettle for gold deposits once a week." The downturn in her sprightliness suggests that her positive outlook was somewhat strained and more than a little insincere.

Helen Hunt Jackson claimed to be much perplexed by the need to identify them as two separate towns. She wrote, "To get to Central City, you drive through Black Hawk. Where Black Hawk leaves off and Central City begins seems indefinite." The steepness of the streets and the vertical relationships among the buildings bemused her: "The houses are perched one above another, on the sides of the gulch, as if they were set on the successive steps of ladders. A man sitting on his piazza may rest his feet on the roof-tree of his neighbor next below; and so on all the way down." She marveled that there weren't "derricks for the elevation of families at the corners of all the streets" and found that "many of the cross streets are made chiefly of stairs." She doesn't name her hotel—it may well have been the Teller House—but was struck by the view from her second-floor room from which she "looked across a very narrow street into the basement of the house opposite." Moreover, she wrote that she "saw many small houses built where the precipice was so steep that, as you looked up from the street you saw the hill above the house, apparently making a continuation of the roof. It produced a most curious optical illusion. No house thus placed can stand so straight that it will not have the look of tumbling down." She concluded: "Add to this apparent confusion of toppling houses, intervals of bare, brown, rocky hillsides, dotted everywhere with piles of gray ore thrown up at the mouths of mines, and some conception may be formed of the desolateness of the scene."

The cumulative effect of these commentaries on Central City and Black Hawk is to make the area come alive in the imagination for its vitality, its griminess, its uncertainty and tenuousness, its earnest and possibly ill-considered energy. This was, after all, at one time known as "the richest square mile on Earth" and so much a center of wealth and culture that it boded a fabulous future, one that peaked and dissipated rather quickly. Central City was decimated by fire in 1874, rebuilt at once, and in 1878 completed construction of the Central City Opera House, for a long time an essential cultural destination along the Front Range (and still in business as a tourist attraction, complete with summer season of performances each year). But the mining industry dried up and the towns shriveled as their populations moved on, and what sustained them was eventually a somewhat desultory tourist industry. For a long time it was possible to visit Black Hawk and Central

City and get a sense of what early Colorado was like, because once the mining was essentially over and the population boom stayed closer to Denver and its suburbs, change simply didn't happen here. Colorado has plentiful sites where the promise of mining riches led to a rapid growth and incredible prosperity and then vanished, immediately taking the population with it and eventually, through the slow, moldering work of time, the very buildings themselves.

Both Black Hawk and Central City remained more or less in suspended animation, shriveling over the decades but still offering a window into the past for tourists, until the arrival of the legal gambling industry. In recent decades there's been a transformation as carloads and busloads of gamblers have streamed up the Clear Creek canyons, like miners of the century before, in hopes of striking it rich. Black Hawk, the first town people come to as they drive up from Golden and Denver, has transformed itself so thoroughly into a casino town that it's difficult to prove it was ever anything else; Central City, with less of the gambling tourist traffic, has until now held onto at least the exteriors of its history, though not without a hankering for similar prosperity that may be very much like a death wish for its historic identity.

My first sight of Black Hawk as I rise up the smooth, well-maintained highway is a narrow canyon filled with huge casinos, long heavy structures with names like the Riviera and the Isle, and soon I seem to pass through an entire town of casinos wedged into the canyon. It takes a while to reach a point on the road where late-nineteenth and early-twentieth-century buildings appear. The transformation in Black Hawk helps me decide to keep climbing up to Central City, which, I remember from our visit to the opera the past summer, still looks like an actual town, a community that hasn't yet destroyed the evidence of its past and replaced it with ostentatious casinos and parking structures. Central City's casinos are located in the historic old buildings and around the business district are housing areas that give the appearance of neighborhoods.

I circle around a bit and end up parking in a lot free for casino customers. Traffic is light enough that I doubt I will be found out if I never go into the designated casino. I walk up Eureka Street—and I do mean up; it's a steep hill—to the Thomas House Museum. I know the museum will be closed until spring but I'm not particularly interested in the interior anyway, apparently done up in turn of the century décor, in furnishings a quarter of century later than when it was built. The house, constructed in 1874, is in Greek Revival style, a rectangular box with four plain columns on the front supporting a second-story balcony running the width of the building and protected by an ornate low railing. The walls are pale yellow, green shutters border the windows, and the white of the columns and trim is linked to the low picket fence surrounding it. The whole building, with its long one-story side addition, sits on land anchored in place by a high rock wall that runs along the front sidewalk. By the time the Thomas House was built, Central City had been flourishing for over a decade and a half and it's at least some evidence of the solidity of the community—this is no transient shanty.

The house looks off down hill toward the Teller House, a hotel once celebrated for its elegance. Built in 1872 of local stone, it hosted President Ulysses S. Grant in 1873 and other luminaries, such as Mark Twain and P. T. Barnum, over the years. Next to it is the impressive Central City Opera House, completed in 1878—the devastating fire of 1874 had destroyed its predecessor—and in addition to opera it offered stage productions with such legendary actors as Sarah Bernhardt, Edwin Booth, and, much later, Lillian Gish (in *Camille*). The view the rest of the way down the hill, until the turn in the street closes it off, is one of solid and tasteful stone buildings.

I drift down Eureka Street, pausing at St. James Methodist Church, an imposing stone building completed in 1872. Beyond the church are several restored small houses dating from the 1860s and across the street a flat square building, the Festival Hall, dating from 1864. The buildings give a sense of the historic past, at least in architecture, but the quiet of the street, with only a few local citizens moving about and only a handful of tourists strolling from the parking lots on their way to the casinos, is a far cry from the grimy, bustling, crowded town it must have been in its glory days, when it was the center of the "richest square mile on Earth."

I wander through the Teller House, moseying through room after room after room filled with slot machines, nothing but slot machines, in place of historic décor. In a narrow barroom, a bartender and a waitress glance at me with disinterest, then continue their conversation; it's early in the day, and I give up the thought of having a drink at the Teller House bar and toasting the past. Instead, I glance at the famous Face on the Barroom Floor, a portrait of a woman painted on the floor in 1936 by a Denver newspaperman. It's the kind of artifact you wish had more of a story to it, more resonance, more context, but so far as I can tell it is simply a painting on the floor of a barroom, now protected by a glass covering and a little surrounding fence to keep people from stepping on it or washing it with beer.

The rest of my walking tour of Central City takes me past casino after casino, a few antique and craft shops, not much except gambling machines filling the buildings and, at this time of year, not many people entering any of them. Black Hawk, the first stop on Highway 119, home of the massive casinos, gets far more business than Central City does. The downside of that is a lot less revenue for Central

City; the upside is that Central City still has a certain amount of exterior charm, until you step into the casinos, where nothing is particularly charming, merely as many slot machines as can be crammed into the hollow rooms. The pace of the town is quiet, little in the way of business being transacted anywhere, the clientele overwhelmingly senior citizens.

Cruising a little before leaving town, I blunder onto the dirt road to Nevadaville, narrow and dotted with patches of snow and ice. There's little to see. A former boomtown that once swelled to several thousand inhabitants, it's shrunk to ghost town status. On the south side of the road I see lots of evidence of mine tailings, suggesting something of how prosperous the town must have been. Otherwise, only a few houses look as if they might still be occupied, perhaps by people who really like to get away from populated areas. Here's a good example, I suppose, of what happens to towns in the West when the population stakes everything on one project and then folds when the industry runs out.

Coming back down from Nevadaville, I take a turnoff that promises a vista over the North Clear Creek valley and discover an old cemetery too protected by a high fence and chained gates for me to wander through. Right near the cemetery is a mound of tailings and a cluster of rotten wood that perhaps indicates a mine site. Remembering warnings against wandering around because of the dangers of unsealed old mines, I make certain I'm on solid ground. I can see a long way down the valley, toward the fir-studded hills above the canyon, across the way to a gigantic housing development of apartments or condos up on the top of the hill, in the direction of the new Central City Parkway. Tired of waiting for the overflow from Black Hawk to reach its casinos, Central City has built a wide, clear expressway of its own from Interstate 70, and whatever growth the city suddenly inspires is likely to be accessible from that highway.

Farther down, I find an empty parking lot with a panoramic view. I recognize St. James Church and the house beside it, the roofs of the opera house and the Teller House, and I see the houses scattered across the south-facing north slope of the canyon, the neighborhoods thinning out the higher they go and the uppermost reaches empty, barren even, with brown earth and scruffy growth, before the rise beyond it begins to darken with trees. Above all is a pale blue sky, with only a few light lazy clouds drifting through it. Central City seems merely wizened and tired and indifferent from this perspective,

Still farther down the road, I pass a sign reading "Lady Luck," and I notice a chain across the entrance to a parking lot, which is entirely overgrown with weeds coming up through the pavement. It seems like someone's effort at ironic commentary, the forced optimism of a gambling town juxtaposed with its undercurrent of inevitable gloom. So much for the richest square mile on earth, the sign seems to say.

The transformation from mining district to gambling district dismayed Boyd and Barbara Norton, authors of a pictorial guide, *Backroads of Colorado*. First published in 1978, their revised edition of 1995 adds to the title of the Black Hawk and Central City section the subtitle "In Memoriam." They claim, "This region represented an important part of Colorado's colorful history," and they lament that the "sense of history and the charms of the region are gone, replaced with sleazy gambling joints." In a book promoting Colorado sightseeing, they urge people to stay away and they reprint their earlier enthusiastic description of the town to let readers appreciate what they can no longer experience.

I understand their outraged sense of loss and, like them, value historic preservation over entrepreneurial reconstruction. When a place can no longer be what it once was in the past, it may still be worthwhile to show people what that past was like; in Colorado the mining district had a far-reaching impact on the development of the territory. The question is whether the transformed district is now worth seeing as an example, like it or not, of transformation itself. Would Taylor, Bowles, Greenwood, Bird, and Jackson come here if they were touring Colorado now? I think they would feel obligated to include these towns in their tours.

Despite my own affection for the Central City Opera, whose superb productions of rare gems like Massenet's *Le Jongleur de Notre Dame* and the world premiere of Guo Wen-jing's *Poet Li Bai* are exhilarating, I have to hurry out of the area after such performances to evade the melancholy that settles on me in Black Hawk and Central City. However prosperous the gambling makes the district, like the Nortons I still prefer preservation over transformation and can't help taking away with me a sense of loss.

iii

This Idaho valley, now so bare of all verdure and foliage, was once grassy and thickly wooded. It has been wasted and despoiled of all such beauty by the gold-seekers, principally gulch-miners. In one place the golden stream had been so severely dealt with,—its very bed taken out from under it, pits dug beside it, rocks tumbled about,—that I exclaimed, "Surely, mining did not do all this; it looks like a convulsion of nature!"

"A convulsion of human nature, madam," said a fellow-traveller.

Grace Greenwood, *New Life in New Lands*

By leaving the train at the confluence of North Clear Creek and Clear Creek, Isabella Bird turned away from Central City and Black Hawk and instead took a coach up Clear Creek to Idaho Springs. She commented only that Idaho Springs was "a fashionable mountain resort in the summer, but deserted now"—she passed through on November 11—and that they continued on to Georgetown with "a superb team of six horses." Helen Hunt Jackson, a few years later, went on from Central City to Idaho Springs by following a route that is probably the one now known as Oh My God! Road. She and her companions left Central City by way of Nevada Gulch, "a steeper, narrower, stonier, dirtier gulch than we had yet seen, more riddled with mines and crowded with more toppling houses." They then passed through "an interval of lesser hills and canyons" where she noticed plentiful deserted mills, mines, and cabins. They took a road "so stony, so overgrown, it seemed hardly possible it could be the one we had been told to take" to the summit of Bellevue Mountain for "a magnificent view of the Rocky Mountains" and then they went "three miles, downhill. Not downhill in the ordinary acceptation of the word, not such downhill as one may have three miles of any day in northern New England; but downhill in a canyon,—that is, downhill between two other hills so sharp that they wall the road."

In *Backroads of Colorado* it is said that Oh My God! Road "twists in tortuous switchbacks down steep hillsides. There are no guardrails, and in places the road is so narrow that from the passenger-side windows you can see the steep drop-offs." The authors claim, "On a white-knuckle scale of one to ten, [it] ranks about eight in places." Helen Hunt Jackson traversed the road in a private carriage in June: "Good horses, an open carriage, bright skies overhead; beloved faces,—eager, responsive, sympathetic,—on either hand; constant and an unrestrained interchange of thought, impression, impulse,—all this, and the glorious out-door world added! Is there a way of being happier? I think not." She insisted that readers touring the same region must seek out "this wild path."

I, however, am driving a compact car at the end of March and have just encountered ice, snow, and mud on the Nevadaville Road. I'm also aware that some roads at elevation, especially the more lightly traveled and less regularly maintained ones, are likely to stay closed by snow until spring—or even summer—thaw. Since Isabella Bird never traveled Oh My God! Road, I don't feel compelled to either (Thanks, Isabella!). Instead, I opt for the smooth, swift sweep of the newly opened Central City Parkway to get me from Central City to Idaho Springs. It's uneventful but not unattractive because it flows through largely unpopulated terrain and over ridges and through gulches that hadn't been completely overpowered by mining.

Grace Greenwood and Helen Hunt Jackson visited Idaho Springs in summer, when its resort business was blooming. Greenwood described it succinctly: "Idaho is cosily ensconced in a most picturesque valley, on the south branch of ubiquitous Clear Creek. It is still a modest little place, but it has two excellent hotels, and the sulphur springs and soda-baths are making it a most attractive point for invalids." Jackson viewed it more imaginatively: "In a hollow made by the mouth of the canyon down which we had driven, and by the mouths of several other canyons, all sharp-walled and many-curved, lay Idaho. From the tops of the mountains which circle it, the little handful of houses must look like a handful of pebbles at the bottom of an emerald-sided well."

As it happens, it's possible to recover a sense of what Idaho Springs must have looked like from the top of a mountain by viewing William Henry Jackson's photograph from around 1885. It looks west down the valley and

has an intriguing composition that may be merely recording an overview or perhaps commenting on a location. The
foreground of the picture is largely rock-strewn hillside,
devoid of plant growth, especially rocky on the bottom left
of the picture. The dominant feature of the background is
a steep mountain on the upper right, sparsely covered with
scruffy bushes and trees. The sky that stretches across the
top of the photo is a hazy gray-white and descends to the
valley in the middle left to meet a rising cloud of white
smoke that brightly silhouettes the distant outskirts of the
town. Idaho Springs stretches across the center of the
photo, getting smaller as it gets more crowded in the farther end of the valley; the more distinct buildings at the
end closest to the camera are widely spaced and undistin-
guished except for an odd castlelike stone structure on a
knoll apart from the town. The compressed and indistinct
image of the town may be a result of the perspective or may
be the photographer's comment on its circumstances, but
even at a remove of a dozen years the photo seems to rein-
force Grace Greenwood's initial reaction to the desolation
wrought on the landscape by the mining industry. The picture gives us little reason to think a charming resort community is crammed into that valley.

In the time since Jackson's photograph, vegetation has
made something of a comeback, the mountaintops more
thick with trees, the valley slopes more fully wooded.
Smoke no longer rises beyond the town. The town has
more buildings now and a number of the old buildings are
still there, especially in the business district, including the
little castle. The dominant feature of the valley now is the
interstate highway. It has altered the terrain, leveled and
flattened the south side of the valley, and scrunched Idaho
Springs into a narrower space than it had before.

By taking the sleek new four-lane parkway from Central
City, I have been traveling virtually alone through the

newest highway-altered terrain in Colorado, the roadbed flawless beneath my auto, the roadsides shorn and clear. It rushes me out west onto Interstate 70, where the four-lane highway is thick with cars taking the altered terrain for granted. There are those who commute east to Denver from Idaho Springs and the interstate is also a funnel west into the high country where the long ski season lures tourists, particularly at times like March Spring Break. Idaho Springs is poised to catch them coming and going for snacks or meals or in-transit lodging. I exit on the first ramp into Idaho Springs and emerge on Colorado Boulevard, a long commercial strip, all gas stations and restaurants and fast food joints and motels and hotels, and Clear Creek running parallel to the north.

Crossing Clear Creek, I backtrack down Riverside Drive to the Argo Gold Mine and Mill, a tourist site closed for the season. The Argo is centered on a red wooden building rising in tiers up the slope, the angled roofs set like tilted stairsteps one below the other. A line of ore cars stands on a raised rock railbed that forms a barrier along the front and two huge engraved boulders stand sentinel duty in the open spaces in the railbed. Glancing up at the hill beyond the mill, I see little glistening lights in the rocks, apparent indicators of gold or silver but more likely strategically placed bits of tinfoil or polished metal blowing in the wind. At the bottom of the slope a long massive mound of tailings spreads out for a long way along the road. The slope on this side of the creek has been pretty thoroughly carved out by the mill, and gives me a good indication of the effect of mining on the landscape.

I cruise through town slowly, finding the buildings of the historic district attractively restored but filled only with gift shops and coffee shops and souvenir shops. Circling back toward the northern mountains, I detour up Virginia Canyon Road far enough to see where Oh My God!

Road would have come out. When I spot the dirt track angling sharply up the mountainside, apparently clear of snow, I have no regrets about not having taken it. There may have been less anxiety in traveling on a horse or a mule, or even in an open carriage, but it is still steep, narrow, and, to my mind, anxiety-inducing enough.

Idaho Springs stretches for a long way along I-70, but it's a very narrow town, hemmed in between the highway and the steep hills on the north. It doesn't take long to see enough of it and to find little there that can't be found in almost any small town along any interstate. I continue on toward Georgetown.

*   *   *

> . . . a descent of 1,000 [feet] took us into Georgetown, crowded into as remarkable a gorge as was ever selected for the site of a town, the canyon beyond *apparently* terminating in precipitous and inaccessible mountains, sprinkled with pines up to the timber-line, and thinly covered with snow. The area on which it is possible to build is so circumscribed and steep, and the unpainted gable-ended houses are so perched here and there, and the water rushes so impetuously among them, that it reminded me slightly of a Swiss town.
>
> Isabella Bird, Letter XII, November 16

One of my favorite photographs by William Henry Jackson is his overview of Georgetown from 1901. Granted, that's a quarter-century after most of the travelers I've been consulting were there but, unlike the dark and hazy Idaho Springs picture, the portrait of Georgetown is clear and sharp, the town tumbling across the foreground and middle ground of the picture, minimizing the effect of the mountains that are shown ascending sharply from the valley floor and extending off into the distance beyond the valley where the town is firmly settled. The buildings by this time are substantial and tightly clustered, made to last and clearly part of a community. In the right foreground corner, almost out of the picture, is the bright steeple of a church, and though there's considerable open space between it and the town at the center of the picture, the church doesn't seem isolated. I can pick out other churches in the town and a number of very solid, substantial buildings. Georgetown looks prosperous and not at all fly-by-night, the way some other towns appear in Jackson's photos. The slopes around the town are scarred and battered, of course, still largely denuded and rough, but the town looks enduring and well established.

John Fielder's parallel picture from around a hundred years later is remarkable, by comparison, for how obscured the town is from the view. The surrounding mountains are particularly dark, full of apparently flourishing forest growth that hides a multitude of scars and incisions made in the terrain. Trees have also grown plentifully in the town and the number of houses and buildings has declined—the church in the corner is missing, some houses beyond it have been displaced by tailings. Georgetown is less prominent in the picture than it was a century earlier. The right center of the picture, though, is starker and more ravaged than before. A considerable portion of the mountainside has been decimated to make room for the interstate, which passes high above the town, midway on the slope. It was not so easy to bypass Georgetown a hundred to a hundred and thirty years ago.

Indeed, the approach to Georgetown up from Idaho Springs seems to have made an impression on everyone. As he had found it in Black Hawk and Central City, Samuel Bowles thought the terrain around Idaho Springs ravaged but considered the drive up the valley "quite the nicest bit of the inhabited portion of the mountains . . . a constantly varying but ever beautiful scene." Grace Greenwood, who drove up from Idaho Springs with friends on a summer day in 1871, observed, "The valley of South Clear Creek is, between the Springs and Georgetown, peculiarly picturesque and lovely." She liked the way "it opens out into miniature parks, green and flowery" and thought Clear Creek "suggestive, with its alluring shine and silvery tattle, of vast treasures hid away in the wilds from which it comes." Since she was visiting Georgetown in its boom days as the "Silver Queen," her barely veiled hint at the mineral riches that inspired the creation of the town is probably unsurprising. She found Clear Creek to be "a marvelous, enticing stream," but the modern traveler has only occasional glimpses of it from the interstate.

It was mid-November when Isabella Bird descended into Georgetown, the days shorter than they are in July or August, the weather colder and the wind harsher, the hills tinged with snow. She noted, "It is the only town I have seen in America to which the epithet picturesque could be applied," but perhaps the season or her own particular outlook made her perceptions of the place less cheery than those of other travelers. Greenwood was enthusiastic and forgiving, casting the setting in the most positive light: "Georgetown nestles like a darling close up against those great mountains, that tower protectingly above her some two thousand feet. It lies most of the day in shadow. . . . Here we see neither sunrise nor sunset. I miss the latter; the former is not of much account." Bird was less cheerful about Georgetown's location: "But truly, seated in that deep hollow in the cold and darkness, it is in a terrible situation, with the alpine heights towering round it. I arrived at three, but its sun had set, and it lay in deep shadow."

Helen Hunt Jackson captures the approach to the town most vividly: "Georgetown is a surprise at last. It has no straggling outposts of houses, and you have become so absorbed in climbing the canyon, watching the creek and the mountains, the trees and the flowers, that you forget that a town is to come. Suddenly you see it full in view, not many rods ahead, wedged . . . crowded, piled, choked in at the end of the narrowed rift up which you have climbed." She liked the way the creek ran through the town and found the houses neat and comfortable, "quite unlike the untamed and nomadic look of Central City." In this last comparison her perspective and mine largely agree. She stayed at the Barton House, a hotel with a view over the town and across the valley. Although the "towering mountain sides, dotted wellnigh to the tops with the shining pyramids of the gray ore thrown up by mines," were thoroughly "honey-combed by galleries and shafts," she felt they looked "still and peaceful and sunny as the virgin hills of the Tyrol."

Bird's view of the landscape was less sunny in either actuality or attitude. She wrote, "I shall forget many things, but never the awfulness and hugeness of the scenery. I went up a steep track by Clear Creek, then a succession of frozen waterfalls in a widened and then narrowed valley, whose frozen sides looked 5,000 feet high." The terrain provoked a passage, in the opening pages of Letter XIII, as vivid and pointed as any in her book. She refers to the mines, mills, and smelters "fill[ing] the district with noise, hubbub, and smoke by night and day." and then tells us:

I had turned altogether aside from them into a still region, where each miner in solitude was grubbing for himself, and confiding to none his finds or disappointments. Agriculture restores and beautifies, mining destroys and devastates, turning the earth inside out, making it hideous, and blighting every green thing, as it usually blights man's heart and soul. There was mining everywhere along that grand road, with all its destruction and devastation, its digging, burrowing, gulching, and sluicing; and up all along the seemingly inaccessible heights were holes with their roofs log-supported, in which solitary and patient men were selling their lives for treasure. Down by the stream, all among the icicles, men were sluicing and washing, and everywhere along the heights were the scars of hardly-passable trails, too steep even for pack-jacks, leading to the holes, and down which the miner packs the ore on his back. Many a heart has been broken from the few finds which have been made along those hill-sides. All the ledges are covered with charred stumps, a picture of desolation, where nature had made everything grand and fair.

Isabella Bird had little patience with progress as demonstrated by commercial enterprises and unharnessed development, and, although she was not alone in noting the effect of mining on all the canyons where it had been at all profitable, she only occasionally allowed herself outbursts of censoriousness or more than passing commentary on the mining, ranching, and farming industries. For the most part, she nimbly steers herself toward the less populated regions and seems content to take them in with as little company as possible.

Isabella seems to have barely spoken to anyone in or out of Georgetown. The more typical tourist behavior among writers tended to involve exploring the central interest of the community as fully as possible. Helen Hunt Jackson, for example, toured the Terrible Mine while she was in Georgetown, not merely walking into the main tunnel, as modern tourists do at the Lebanon Mine during a ride on the Loop Railroad between Georgetown and Silver Plume. It's good to know what the mining conditions were like and the brief tour is informative there, but designed for safety and protection from liability; Jackson had somewhat more of an immersion experience. In miners' jackets, carrying candles, "facing an icy wind and breathing the fumes of gunpowder," she and her companions walked along a "wet and slippery" track in the tunnel "down which cars loaded with ore came constantly rumbling out of the darkness." Eventually, she reached a vaulted chamber where a steam engine was at work and was invited to descend the mine shaft. Though frightened, she assented. The bucket in which she was to ride was "an extra-sized water-pail, with high sides,—sides coming up just to the knees of them who stood in it." Only two people could go at a time. Jackson observed, "It was odd how much it felt like being lowered by the hair of one's head, the going down in that bucket. It is odd how very little consciousness one has of any thing solid under one's feet . . . It is odder still what a comfort here is in a bit of lighted candle in this sort of place." She could see only "the slanting wooden wall, against which we bumped with great force every now and then." She said that, "during the hour—three minutes long—which we passed in that descending, swinging, twisting, bumping bucket" she fixed her eyes on the candle flame and looked nowhere else. Then she was guided around the lowest level of the mine, after which the promise of the ascent in the bucket was welcome and reassuring.

I've been in mines, the Lebanon among them, and a number of others in the Upper Peninsula of Michigan, and respect the dangers and difficulties of mining, particularly in those early days. I can handle the cold and the damp and the awareness of tons of rock overhead and the total darkness that comes when the only candle is snuffed out (or flashlights and lighting systems are turned off, as so often happens on mine tours I've taken). However, to have toured a working mine under relatively crude conditions, ore cars shuffling by, gunpowder in the air, the clank of machinery echoing all around, is considerably more daunting a prospect. I can appreciate Jackson's rising to the challenge and value the picture of the mine she records. We don't know if Isabella was ever offered the opportunity to take a similar tour but, given her circumstances and sensibilities, it's not surprising that she expresses no interest in having that experience.

When I leave Interstate 70, I head away from Georgetown toward the Wildlife Watching Area on Georgetown Lake. The gravel road takes me past a park and a skating rink and a warming shed for skaters and on down to a muddy parking lot near a low concrete tower. The brown of the tower matches the brown of the hills on either side of the valley. Georgetown Lake is frozen over and hemmed in and devoid of wildlife, but the tower is really just a two-story concrete platform with some level space to watch from and some enclosing walls that provide a little concealment. The wind is sharp enough that I'm happy to have the solid walls around me. The idea is that tourists can stop here, watch waterfowl on the lake, and catch sight of bighorn sheep feeding. I sweep the hills slowly and carefully with my binoculars but find no signs of wildlife of any kind (though I've actually seen a handful of sheep near Idaho Springs and another handful minutes away from Georgetown, in either case grazing the dry grasses close to the westbound lane of the interstate). But I take a moment to look at the steep scruffy arid slopes on either side of the canyon and survey the valley floor up and down. In an earlier age, I would have approached Georgetown close to the valley floor, moving at a walk or a trot, more completely aware of the scale of the town against the scale of the valley.

Whatever the changes in its fortunes have been, Georgetown seems to have been able to maintain a sense of itself. Together with Silver Plume, two miles west up the valley, it has been declared a National Historic Landmark District and seems to have been conscientious about keeping buildings intact and, despite changes of use—the early miners were probably not much interested in fudge, cappuccino, and crafts shops—and the occasional paved street notwithstanding, the town has an atmosphere redolent of an earlier era.

I drive back into Georgetown from the lake, find a parking place, and start ambling. I know that the tourist stops will be closed—the Georgetown Loop narrow gauge railroad, now operated by the Colorado Historical Society, only runs between Georgetown and Silver Plume from Memorial Day to Labor Day, and the 1879 Hamill House is only open in the summer—so I concentrate on well-kept houses and businesses. Rose Street, the main business street, is lined with antique shops, craft shops, gift shops, restaurants, art galleries. The Fort Mackinaw Candy Shop, where I pick up a few pieces of hard licorice candy, reminds me, by its name, of the plethora of fudge shops at Mackinac Island and Mackinaw City. Both Michigan communities depended on the eminently disposable income of tourists. Georgetown may have aspirations to that kind of lucrative shopping district but the area seems modest now. I can't really tell how much business it picks up from vacationers bound to or from the ski areas to the west and wonder if the businesses thrive more in the summer tourist season.

Returning to my car, I roam the town toward its southern end, where the streets rise and a mountainside closes off the valley. Clear Creek runs northerly along the west side of town but it enters from the west, and the valley and the creek and the interstate all turn sharply at the south end. What impresses me the deeper into Georgetown I go is the fact that there's a town here. It seems very much a place where people live, not simply a place pretending to be a community for the benefit of tourists.

I don't know where Colorado ranks among the states in the number of ghost towns, but I suspect it's ranked high in regard to the mountains where the boom-and-bust nature of mining—the Upper Peninsula of Michigan, settled by copper miners, iron miners, and loggers, has a similar history I'm very familiar with—launched and sank any number of potentially or momentarily prosperous communities. The questions are whether those gaudy and frantic first acts turn out to be unexpected one-act plays and what those who continue their community dramas do for a second or third act. Golden, Boulder, Black Hawk, Central City, Idaho Springs, Georgetown—all in their own ways still endure but how and whether they thrive is what distinguishes them, while Nevadaville, Mountain City, Sunset at the top of Boulder Canyon, and hundreds of others have only the evidence of whatever has decayed or rusted most slowly to prove they ever existed.

* * *

At a height of nearly 12,000 feet I halted on a steep declivity, and below me, completely girdled by dense forests of pines, with mountains red and glorified in the sunset rising about them, was Green Lake, looking like water, but in reality a sheet of ice two feet thick. From the gloom and chill below I had come up into the pure air and sunset light, and the glory of the unprofaned works of God.

Isabella Bird, Letter XIII, Boulder, November

From what Isabella Bird says in her letters and in the text of her book, Green Lake was "the goal of my journey" on this portion of her travels all along. While other visitors took advantage of the opportunity to descend into gold and silver mines, as part of their emphasis on the burgeoning enterprises of Colorado Territory (this was, after all, exotic terrain to sedentary readers and potential settlers and entrepreneurs), Bird was almost begrudging of her time spent gazing at industry and commercial ventures and architecture she had no interest in occupying. Her disinterest in Georgetown is such that her description of it, once she's actually in the middle of it, is crammed into a sentence which ends with her efforts to get out of town: "We drove through the narrow, piled-up, irregular street, crowded with miners standing in groups, or drinking and gaming under the verandas, to a good hotel declivitously situated [probably the Barton House, where Jackson stayed], where I at once inquired if I could get to Green Lake."

Though the landlord told her that no one had been to Green Lake for five weeks and that the snow was very deep, he had some one go ask at a stable. "The amusing answer came back, 'If it's the English lady traveling in the mountains, she can have a horse, but not any one else.'" Letter XII ends on that line in the book and Letter XIII begins by picking up the consequence of the remark; the original story is told in a single letter to Henrietta datelined "Georgetown deep buried among huge mountains Tuesday night. November 11." In this letter there is no direct quote from the stablekeeper; instead, she writes: "The answer came that no lady could go up, but if it was the English lady who was travelling in the mountains they would saddle a horse for her for she was said to be the boldest rider in Colorado." The published version is clearly more dramatic but also more modest.

From time to time, mention of Isabella's travels reached newspaper readers in several communities and word of mouth seemed to travel with some speed as well. The landlord, confirming the stablekeeper's offer, asked if she was "the lady who had crossed from Link's to South Park by Tarryall Creek." Though she never sought or exploited her brief celebrity—Anna Dickinson and Grace Greenwood in the same period were drawing crowds to their lectures and public presentations—it occasionally opened doors that general letters of introduction might not. Here she owned up to being "the English lady" and took advantage of the opportunity to ride up to Green Lake. She confided to Henrietta, "This is the only 'mad bad' thing I have done." Her arch allusion to Lady Caroline Lamb's scandalous description of Lord Byron is amusing but hardly apropos, since Isabella was probably never, as the poet was, "dangerous to know."

As she observed, Georgetown was already in shadow by midafternoon and, following directions given her in town, she climbed toward Guanella Pass. She had a brief opportunity to see a spectacular sunset but "the sun was fast going down, and even as I gazed upon the wonderful vision the glory vanished, and the peaks became sad and gray." She wrote, "It was strange to be the only human being at that glacial altitude, and to descend again through a foot of untrodden snow and over sloping sheets of ice into the darkness, and to see the hill sides like a firmament of stars, each showing the place where a solitary man in his hole was delving for silver."

Like Bird, though in summer, Grace Greenwood had gone up on horseback from Georgetown to Green Lake, which she described as "a pleasure resort, with nice buildings and boats, at present in charge of three young miners resting from severer labors." She thought the lake to be "a beautiful and unique sheet of water, lying high up among the mountains in a deep, dark privacy of rock and pine," and found the young miners to be "remarkably cultivated and courteous young gentlemen." The highlight of the excursion for her was being rowed across the lake to see "[f]ar down under the clear, green water . . . large round rocks, covered with a peculiar kind of moss, which gives them a remarkable resemblance to the lobes of the human brain." Isabella Bird saw only the frozen lake and no sign of activity or human presence, and soon returned to Georgetown in growing darkness, through snow and over ice.

I myself have reservations about heading up towards Guanella Pass to get to Green Lake. For one thing, not every map identifies Green Lake and at first I'm nervous that I'll have to go *over* Guanella Pass—11,669 feet of elevation and the trailhead for 14,066 Mt. Bierstadt—to reach it. Isabella herself had claimed she reached "a height of nearly 12,000 feet" before she spotted Green Lake below her, reflecting the sunset. A better map reassures me that I'll reach the lake (9,916) long before the pass and without the need to ascend to the elevation Isabella thought she had. I also read that the road is steep, narrow, without guardrails, and when I begin the climb I can tell that all that is true. Signs warn travelers not to take the road. One reads: "Road closed 8.2 Miles." Another reads: "Construction starts 14 miles." Another says: "Dangerous. Road Closed to Through Traffic." I'm uncertain whether Green Lake is more or less the distance mentioned on any of those signs, and well aware that the roads over other passes—Boreas, for example—or at similar elevations—the Trail Ridge Road in Rocky Mountain National Park, the Mt. Evans Highway—have been snowclogged and unplowed since November. So I am, undoubtedly, overly cautious as I drive up the first few switchbacks, run into a few patches of ice and unmelted snow, particularly on the northern or shady side of the road, where the sun has had little effect, and think that, even where the snow and ice have melted, each evening they would refreeze. Not certain about my prospects for turning around farther up, I make a U-turn at a wide spot and come back down to a good vantage point where I can get out and photograph the valley. While I stand at the overlook, five or six other cars come past me, heading up the mountain. Well, gee, I think, they seem to be pretty confident about this; maybe they're locals and maybe they know where they're going. None of them come back down in the few minutes I take my pictures, so I turn around again and follow them up the mountain. The road, while still narrow, steep, and sans guardrails, is not as bad as Oh My God! Road—more of an Oh! road.

Green Lake, as it turns out by my calculations, is only six or seven miles up beyond Georgetown, and it's a pretty little spot, although nothing I see suggests a motive for Bird or Greenwood to have made the ascent. As it was when Isabella Bird saw it, the lake is mostly ice covered and frozen over, with a little bit of open water at the north end, the part that gets the most sun, surrounded by trees and, above them, mountains rising past timberline, over 11,000 and 12,000 feet. I'm uncertain if the most distant one I see is Mt. Bierstadt or not, but I know the valley stretches a long way south in its direction. A sign announcing "Private property" keeps me from lingering, but I'm content to see a pretty little frozen lake, the highway arching around it and disappearing over a rise to the south, and head back down to Georgetown. I've come as far as Isabella Bird had, and Guanella Pass and Mt. Bierstadt can wait until summer, when I'll reach them for fun and not claim the need to go up them for research.

When Isabella Bird returned to Georgetown, it was an unnerving journey. "The view, as long as I could see it, was quite awful," she wrote. "It looked as if one could not reach Georgetown without tumbling down a precipice. Precipices there were in plenty along the road, skirted with ice to their verges." She claimed—and this is something of a statement for a woman who had been several weeks traveling alone on horseback around the Front Range—"It was the only ride which required nerve that I have taken in Colorado, and it was long after dark when I returned from my exploit."

In her corresponding letter to Henrietta, she was less self-effacing. She wrote, "There was one steep ice sheet which the horse could not go over, and there were only a few inches of bare ground between that and the loose crumbling edge of a tremendous precipice. Think how strong my head has grown with practice that I guided him for about 50 yards along that edge." She also opined, "This was the only ride which involved real riding since I left Hawaii and it was shocking to be taking it on a sidesaddle." The changes from correspondence to publication help distinguish between Isabella's private and public personas.

Despite newfound confidence in my ability to navigate the road and the happy circumstance of returning in the middle of a sunny day, rather than at nightfall, as Isabella had, I drive slowly down the switchbacks leading back to the valley. It is less a matter of nerve than one of prudence, but I also relish the final chance to see the valley again from the heights. If I had a wide angle or panoramic lens I could fashion a Clear Creek Valley mural: unblemished light blue sky across the top, a long rising brown canyon wall, green-tinted with trees along the ridge line and a combination of reddish-brown and gray at the nearer end of the valley, where the walls are craggy and jagged with boulders, a dark tan stripe of lifeless soil running evenly below that and holding up the interstate it was constructed to buttress, then the town, not always visible among the trees that have grown up below the switchbacks on Guanella Pass Road but filling the flat valley floor from off the end of the frame on the left down as far as Georgetown Lake, a blue-white smudge in the distance. At the end of the valley, where the slopes seem to descend toward each other, are snow-capped peaks and more densely wooded mountains. From this distance they look unspoiled and undeveloped, like the landscape that the Clear Creek Valley once resembled.

*   *   *

From Georgetown down to Idaho at sunset is more beautiful even than from Idaho up to Georgetown of a morning.

Helen Hunt Jackson, *Bits of Travel at Home*

Helen Hunt Jackson, ever the appreciative traveler, gave a vivid picture of her departure from Georgetown. "Full speed; sunlight gone from the left-hand wall, broad gold bands of it on the right; now and then a rift or canyon opening suddenly to the west and letting in a full flood of light, making it sunny in a second, afternoon, when the second before it had been wellnigh twilight again; red, gray, and white clouds settling down in fleecy masses upon the snowy mountain towers of the gateway of the valley— this is sunset between Georgetown and Idaho." The final image in her essay on Georgetown, following the glories of the sunset, is a simple appreciation of "the Rocky Mountain columbine," allowing her to end not on the rigors of the mining life but on "the solemnity in its beauty" and a fellow-traveler's remark that it was "the gladdest flower I ever saw."

Isabella Bird left Georgetown at eight in the morning, in shadows; she noted that the "sun does not rise until eleven now; I doubt if it rises there at all in the winter." She rode the stage to Idaho Springs and, "after four hours' fearful bouncing," transferred to the train to return to Golden. Instead of having to sit at the door of the baggage car, as she had on the way up, she was given a chair on the platform by the conductor, "so that I had an excellent view of that truly sublime canyon."

I leave Georgetown on the interstate, watchful more of traffic than of scenery, and soon buzz by Idaho Springs, then turn off on Highway 6 to travel Clear Creek Canyon all the way back to Golden. It's a beautiful drive, partly impressive for the highway engineering involved—I traverse five long tunnels beneath masses of rock and skirt a sixth no longer in use—but mainly impressive for the massive canyon walls. It makes me wonder how anyone could understand a canyon traveling the way we do, roaring down superfast roads, traffic piling up behind the slower drivers, attention focused on the hairpin turns and the cars braking or accelerating ahead of us. People zip through the canyon and it's hard to take it in going so fast. Nonetheless, when traffic seemed light enough, I tried to imagine going through Clear Creek Canyon slowly, on horseback at a trot or a canter or walking through at an easy pace, being just a small figure, a small person, with that mass of rock overhead all around me.

No matter what becomes of the towns, the canyons seem to still keep a timeless sense of scale.

The Last Canyon

The more canyons one sees, the more this truth sinks in, the more vividly one realizes the intense individuality of each canyon. Carried blindfold into any one of them and set down midway, one knowing them could never mistake or be in doubt. But it is hard to find words in which these differences shall be distinctly set forth, harder even than it is to tell just how one human voice differs from another; yet who ever mistook a voice he knew?

Helen Hunt Jackson, "Bowlder Canyon"

Helen Hunt Jackson claims that "there is a right way to take a canyon, as there is to take a person. One must not be driven through,—no, not if a broad turnpike ran its whole length. Only by slow and humbling toiling on foot can one see its beauties. Another is made for a swift and royal dash on wheels, or on horses' backs; as distinctly 'set' to an allegro movement as was ever a joyous outburst of the soul of Beethoven or Mozart." In order to "keep time" with nature, she asserts, "If we live in Colorado, we shall take our canyons right end foremost and be absolutely certain which way they were meant to be read."

I am out trying to read a canyon—specifically, Boulder Canyon, the one that inspired Jackson's reflections. In Colorado, where it's easy to be overwhelmed by the view of the mountains from the plains, easy to be awed by the view of the plains from the mountains, we tend to forget that the passage between the plains and the mountains is through the canyons. It's also easy to be astonished by the canyons once you're in them.

At last in tracing Isabella Bird's travels I've reached an area with which I'm a little familiar. Boulder Canyon, as well as the city of Boulder itself, is close to home turf. At the moment we live ten miles due east of the city. To get to Boulder we take one of three roads—South Boulder, Baseline, or Arapahoe—directly west. On any of them, though we may sink into low points that limit our horizons, we soon reach the top of a rise where first the Front Range, then the foothills, then the Boulder Valley open up to view. I'm on Arapahoe today, trying to pay attention to heavy early morning traffic while gazing at shining peaks pristine with snow. Longs Peak is a flawless white study in geometric shape rather than rugged geology. The Flatirons, those upended slabs of sandstone, display contrasting red and white patches, and the browns of the foothills show through the melted snow on slopes facing south or east.

To get to the backcountry, the trail to Mt. Audubon, say, or the trail to Arapaho Pass and Lake Dorothy, we drive up Boulder Canyon and return the same way. To get to Estes Park, we sometimes traverse Boulder Canyon and sometimes other canyons—the South St. Vrain, the North St. Vrain, the Big Thompson. We've taken the Clear Creek Canyon west of Golden to get to Central City and Blackhawk. Like Helen Hunt Jackson, I find each of the canyons unique; like her, I'm hard pressed to find words that distinguish one from another.

Grace Greenwood felt the same way. She wrote that coming to "Boulder City" the back way, up from Central City and Black Hawk and "over grand heights, through lovely little parks, and wild pine forests, and by the new opened route down the North Boulder Cañon, then thrilled me with wonder and delight, and now fills me with despair. I know it is utterly indescribable. I have seen nothing in America that has so impressed and enchanted me." Her account of what she saw in early September 1871 is brief but enthusiastic: "All the way, height and depth, and the immensity of mountain and gorge,—sheer granite walls, and massive, castle-like rocks,—are softened and shaded and glorified by beauty incomparable; by swift, bright, gurgling waters and silver cascades, and by luxuriant foliage of every imaginable shade of green, touched here and there by scarlet and gold and tints of ruddy brown, while every shadowy place is illuminated with flowers."

Greenwood, who spent August and September in Colorado and traveled in relative comfort, usually takes a positive perspective on her experiences. She wrote, "Boulder is a remarkably pretty town, exquisitely situated, just under the foot-hills, looking out on the prairie. It is well watered, and is in the midst of an agricultural region of great capabilities. The Buttes—sharp, bare, rocky elevations, a mile or so to the left of the town—make a striking and picturesque feature of the town landscape." Her snapshot of it makes it seem to be a delightful destination.

Isabella Bird, after weeks traveling alone, on horseback, often through deep snows and severe cold, and a few social days in Denver, made her circuit through Georgetown, and struck out from Golden for Boulder. She went the wrong way, blundered on the home of an acquaintance (identified in the letters as Mr. Church) four miles from Denver, and the following day rode on to Boulder, arriving a day later than she intended. She claimed she developed "vertigo, headache, and faintness" from riding in "the intense heat of the sun" over the plains. Given all these circumstances, it may not be surprising that her responses to the town and its attendant canyon were as terse and cranky as any reaction she records in her book. She wrote, "Boulder is a hideous collection of frame houses on the burning plain, but it aspires to be a 'city' in virtue of being a 'distributing' point for the settlements up the Boulder Canyon, and of the discovery of a coal seam." After getting up early and renting a horse other than Birdie, she reported that she "went nine miles up the Boulder Canyon, which is much extolled, but I was greatly disappointed with everything except its superb wagon road, and much disgusted with the laziness of the horse." That was all she had to say. So much for Boulder and Boulder Canyon.

The canyon seems to me to merit more attention than that, and I find support for my position in Helen Hunt Jackson's essay about it. Here Jackson and I both view the terrain as the Colorado residents we've become (or are becoming), not as transients in a hurry to pass through. Jackson rode through the canyon a few years after Bird did, traveling gregariously and comfortably. She frequently extolled the western landscape, particularly its canyons. One of her essays began: "There are nine 'places of divine worship' in Colorado Springs," then named eight Christian congregations and Cheyenne Canyon. Her exuberant description of Boulder Canyon is worth quoting at length: "Bowlder Canyon," she asserts, "is one of the 'allegro' movements. It is sixteen miles long and one should ride swiftly down it,—race, as it were, with the creek, which has never yet drawn a long breath since first it plunged into the gorge." Later she makes a run for it:

Now between walls made of piled bowlders, piled as if storms had hurled them where they hung,—bowlders poised, and bowlders wedged, and bowlders half welded together; with great fir-trees crowded in among them, shooting out of crevices like spears thrust through from underneath; clasping gnarled roots like anchors round edges of precipices.

Now a high pyramid of rock, only a few rods ahead, walled the way, and we said, "Where do we and the creek go? Surely, to the left." No; to the right, and under rather than around the rock. Like a huge sounding-board, it ran out above our heads, its seams like rafters and its rifts like groined archways, mossy with age and now shining with the dripping water. We and our carriage and our horses could have been safely housed under it, with room to spare.

Round this, sharply to the left, and another just such wall juts out on the right; and between the two we cross the foaming creek on a narrow bridge.

Fir-trees high up on the sides; fir-trees walling the topmost edge; fir-trees standing with their roots in the water; fir-trees bent out across the stream, as if they had sought to clasp hands—the air itself seemed of a verdurous color, from their masses of solemn dark green.

Now through the wider spaces, where one or other of the walls recedes, and the broader slopes are green as meadows. Now through narrow passes, where the walls are straight hewn, and the narrow strip of sky overhead is like a blue line drawn on gray, so closely the rocks approach each other. In these rock-walls are ravines, packed full of fir-trees. They look only like fissures filled with bushes. Mid-way up these rock-walls are jutting projections which look like mere ledges. They are broad plateaus on which forests grow.

Meantime the creek never slackens. Amber and white and black in the arrested spaces, it whirls under the bridges and round the corners, doubles on itself, leaps over and high above a hundred rocks in a rod, breaks into sheafs and showers of spray, foams and shines and twinkles and glistens; and if there be any other thing which water at its swiftest and sunniest can do, that it does also, even to jumping rope with rainbows.

And I must not forget that there are gardens all the way down. In the bends of the creek, round the butments of the bridges, in sheltered nooks under the overhanging rocks, wherever there can be a few feet of ground, there spring all manner of flowers,—white spiräas and pink roses and blue larkspur, and masses of yellow for setting.

Sixteen miles, such miles as these, and never once the creek slackens!

This, of course, follows her assertion of how difficult it is to find words to describe the canyon.

I don't expect to do half so well describing Boulder Canyon, but then, in my time, it's quite a different creek that I'll be following. The Barker Dam impounds the Middle Boulder Creek at the high western end of the canyon and the regulated flow is nothing so tumultuous as the one Jackson describes—snowmelt and mountain rain-fed creeks and rivers have generated devastating floods along the Front Range, and most of the mountain waters entering the plains have been dammed and diverted and in some cases drained to dryness. A well-maintained blacktop highway winds through the canyon on a raised bed often lined with a concrete wall. It channels the creek against the canyon wall on the opposite side from the road and limits its options. The creek that flows through the city on its way to a quiet rendezvous with the St. Vrain and then the South Platte is placid and picturesque, the paved walks along it a pleasant passage for the joggers, walkers, hikers, bikers, rollerbladers, and rollerboarders—and their dogs—that often seem the main population of Boulder. The city has a kayak park on the creek and in the summer children gently tube the stretch near the library. Boulder Creek itself doesn't inspire much reflection on the sound of mountain water these days.

Still, I am a "canyon-lover," like Helen Hunt Jackson, and I thought that my local canyon deserved closer attention than I'd been giving it.

*   *   *

I know Boulder mostly for its bookstores and libraries, its organic markets, the occasional concert or play or reading, the hiking trails in the open spaces along the Flatirons, the biking path along Boulder Creek. It reminds me often of Ann Arbor, where our daughter attended the University of Michigan—the similar cultural events and venues, the similar intellectual atmosphere, the similar grating sense of privilege and ardent affluence mixed with earthy asceticism, the class gap crossed by shared self-indulgence. There was only so much of Ann Arbor I could take in one visit and my threshold is only slightly higher in Boulder.

After a solitary cup of coffee in a café adjoining a used bookstore near the foothills end of Pearl Street and a leisurely review of the comments of earlier writers, I leave the grooviest part of Boulder and drive west into the canyon, heading up toward Nederland. I quickly find myself channeled between high rocky walls. Little traffic leaves Boulder at that hour of the morning and I have the opportunity to ride slowly and look around. It's been months since I've traversed the canyon, not since autumn at least, and the blending shapes of snow and rock and trees captivate me. The canyon is deep and the sun in early February barely affects the ranks of firs clinging to the steep slopes. The heavy snow grips the overhanging rocks at so sharp an angle that I won't be surprised to see it slide off at any moment. The glimpses I have of the creek reveal a boulder-strewn bed mounded and blanketed with snow, the clear dark water seldom visible.

The road winds through sharp curves that often run close to the walls of jumbled gray rock, some draped with wire nets to hold them in place. Though the road is sometimes wet or slick where the angles of the walls are too steep or the trees are too dense to let the sun filter through, for the most part it's dry and traction-sure. Nonetheless, I navigate the curves carefully—accidents are frequent enough here that, according to a friend, the local police refer to one curve simply as the "usual place" whenever reports come in, and the flow of traffic is often too zippy and too daring to suit me. The double solid yellow lines in the center of the road are grooved to alert drivers when they've taken too narrow or too wide a turn on a curve and drifted off into the opposing lane.

I keep a steady pace, noting places to pull off on my way back down, but not really getting much chance to appreciate what I'm seeing—or might see at a more leisurely rate of travel. I've done a little twentieth-century research, and found a book with an extensive section on Boulder Canyon, but it's neither geological nor historical. Instead, it's a guide to area rock climbing, *Boulder Climbs North*, by Richard Rossiter. *Climbs* is a noun in this title. The times my wife and I have driven through the canyon, or ridden on our bikes from 30th Street along the Boulder Creek Pathway out to the end of the trail, at Four Mile Junction, or walked along the same path from a parking area in the canyon—during those times we not only gazed at the rock formations and the trees but also gaped at the sudden discovery that people were clinging to the vertical surfaces of the rocks, often with no visible means of support. For a flatland midwesterner like me, this need to challenge gravity is largely a mystery, an impulse that no reduction in my acrophobia and no expansion of my upper-body strength is likely to raise in me. It makes me apprehensive simply to see others doing it, so I tend not to watch for very long. And, indeed, in the few months we've been in Colorado two unprepared young men fell to their deaths climbing for fun above Boulder Falls, farther up the canyon, and an experienced and much-admired climber died in Eldorado Canyon, south of Boulder, the first canyon we'd ever visited in Colorado. These were not the only climbing deaths and injuries we'd heard about, and it often seemed to me that "sport" might not be the right word for so potentially fatal an activity. In Boulder County, though, mine may be a minority opinion.

Though the climbing guide mentioned the possibility of climbing up ice-coated Boulder Falls, the heavy snow cover on the flat and lightly angled surfaces throughout the canyon makes winter climbing problematic. In the glimpses I take as I drive I see no one clinging anywhere. I'm also unable to distinguish the particular sites the climbing book mentions, though I think I must have seen Goofy Spire, a "small pillar" near the Boulder end of the canyon. The rock formations are distinctive enough and stand out sufficiently from the canyon walls that climbers over the years have not only named most of the climbable ones but also recorded the various routes they've taken to the top. For example, not far from Goofy Spire are the four Elephant Buttresses and beyond them is a formation called the Dome. Rossiter lists sixteen routes up the Dome, not only numbered but also named—Evening Stroll, Gorilla's Delight, Supersqueeze, the Umph Slot, Prelude to King Kong (which leads to "the belay niche" on Gorilla's Delight), Cozy Hang, Cozy Overhang. The individuals who named the routes, often the first people to climb them, are fond of puns and sight gags and plays on other titles. Candelaria's Groove on the Fourth Elephant Buttress and Candelaria's Crack on Highway Island are named for first climber Rob Candelaria; Rossiter comments about the second route, "As one might guess, this is not too far from Anus Great," a route on nearby Three Buffoons. Cob Rock is just before Blob Rock (with grim pop cult-named routes like Night Stalker, Wounded Knee, The Radlands of Infinity, Silent Running, and the Gathering Storm). The Berlin Wall, about eight miles up the canyon, has route names following the German theme—Walpurgisnacht, Dachau, Blitzkrieg, Weinachtsfest, and Himmelbruch—and the rappelling point at the top of the wall is called Checkpoint Charlie. The Boulder Falls Wall has seven established routes, though Rossiter disparages the tourist appeal of the falls itself (at least when no one is ice-climbing it); he calls it "an ideal location for throwing trash into North Boulder Creek, falling off the rocks, and for outdoor sexual activity" and warns those interested in rock climbing about "taking care not to lose footing on empty beer bottles."

I suspect that, unlike, say, the outline of Sleeping Ute Mountain in the Four Corners or the Kissing Camels formation (formerly Nun Kissing a Seal) at the Garden of the Gods, which more or less anyone might discern, the names of the formations in Boulder Canyon are ones you had to have been there, climbing, to appreciate. Particularly passing them on the highway, they evoke no such identifications in me. Nor are they meant to.

I tend to take for granted the complete immersion in physical activity I see all around me—the steady stream of bikers, walkers, joggers, rollerbladers, climbers, long-distance dog-strollers we meet on the trails and paths and highways all around us; the kayakers, rafters, and tubers (tubists?) we spot on creeks and rivers and reservoirs; the patrons testing climbing walls in sporting goods and outdoor equipment stores; not to mention the anglers and horseback riders enjoying the outdoors in their own ways. Like the miners, ranchers, farmers, and tourists of the picturesque of an earlier day, these are all people trying to define and exploit the outdoors on their own terms. Like the miners and ranchers, they have their own vocabulary, their own specialized equipment, their own special purposes. The chief difference may be that they don't particularly want to change the land and, instead of greater wealth, for the most part seek only greater health, greater amusement, a moment of enhanced emotion.

It strikes me that these are not thoughts I would likely have in any other canyon than the one that leads up from Boulder.

And yet, as the road twists and turns relentlessly up the canyon, at first seeming level, then reaching what geologists call a knickpoint and beginning a more pronounced rise, I find myself thinking more and more about the canyon itself. The curves demand attention but, a few miles into the canyon, the road seems only a thin stripe of civilization. Dark spearpoint-shaped firs climb in thick ranks up the steep slopes, except for the places where sheer rockfaces rise from the side of the road, its shoulder often littered with fallen rocks, or the places where spires and towers of stone loom above the trees, gray granite piles of boulders balanced precariously hundreds of feet high. The narrows here are mid-canyon and a good many turns arc around and beneath massive overhangs. Only toward the top of the canyon does it open up enough for a valley and a ranch far below the shelf on which the road runs. In a field close by the highway, remains of mining shacks slowly decay in the sun and the snow.

Though the creek begins as far away as the Continental Divide, the canyon ends at the high, red Barker Dam and the huge man-made lake behind it, just east of Nederland. The reservoir fills the long last stretch of canyon to a great depth. Though all the snow is long gone in Boulder, up here the snow is still deep. The broad flat frozen surface of the reservoir gleams with an unblemished blanket of snow.

Across from the Barker Dam, I slow and turn onto Hurricane Hill Road, which jogs first east, then north up a hill. I drive a little way up and park at the top of the rise, lean my notepad against the steering wheel, and record some thoughts—or at least some words—about the uphill portion of the drive. From time to time other vehicles, mostly SUVs, Jeeps, and pickup trucks, rush down the other side of the road and slow abruptly as they reach the sharp curve behind me or they come up off the main road, as I did, straining on the first part of the rise, then gunning it as they come out of the curve onto the straighter stretch uphill. Sometimes I look up, sometimes I don't.

I have no particular reason to think much about the dwellings at the start of Hurricane Hill, but in casual glances up from my notepad, I register the closest ones: on the left side of the road, a large, one-story structure with plenty of windows, a big porch and a winding driveway down to the road; above it a brown house with wooden siding at the top of a dirt drive; on the right, a rustic-looking chalet-style home, its front enclosed in glass. Though this section of the road is mostly clear and dry, the snow is deep in the yards. A quiet, out-of-the-way spot.

Two vehicles, one a SUV, one a van, labor up the hill behind me and, hearing their engines, I glance up ahead of them at the empty road. It isn't empty. A long lithe sandy shape lopes across, unhurried but purposeful. Its ears are up and its stride relaxed. It seems to have come from between the buildings on the left. It swiftly crosses the road and vanishes behind the chalet on the right. The driver of the SUV must see it but neither vehicle slows and all at once they fill the road in front of me and then race out of sight around the curve. I keep looking at the empty road. I can hardly believe that I've seen what I've seen.

I sit there stunned for only a few seconds, then drop my notepad and pen onto my lap, start the engine, and lurch up the hill, steering more by instinct than design and looking frantically for a second glimpse of the mountain lion.

The cougar is by now, in half a minute, long gone, but I see its tracks in the snow, veering off around a second house previously hidden from my view behind the chalet, leading into the trees behind it. I go a short distance up the road to a clear stretch where I can make a quick Y-turn, and drift down slowly, scanning the woods, but the chance to see the cougar is already long over. Those few seconds of exposure allowed the only sight of him I will get, and I struggle to keep the image in my head.

If I hadn't heard the cars or if they hadn't arrived just then, I might have kept my head down, working on sentences, and missed that mere instant of sighting. Sometimes I think everything I learn depends upon inadvertence and chance.

I stay in motion and pause when I reach the intersection of Boulder Canyon Road and Hurricane Hill Road. Earlier, when I looked off at the flat snowy surface of the reservoir, I saw a tabula rasa of pristine, unruffled whiteness. This time, I see a single set of tracks leading from the far side of the reservoir to the side along the road. Did the mountain lion cross the Boulder-Nederland road after clambering out of the reservoir and then mount the hill behind the intersection or was it traveling down from the woods behind the houses? I know it can range as much as 120 miles over the course of ten days or so and may not be back in the area for at least another week.

Signs warning hikers that they are in mountain lion country abound at all the trailheads. A controversial book by David Baron, *The Beast in the Garden*, about sightings around Boulder and the death of a jogger killed by a cougar in the hills near Idaho Springs, focused attention on their proximity to civilization. Reg Saner, who daily walks Table Mesa, has written of an encounter with three cougars as he walked a trail near his home at dawn and also about his concerns for the safety of children playing in their yards in neighborhoods like his, bordering the wild. As a consequence of these warnings, I sometimes pack my Swiss army knife on the trail, as a perhaps futile precaution, and I occasionally reread the pamphlets about recommended human behavior when encountering cougars. I've imagined what it would be like to see one lurking or lounging or padding along the trail, and been on the alert for them while hiking. But, despite all I've read of their likely predations on backyard pets, I hadn't associated them with houses. All the times I've looked for signs of them in the woods, near the trails, and my actual sighting comes on a populated, somewhat busy country sideroad, unexpected and momentary—if I hadn't looked up, I'd have never known a mountain lion had been fifteen yards away, in clear view.

Before I put the car in gear, I sit at the intersection, trying to lock the cougar's image in my brain. Long tawny body, thick rope of tail, head up, looking ahead. Strides long, effortless, graceful, already emerging, front paws outstretched, onto the pavement, back legs propelling its body forward, front paws touching down a second time, now on the opposite shoulder of the road, pulling it forward so that the next push of back legs will be on snow. The torso contracts, then expands, then the cougar disappears behind a house. I'm trying to replay an instant in slow motion and recognizing how little detail I can accurately recall within minutes after the event. The instant is over, irretrievable, unrepeatable, and, although I know I will not see the cougar again, no matter how long I stay in the area, it takes an act of will for me to put the car into motion and head back down the canyon.

* * *

My sense of Boulder Canyon as, in Helen Hunt Jackson's phrase, "an allegro movement," a place where "one should drive swiftly down it" and "race . . . with the creek," comes less from the sight of the stream, flowing under long stretches of snow than from the press of traffic behind me. Other vehicles rush up behind me, then slow and keep their distance, their drivers no doubt seething at my pace and wishing they could hurry to "the usual place." Even at my speed the continually curving highway enhances the feeling of hurtling with centrifugal force. Nonetheless, I take notice of the pinnacles rising above the trees, the jagged outlines of stone walls hanging above the road, the occasional impression of faces in the boulders, one looking like an elongated Easter Island head near the top of one rock tower. The creek and the highway bounce around barrier boulders like a pinball around its bumpers. Definitely allegro, I think.

I reach the Boulder Falls turnout and veer right, into a partly plowed parking area. The cars I've been leading plummet past in a series of whoomps.

The path to Boulder Falls, across the highway, is pretty well snowed-in on this February weekday. To reach the fence above the creek, I step into the tracks of others who post-holed through the wide, deep bank of snow a day or two before. I face a wall of rocks, trees growing from the barest toeholds of crevices, living monuments to tenacity, and below them a track of piled snow covering the trail to the falls. Even here where the North Boulder Creek plummets over the falls and meets the Middle Boulder Creek (to become simply Boulder Creek—the South Boulder Creek joins it on the east side of Boulder), I hear gurgling water but have trouble seeing any. I retrace my footsteps and recross the dry pavement. In a brief lull in the traffic, at the start of a windless afternoon, closer now to the main channel of the creek, I pause and listen outside my car; the sound of the gurgling fills the canyon.

I remember coming to Boulder Falls on a warm April day, somehow lucky enough to be the only one there for the better part of an hour. Sitting in the roar and the spray of the falls, not high but impressive enough tucked away in a crevice of the canyon, I watched the swift current at its base tumble down to a tunnel under the roadbed. The falls drowned out the traffic sounds and gave me the deceptive sense of being farther away from civilization than I was. To get deeper into the moment, and into the nullifying sound, I strolled down close to the water, stepped out onto a flat rock, and sat down. For several minutes I meditated quietly, eyes closed, hearing the steady roar of the falls and the barely discernable whoosh of the rapids, feeling cold spray and cool breeze and warm sun on the back of my neck. Then I opened my eyes and watched the clear green water foaming white in its rush downstream and lifted my gaze to the falls. The water poured off the lip of the falls in thick braids on the sides, a thinner flow at the center, surged over the lip, plunged and pounded the rocks below, bounced and sprayed in foaming white sheets and bundles. How does so much pure white come from so much green? I put my hand in the water—it was still as icy as the snows where it began.

I drive farther down into the canyon, somewhat less allegro, the walls rising higher above me, and pull over into a wide parking turnout on the inside of a long curve. Behind me in the rearview mirrors, I see a stark slope with only black sticks of trees standing on it, a barren burned-over area. Glancing across the road at the houses above the north side, I remember what a friend said about building homes in tree-dense canyons: "The question isn't *if* there will be a forest fire—the question is *when*." As long as lightning ignites dry timber at random, fires will flare in the mountain canyons, and the homes—and sometimes lives—of the people who build and buy there will burn with the forest. It must have been terrifying to be the people living in this Boulder Canyon house, watching a fire consume the slope not more than a hundred yards away, a slope adjoining the one they'd perched their house upon. Another house, with a pickup truck parked above it, nestles at the base of the burned-over slope. A few green trees still grow around it, but the stretch of scorched tree trunks and shadeless ground begins only a few yards above it and continues beyond and over the summit, in every direction. This, I've begun to learn, is a persistent feature of the western landscape, the burnt-over region. It's always a stark and sobering sight.

I continue on and, near the end of the canyon, watch the number of buildings rapidly increase. I pass Settler's Park, location of the first settlement in Boulder, where miners came in 1858 looking for gold. When mining moved farther up the canyon, the settlement became a supply depot for the miners, and gradually evolved into the city of Boulder. In the center of the park are the Red Rocks, tall sandstone formations at the top of a steep hill, made of the same material as the Flatirons and providing ready places to perch for a view of the Boulder Valley and the plains beyond.

And then I'm in Boulder and soon even looking in my rearview mirror gives me no view of the canyon or the foothills. It's a crowded, expensive city, filled with high-tech firms and college students at the University of Colorado and Naropa University and the remnants of a beat generation–flower child sensibility that still generates art and literature and popular culture, still supports bookstores and coffeehouses and stores selling items from Tibet and maps and gear for biking and skiing and rockclimbing and running. In my first year in the area, the big issues revolved around the university—the use of prostitutes in recruiting athletes, the binge-drinking deaths of students, the controversial speech acts of an activist professor—as well as the economy and the crime rate and the rising cost of real estate. Boulder has become a twenty-first-century city like so many others, with little memory of the frontier town it once was.

Unlike Helen Hunt Jackson's race with the creek, my swift descent of Boulder Canyon has taken me not only through the canyon but also across time. At the top of the canyon, I encounter the mountain lion, the embodiment—the very essence—of the wilderness; coming down I pass through the dark trees and the granite walls of the canyon, evidence everywhere of the power of mountain water, and cross regions of fire and commerce and recreation into the center of population. The stages of the canyon's history over a century and a half reveal themselves in a half-hour drive. The changes also appear at an allegro pace.

Given my inclinations toward a wilderness aesthetic and my exposure to as many Front Range canyons as Helen Hunt Jackson found "places of divine worship" in Colorado Springs, I tend to think of other canyons first—the Big Thompson, the Clear Creek, the South St. Vrain—when the lure of canyons arises in me. But I see now that the Boulder will always come to mind as my home canyon and that the cougar's image will always flash indistinctly across my memory whenever I speak of canyons. It only takes an instant to see the world differently—or to realize that you've already been seeing the world differently for quite some time.

*　*　*

You can form no idea of what the glory on the Plains is just before sunrise. Like the afterglow, for a great height above the horizon there is a shaded band of the most intense and glowing orange, while the mountains which reflect the yet unrisen sun have the purple light of amethysts.

Isabella Bird, Letter XIII, Boulder, November

The morning that Isabella Bird rode from Mr. Church's house to Boulder, she was struck by the beauty of the dawn and wrote about it in her letter to Henrietta; the passage made it verbatim into the book. Her description of "glory on the plains," the "shaded band of the most intense and glowing orange," "the purple light of amethysts" stays with me because it captures so well my own experience of sunrise from where I live on the plains near Boulder. Helen Hunt Jackson felt the same way; one of her most delightful essays is titled "A Calendar of Sunrises in Colorado" and describes five sunrises she witnessed in 1876. Her devotion to watching sunrises is echoed in Reg Saner's "The Dawn Collector," the title essay of a collection that also contains two magnificent photographs of dawn from his mesa. If living in Colorado has done nothing else, it's convinced me that painters like Albert Bierstadt and Frederic Church, so often dismissed as Hudson Valley School romanticists, were actually photorealists when it came to picturing the sky.

Especially in the winter months, when the days are shorter, I often check on the sunrise from my bedroom window after my wife has left for work and I've started my own chores or projects around the apartment. In the evenings when I drive to meet her at the bus stop I often catch the early sunset and watch it over the distant mountains until her bus arrives. The sky in Colorado fascinates me and the interaction of sun and clouds at dawn and dusk has endless variety. The book that I will never be able to write, the one that would be my masterpiece, would be *The Book of Colorado Clouds*.

This morning, when I go out to warm up the car for our short ride to the bus stop, the sky is dark, an inky blue-black, and almost starless. Yet in the ten or fifteen minutes it takes us to drive a few blocks and wait in the parking lot for the Denver-bound bus from Longmont to pull in, the day has visibly begun. It is just after six o'clock and the sky in the east is already lighter, a gleaming beam of blue-white radiating outwards from a point beyond the curve of the earth, pushing back the darkness on either side. I know at once it's a morning to watch the sunrise from a higher perspective. I rush home for my driver's license, coffee, pen, and notepad, and race off toward Boulder and a higher vantage point.

For a few moments on South Boulder Road the night lies ahead of me in the west, and in the east that pale blue ray, visible in my rearview mirror, widens. Then a large pickup truck pulls into my lane and begins following me, its headlights even with my back window, and the view in the east is gone. I scurry ahead of the truck and when it turns off I see in my mirrors that I will have to hurry to beat the sunrise to the foothills.

I cross the ridge at McCaslin Boulevard and start my descent into the Boulder Valley, still dark but arrayed as far as I can see from south to north in bright pinpoints of light. The vague shapes of the foothills, partially illuminated by light on the snows in the upper reaches, appear out of the darkness, and lighten the closer I drive. Luckily, traffic is sparse and the traffic lights are with me most of the way. South Boulder Road turns into Table Mesa Drive and I hurry up the other side of the valley to Table Mesa and the parking lot in front of NCAR. I look for an open view across the valley, especially clear to the horizon, and park my car to face the sunrise.

I can scan the entire valley, from the distant foothills to the north arching out into the plains, past the ridges succeeding one another out toward the east, to the distant lights of the Denver suburbs to the south. Without taking my eyes from the horizon I open my notepad, take out my pen, and start to write.

By 6:40, I realize the light is changing minute by minute. A moment before the sky was fiery and the plains still a deep hazy blue, clear chains of moving lights on the freeway from Denver and the highway descending from Louisville and Lafayette, marking the trajectory of my own rapid transit down from the ridge and across the valley. What have been beads of yellow light sprinkled in the darkness of the valley keep morphing into increasingly distinguishable structures and shapes, outlines of buildings, clusters of trees, the gleam of the reservoirs. The eastern light grows paler still. Behind me the Flatirons are clear, speckled with snow, and the mountains beyond them are sharply detailed. The eastern sky diffuses a pale rosy glow, except for one brilliant golden patch where the sun's orb will soon be appearing. Translucent smudges of cloud, dark streaks in the sky, grow steadily more transparent. The thin cloud cover in the east has one squarish hole in it where a light turquoise sky shows through, and the golden radiance burns more brilliantly, more intensely.

The day is light enough now to make the streams of headlights more difficult to discern, and still the sun hasn't cleared the horizon. The glow brightens and brightens, straining to burst through the gauzy atmosphere, and then the curving top of the sun emerges, a fiery gleam rising above, refracting its own intense presence, until the two light sources merge, as if the sun has risen into the gleam above it. Now the light is too intense to look upon directly and still the ground is hazy and the headlights so dim that from Table Mesa there sometimes seems to be no movement on the black strings of highway. The smears of cloud that have been gray and dark change suddenly to powdery, chalk-white smudges radiating outward from the east, and above them the sky has become brilliantly blue. Only close to the distant horizon is there a layer of reddish-brown sky and only the thin clouds keep me from peering at a dazzlingly white sun. The fingers of white clouds that stretch overhead dissipate by the time they reach the foothills, so clearly delineated behind me, and when I look north along the Front Range the distant mountains are still blue. It has been day for fifteen minutes.

A quote from the ornithologist Don Kroodsma comes to mind: "One of my favorite images of our small, beautiful world is of morning's first light sweeping around the globe, continuously, relentlessly, forever circling and returning to repeat the cycle. Always, somewhere, it is dawn and always, somewhere, the birds are singing." By the time I get back home, all the glory of the sunrise has evaporated and only a typical, radiant day is left. But images of the sunrise stay with me. As Reg Saner has said, "Still, each dawn is a gift." It is indeed.

The Park in Winter

Every day some new beauty, or effect of snow and light, is to be seen. Nothing that I have seen in Colorado compares with Estes Park; and now that the weather is magnificent, and the mountain tops above the pine woods are pure white, there is nothing of beauty or grandeur for which the heart can wish that is not here; and it is health-giving, with pure air, pure water, and absolute dryness. But there is something very solemn, at times almost overwhelming, in the winter solitude.

Isabella Bird, Letter XIV, Estes Park

In winter the mountains act, from the perspective of those of us living on the plains, like a 12,000- to 14,000-foot snow fence. We live in what is generally termed a "rain shadow," an area to the leeward side of the mountains where rain and snow seldom fall, no matter how much saturates—or, alternatively, accumulates on—the western slopes and the central mountains. In winter we sometimes see thick, cottony-white snow clouds frothing beyond the peaks, peering over their summits and around their shoulders without being able to rise above and tumble across them. At other times, reinforced by strong winds backing a moisture-laden front, they overwhelm the mountains and soar ominously above them, like a broad gray inverted waterfall, like tumultuous waves of cloud breaking fiercely on a coastline of mountains. The Continental Divide disappears beneath snow clouds that seem to reach heights double or triple those of the highest peaks; a stranger, unable to see beyond the low foothills, might be intimidated by that looming snow-filled sky. But those who live on the high plains know that very little of that impressive display will leave the mountains or, if it does, fall within the rain shadow. Rather, it will likely arch above us, o'erleap us, and drop upon the lower plains to the east, closer to Kansas or Nebraska. By nightfall the sky will be clear again, and the temperature at midnight will lower thirty or forty degrees below the earlier afternoon's high, and in the morning the mountains will wear a brighter mantle of white and the sky beyond them will be empty, already turning an unblemished blue.

Winter is a different country in the mountains than on the plains, we are reminded by every westward glance as we run our errands on the plains. For me at least—for now at least—the mountains are hard to ignore, hard to be complacent about, and yet the sight of them so often startles me, stuns me, as if I'm repeatedly discovering them anew.

So it is today. I top the ridge to start my descent into the Boulder Valley and suddenly see the Continental Divide sprawling across the distant horizon, deeply coated in snow. The Snowy Range indeed. Across the valley the Flatirons are only lightly flecked with sprinkles of snow, but the distant mountains, including Longs Peak, are thoroughly and thickly covered. Foaming billows of clouds rise beyond and between the mountains, obscuring some slopes and attempting to squeeze past them rather than flow over them. Above the peaks and the clouds that form a roughly even line with them is limitless bright blue sky, clear, cloudless, open, unruffled. As I drive, my gaze centers on those pristine and beautiful mountains and I am both drawn to and unnerved by their white-capped serenity. I find that expanse of unbroken high altitude intensely inviting and intensely forbidding at that same time. As much as I can while safely negotiating heavier traffic approaching Boulder, until the intervening foothills and buildings shut off the view, I keep looking at the mountains with a longing like that of someone who's never been among them.

*   *   *

Long's Peak rises in purple gloom, and I long for the cool air and unfettered life of the solitary blue hollow at its base.

Isabella Bird, Letter XIII, Longmont, November

Readers of *A Lady's Life in the Rocky Mountains* have little inkling in the chapters reporting her tour of the Front Range that Isabella Bird has every intention of returning to Estes Park. Indeed, the places she ends up going throughout the book all seem, generally speaking, adventures in inadvertence. For example, we don't know in the beginning, until she gets off the Denver-bound train in Greeley and heads first to Fort Collins and then to "Canyon," that for some time she's intended to visit Estes Park. Her setting off for it seems more like a whim, a lark, so impromptu that, when she fails to reach it, she's willing to abandon the effort, until her landlord in Longmont suddenly arranges for her to accompany Downer and Rogers up to Evans's ranch. Similarly, after she returns to Denver from the southern part of her tour, she seems to simply launch herself off to Golden and Georgetown without warning and with merely a mild complaint about the "wearying world" of social Denver to motivate her. To read Letter XIII, when she's finished the northern part of her tour and ended up in Longmont again, you'd think that, but for the $100 she needs to receive from Griff Evans and the temporary poverty occasioned by a bank panic, she would have readily headed east to New York and home to Scotland instead of making her way to Estes Park "where [she] can live without ready money, and remain there till things change for the better."

However, given the evidence of letters to Henrietta that survive from the end of her Colorado trip, Isabella intended all along to return to the ranch after her ride up to Green Lake, to remain in Estes Park for three weeks, and to depart on December 1. She recorded this plan while still in Denver, claiming that she needed to retrieve luggage and fetch waiting mail. Even before setting out for Golden, she apparently loaded up the mailbag—in the book she seems to acquire it in Longmont—and purchased gifts to bestow upon her friends in Estes Park, including "sweeties" for the children and "a very nice russia leather diary for Mr. Nugent." Though in the book she expresses surprise in Longmont to find that the Evanses and Edwardses have come down to Denver, in the letters she walks on the streets of Denver with Mrs. Edwards and Mrs. Evans before she heads out toward Golden. The letters also indicate that Evans owes her $55, not $100.

Why the discrepancies between the two accounts? Lacking Isabella's own explanation, we can only surmise. Certainly the revisions to the original letters make the book's narrative current flow more smoothly; the letters are much more random and prone to abrupt changes in subject, offhand remarks, and explanatory backtracking, but the book moves steadily forward. Some changes can be attributed to the shift from a private, personal interchange to a public presentation, requiring alteration of voice and persona. The voice of the letters is conversational and intimate, that of the book more informative and neutral. Yet none of that explains her troubling to mute her intentions, to emphasize necessity instead of desire as the impulse behind her return to Estes Park, and to postpone the revelation that the communal group previously at the ranch had scattered. Perhaps she was modifying the perception of her own behavior to seem less objectionable and more prudent than it might appear to readers other than her sister—she was, after all, about to go into the mountains to lodge alone with two unknown young men tending the ranch; for a woman who occasionally shifted from riding astraddle in "full Turkish trousers" to riding sidesaddle in a skirt when she approached a sizable community, such a concern about propriety is not unimaginable. From the evidence in the letters of material toned down or excluded from the book, she also underplayed the role her attraction toward Jim Nugent played in her decision to return to Estes Park.

In her letter to Henrietta datelined "Denver Sunday November 9," she writes: "Regarding a place one likes one always thinks (in spite of all lessons) 'tomorrow shall be as this day and much more abundant'. All my tour I have been reveling in the thought of returning to Estes Park to explore its glories and stay 3 weeks." Her point, of course, is that such a thought has been exploded by circumstances. Yet in the book she makes her argument for return solely on the basis of need, then shifts focus disingenuously to the landscape and "the cool air and unfettered life" she'd enjoyed earlier in Estes Park. It would turn out that her days in that place she liked would be quite different on virtually every level.

In the few weeks that Isabella had been traveling, conditions had changed in the mountains, a circumstance that became apparent to her on her solitary ride from Longmont to Estes Park, which she recounted in the November 20 section of Letter XIII. Two familiar ranches on the way were now deserted, and only the last house she reached had occupants. She found Nugent's cabin dark but soon encountered him and another man returning with a load of furs. Nugent accompanied her to the Evans Ranch, where she met the two young men staying there (identified as Kavan and Buchan in her book, Kavanagh [the correct spelling was probably "Cavanaugh"] and Buchanan in her letters; Chubbuck identifies the latter as John Buchanan, who married Griff Evans's niece). She found her cabin and other outbuildings dismantled and supplies low, and set herself up in an unoccupied room in the main building that had been used by the Dewys when they were at the ranch.

The young men, it turned out, were amiable enough, and Isabella volunteered to maintain the house and share the cooking, thus freeing up the men for hunting, procuring provisions, and keeping track of cattle. Within a few days they had established a routine—breakfast at nine, dinner at two, supper at seven—and an unvarying menu. In the evenings, around an intense fire, the men smoked, Isabella wrote letters and mended clothing, and they all talked or read aloud. She noted that "our circumstances, the likelihood of release, the prospect of snow blocking us in and of our supplies holding out, the sick calves, 'Jim's' mood, the possible intentions of a man whose footprints we have found and traced for three miles, are all topics that often recur, and few of which can be worn threadbare."

Her situation was congenial but confining. Before she left on her tour, there had been a lively community at the ranch, including several other women; now she was left alone quite often, frequently unable even to go riding because the horses were unfit or had wandered off. Instead of the robust life she had led when cattle round-ups delayed her departure, she now endured a more sedentary existence, her activities centered on domestic chores. In Letter XIV, she wondered "if all [her] life is to be spent here in washing and sweeping and baking." Though Isabella Bird seems to have been a resilient, adaptable individual, though the passages recounting her winter weeks at the ranch are often lively and amusing, clearly the privations of her current life and the lack of communication with the outside world affected her.

Once, coming back from a ride toward Longmont, Isabella recognized her view of Estes Park as the same one she had had when she first arrived in late September. The alteration of the scene struck her. "Life was all dead; the dragon-flies no longer darted in the sunshine, the cotton-woods had shed their last amber leaves, the crimson trailers of the wild vines were bare, the stream itself had ceased its tinkle and was numb in fetters of ice, a few withered flower stalks only told of the brief bright glory of the summer." To her the park seemed "utterly walled in" and "fearful in its loneliness," and she felt that "the world was absolutely shut out." The isolation of the landscape, so invigorating in autumn, could be oppressive in winter.

Isabella Bird wasn't unfamiliar with the bleak midwinter—she was an Englishwoman who resided for long periods in Scotland—but I suspect there was something more to her winter of discontent than weather and the change of seasons. Whatever her motives for returning to Estes Park, that place she liked, her discovery that her days were not as they had been or "much more abundant" was likely tied up with the realization that her role had changed, her identity been altered. It's notable that, though Isabella is often sympathetic towards the women she meets and the conditions in which they live, she never really identifies with them, even on occasions when she pitches in to help them manage their domestic chores. At Evans's ranch in the autumn she alternated between being a guest and being a volunteer wrangler; she could choose her commitments and still be free to ramble and explore. At the ranch in winter, however, her role was reduced and redefined; she became, as a female and as a woman older than the men she lived with, a kind of maiden aunt/housekeeper/den mother. Her daily life was centered not on her excursions into new terrain and opportunities for new experiences but on her daily living, on a repetitious round of mundane routine.

If you stay too long in one place you can no longer call yourself a transient or a traveler. You've become an inhabitant and you spend your time learning how to dwell there, day by day. For most of us, perhaps, this inevitable change is not only expected but anticipated. For Isabella Bird, it was frustrating and unacceptable.

* * *

It looked icily beautiful, the snow so pure and the sky such a bright, sharp blue! The snow was so deep and level that after a few miles I left the track, and steering for Storm Peak, rode sixteen miles over the pathless prairie without seeing man, bird, or beast—a solitude awful even in the bright sunshine. The cold, always great, became piteous.

Isabella Bird, Letter XVI, December 4

Exploring the Front Range after Isabella, I haven't given much thought to her final few weeks in Estes Park prior to her departure from Colorado or how they might figure into my own travel plans. I've been to Estes and to Rocky Mountain National Park several times over the past year and a half and feel as if I've covered the territory pretty thoroughly. If I were to isolate myself in a snowbound cabin somewhere it might help me duplicate her experience, which isn't my intention, but it wouldn't necessarily locate me more thoroughly in her landscape, which has been my desire. Nor do I feel the need to cultivate strangers in search of characters equivalent to Kavan, Buchan, and Rocky Mountain Jim. Yet as I settle in to concentrate on her time at the Evans ranch in the end of November and the beginning of December, I can't help but think that, as much as she dreaded the changes that could come to Estes Park once it became well known—and she herself claimed to identify it only because others had already publicized it—she would never have predicted that the mountain landscape in winter could be so populated.

In Isabella Bird's time, people retreated from winter in the mountains. As she observed upon her return, the valley would not see another woman before the following May, when the snows melted and the range was open again. Even as Estes Park developed as a vacation spot, the resorts and the cabins were often designed for the summer months, not for year-round living. Even now, the population of Estes Park shrinks in winter, vacation homes are boarded up for months, and many of the seasonal shops close while their owners retreat to other homes or other seasonal businesses elsewhere. Yet winter recreation is so popular that the hiking trails now under feet of snow are almost as busy as they were in summer.

In Colorado, in the Front Range, it's hard to find an uncrowded trail on the weekend. The trailheads in the national forest and wilderness areas are usually down long backroads that are only plowed up to a point long before the trailhead. Sometimes the winter ski and snowshoe trekkers have the trailheads themselves as a likely final destination. The roadsides are lined with vans, sports utility vehicles, pickup trucks, and station wagons, and the roadbed surfaces have grown smooth and slick from the continual passage of people headed for the locked gate and the piles of plowed snow that close off access to the remainder of the road.

Sue and I are not stylish outdoorspersons, sometimes hiking in jeans, though never, in winter, snowshoeing in cotton clothes ("Cotton kills," my ice-climbing and backcountry-telemarking contacts in the Colorado Mountain Club keep advising me), but I note the array of winter fashions on the people we see. I'm particularly struck by the whippet-thin men and women in skin-tight Lycra® and spandex, as muscular and lean and revealingly dressed as ballet dancers, their only baggage the Camelback water containers with the long drinking tubes and pockets filled with high-energy sports gels and fruit bars. (One hiking guidebook we own advises the reader not to be intimidated by the "aerobic animals" who overtake and pass and disappear ahead of you on steep high-altitude trails, but the only ones who bother me are the ones loudly talking business or personal drama all the way up and back.) Others ski or snowshoe in heavy down snowmobile suits or lightweight down vests and fleece jackets and high-wicking layers of nylon, polyester, acrylic, and trademarked fabric concoctions like Capilene®, Polartec Power Stretch®, Vaporwick™, TechnoWool™, Arctic Insulation™, Synchilla®, and the like, including PCR® (Post-Consumer-Recycled) polyester. All are designed to be lightweight and warm and prevent hypothermia at the same time that they advance stylishness and heighten athletic performance (or at least the appearance of athletic performance). It's a colorful parade on the trail, though perhaps less so than at the downhill ski resorts.

The snowshoes and skis and poles run the gamut as well, from classic antiques or faux antiques in handsome durable woods to various shapes and lengths and combinations of aluminum and high-tech plastics. Some walk on snowshoes barely longer than their boots, others on long elegant shapes with the properties of tennis rackets, still others on versions meant for running or climbing as well as simply hiking. Occasionally, someone comes by hauling a child in an enclosed sled or dragging a trailer of camping equipment, bound for more distant destinations than the dayhiking majority on the trail.

For Isabella Bird and the men in Estes Park in the winter of 1873, the snows were a barrier to be crossed on horseback or not at all; Isabella never mentions walking except as a way to prolong her outing by leading the horse back to the cabin. The question of communication with the outside world preoccupied them; in the November 29 entry of Letter XV, she wrote: "This life is in some respects like being on board ship—there are no mails, and one knows nothing beyond one's little world, a very little one in this case." But in the Colorado of my day newscasters celebrate the snow, cheerily report the depth on the ground at resorts around the state, and inform the public of road conditions so that they can hurtle toward those resorts in throngs. One day, when we went up to Rocky Mountain National Park from the snowless plains, a Park Ranger informed us that Bear Lake had had forty-seven inches of snow so far that winter. This news was meant to encourage us, not alarm us. That was the day we spent hours snowshoeing up toward Lake Helene, passing a group who determined their location by Global Positioning Satellite before they decided which trail to take, and only turning back when blowing snow on open terrain obscured the trail completely. We could measure the amount of time we were ever alone only by minutes.

Yet even while I observe all this, and try to stand aside like a disinterested spectator, I have to acknowledge a simple truth. On these outings we can't claim to be vacationers or visitors; instead, we've become anonymous members of a resident community of recreationists, another couple of a certain age spending another morning enjoying another trail readily accessible from where we live. We greet our doppelgangers, in all their variety, on the trail all the time.

*   *   *

He is a man whom any woman might love but no sane woman would marry.

> Isabella Bird, Estes Park, Rocky Mountains,
> November 18[,] 1873

Though I've hardly mentioned Isabella Bird's relationship with Rocky Mountain Jim Nugent, it's caused much speculation among those who've written about her. Modern biographies routinely highlight it and it has inspired works of fiction, including one fairly erotic romance. Readers of the first four-fifths of *A Lady's Life in the Rocky Mountains* may find such attention surprising. Except for a couple of lengthy descriptions of his appearance in her early days at Estes Park and his commanding role in her ascent of Longs Peak, he is merely the most vivid character but hardly a significant presence in the book until she returns to Evans's ranch in the final chapters. Even then, much of her narrative focuses on the rigors of ranch life in winter, attention to daily living, the activities of the two young men with whom she's living, and the distracting presence of a "ravenous," "wretched," and "vexing" latecomer, called Mr. Lyman in the book (actually James Allen). She mentions marauding wolves and the habits of beavers and occasional rides through the snow. In addition, she recounts emotional conversations with Jim in which she is disturbed by his revelations of his reckless and profligate life. His presence in her thoughts as well as in actual scenes with her provides dramatic tension throughout the end of the book, especially since she alludes to his subsequent death at the hands of Griff Evans months after her departure.

Anna B. Stoddart, Bird's friend and first biographer, whose biography covers the Rocky Mountain adventures in a single sentence, recounts an experience that took place around the time of Jim's death. According to her, when Bird and Nugent parted in Colorado, "they promised each other that after death, if it were permitted, the one taken would appear to the other." The two apparently corresponded over the next six months—Nugent was shot on June 19, 1874—and the version of his death that Isabella received in July led her to "the distressing conviction that Jim had died unrepentant." Actually Jim lingered on for more than a month. Stoddart tells us that, while Isabella was vacationing at Interlaken, Switzerland, "one morning as she lay in bed, half unnerved by the shock of his death and half expectant, she saw 'Mountain Jim,' in his trapper's dress just as she had seen him last, standing in the middle of her room. He bowed low to her and vanished." She learned shortly after that Jim had finally died: "When exact news of his death arrived its date coincided with that of the vision." (At least one scholar who has worked out the chronology of events and variances in time zones has dismissed the claim of precise timing.)

It's a quirky story, quirky in the same way as the evidence that Isabella wore black funereal clothing when she married her late sister's doctor, John Bishop, in 1881, and it adds to the impression that, despite the calm, sensible, occasionally wry but always observant public persona presented in the travel books, the private woman was more complex and problematic. At the same time, it reveals that Isabella's emotional investment in Jim Nugent was considerably greater than the evidence of the book alone would suggest. It's well to remember that the articles for *The Leisure Hour* and the eventual book edition of *A Lady's Life in the Rocky Mountains* appeared roughly five years after she left Colorado and four and a half years after Nugent's death. Time and circumstances were bound to have a mitigating influence on her feelings, whatever they were. The much-quoted line of hers about him, that he was "a man any woman might love but no sane woman would marry" (which comes from her letters, not from her book), suggests that she might well have considered herself to be falling in love with him at the time and explains how her pragmatic side was able to resist the weakness of her romantic side.

The only scene from early in the book that gives us any insight into their relationship is the conversation at the end of the chapter on Longs Peak, when they talk around the fire and Jim "told stories of his early youth, and of a great sorrow which had led him to embark on a lawless and desperate life. His voice trembled, and tears rolled down his cheek." Victorian lady and clergyman's daughter though she was, Isabella reveals a shrewd sense of character in the next sentence, which closes the anecdote: "Was it semiconscious acting, I wondered, or was his dark soul really stirred to its depth by the silence, the beauty, and the memories of youth?"

Since we don't have the original manuscript where she first recorded that scene, we can't know whether her perception at that moment was immediate or retrospective, but it establishes Isabella as canny rather than naïve. However, the letters from her final three weeks in Estes Park do survive and there is where we encounter her most instantaneous and somewhat less guarded reactions to more tempestuous interactions with Jim. The differences between the letters and the book are an interesting study in what an author chooses to conceal and what she chooses to reveal.

Consider one example.

Isabella's first full chapter about her time at the ranch in winter, Letter XIV, opens with an account of her ride up Black Canyon with Nugent, ostensibly to see the beaver dams, during which he tells her the story of his life, which she claims was "one of the darkest tales of ruin I have ever heard or read." The recapitulation of Jim's account of his life that Isabella provides is a remarkable set piece, and presents Nugent as a tormented, forceful and darkly romantic figure of more or less heroic proportions—a grieving lover, a runaway, a trapper, a cavalry scout and Indian fighter. His tale is punctuated with gunplay and violence, dissolution and promiscuity. Isabella, attentive throughout the three-hour-long telling, only occasionally interjects a critical perspective, as when she notes: "Vain, even in his dark moods, he told me he was idolized by women . . . The handsome, even superbly handsome, side of his face was toward me as he spoke." Even as she seems caught up in the moment, Bird maintains a certain amount of detachment, as if she is aware that some of these revelations are enhanced by a flair for self-dramatization.

The speech by Nugent that Isabella quotes is highly melodramatic, including cries of "Now you see a man who has made a devil of himself! Lost! Lost! Lost!" The final three exclamations impress her enough that she repeats them later. Isabella claims that "his proud, fierce soul all poured itself out then, with hatred and self-loathing, blood on his hands and murder in his heart, though even then he could not be altogether other than a gentleman, or altogether divest himself of fascination, even when so tempestuously revealing the darkest points of his character." She declares: "My soul dissolved in pity for his dark, lost, self-ruined life."

It's a striking and highly dramatic moment in the book, one some readers no doubt find tainted with Victorian melodrama: the degraded lost soul worth redeeming, the compassionate and upright woman grieved by his torment. There are echoes of Heathcliff and Catherine, Rochester and Jane Eyre, in this scenario. But those readers also familiar with the letters to Henrietta are aware that the scene in the book is very much at odds with the scene in the corresponding epistle.

In her letter of November 18, Isabella explains that, while she was riding with Jim and another trapper in Fall

River Canyon (not Black Canyon, which she rode into on her own two days later), a snow squall made her turn back and Jim accompanied her a little way. "Then came a terrible revelation that as soon as I had gone away he had discovered: he was attached to me and it was killing him. It began on Long's Peak." The conversation is not a revelation of his sordid past but rather a declaration of his romantic feelings for her. Her reaction is to become alarmed: "I was terrified. It made me shake all over and even cry." Here is where she observes: "He is a man whom any woman might love but no sane woman would marry." She credits him with having the good sense not to ask her to marry him, but clearly her response in the book to what he says is really a response to what she claims in the letter he said: "A less ungovernable nature would never have said a word but his dark proud fierce soul all came out then. I believe for the moment he hated me and scorned himself, though he could not even then be otherwise than a gentleman." Here is the origin of her declaration, "My heart dissolves with pity for him and his dark, lost, self ruined life," but what she adds is more revealing of her actual feelings at the moment: "He is so lovable and fascinating yet so terrible." When she tells him she is too nervous to speak to him, he declares he will not see her again and says "such fearfully bitter things" before he sets off to camp in the mountains. Her reaction to all this is less detached than it appears to be in the book: "I could not bear to think of him last night out in the snow neither eating nor sleeping, mad lost wretched hopeless."

The letters have a good deal more evidence of Isabella's confusion and conflicted feelings about Jim's romantic overtures. She alternately chides his behavior and language and regrets his absence and alienation. She dreams that he enters the ranchhouse and shoots her, claims that one day when he visits she is alarmed enough to think about reaching for a pistol, feels guilty about rejecting him and asserts, "I felt that I had stabbed him," and wishes she could "be kind to him rather than kill him as [she] had done." She describes his demeanor toward her at one point as "freezing, courteous of course, but the manner of a corpse hardly touching my hand" and repeats the phrase "The dead past has buried its dead" in regard to reaching a resolution. The recurring theme of violent behavior, he against her, she against him, is rather striking, and given all her reassurances throughout her letters that Jim is always courteous and that no one believes he would ever harm a woman, it's difficult not to believe that the physical passion her terminology reflects is more erotic than violent.

The situation is resolved on Sunday, November 23, when they meet while riding. "I told him that if all circumstances on both sides had been favourable and I had loved him with my whole heart I would not dare to trust my happiness to him because of whisky." Her statement strikes me as more equivocal than it might seem on the surface, but according to her, both of them are satisfied with the resolution they've reached. "He said he would never say another word of love" and she, on her part, claimed, "I feel quite at ease about him now."

The book offers no hint of any of this. Of this last talk, she says only, "We had a long conversation without adverting to the former one, and he told me some of the present circumstances of his ruined life." Her emotion is detached: "It is piteous that a man like him, in the prime of life, should be destitute of home and love, and live a life of darkness in a den with no companions but guilty memories, and a dog which many people think is the nobler animal of the two." Considering that this was likely not written at the time—certainly not transcribed from a letter to Henrietta—and is presented as her point of view then about a man she knows is already dead, the statement is remarkable for its summing up the circumstances of Jim's life as Isabella came to see them.

After her Rocky Mountain adventures were published, Isabella denied to a friend that she had ever been in love with Rocky Mountain Jim but rather had pitied him and yearned for his reform. The evidence of her letters is open to interpretation but it takes considerable reading between the lines to conclude that her confusion about him was more than a combination of infatuation, reticence, and long habits of both pragmatism and repression. Eventually, of course, she wrote a travel narrative, not a memoir, and in the end, whatever there had been or might have been to the relationship, the book primarily presents us with a character profile of a colorful friend and guarded scenes from a Rocky Mountain life.

*   *   *

December 21, 2005. Winter Solstice. Nine days and 132 years after Isabella Bird left Colorado, I accept the mountains' invitation and return to Rocky Mountain National Park. I leave Lafayette at 7:00 a.m., the eastern sky behind me dully light, the sky above the western mountains still dark with horizontal bands of cloud broken by a band of open sky. Soon the higher clouds begin to glow pastel ruby-pink and red-orange while the lower clouds, closer to the mountaintops, remain a dingy off-white. The colors deepen as the sun nears the eastern horizon and for a while I can estimate the sun's altitude behind me by the way, ahead of me, first the lower clouds and then the mountaintops begin to take on that first glow of dawn. Within fifteen minutes, as I skirt around Boulder, the pastures along the back roads display a pastoral serenity, infrequent trees standing starkly in broad fields where horses, cattle, or (familiar at least in Boulder County) llamas graze. By the time I reach the highway paralleling the foothills north of the city, the slopes to the west and the valley to the east are equally alight, and the bucolic valley scenes give way to wholly western vistas, vast open ranchland, distant horizons. Gusty winds buffet the car and I hold tight to the steering wheel.

By 7:35, I've reached Lyons and the sun is brilliant behind me until I enter the North St. Vrain canyon. The snows of a few days earlier, now largely vanished, left minimal residue on the ground all the way to this point, but in the canyon the north-facing slopes and the narrow passages hemmed in by high walls are still snowy, though the road is mostly dry. Only light traffic comes out of the mountains and, going in, only two cars pass me on the highway. I reach Estes Park at 8:00, thinking as I descend Park Hill that the blinding sun in my rearview mirrors was not something Isabella Bird had to contend with on any of her descents.

The sky has been mostly bright and clear all the way, the few large clouds high and lazy, but as the view of Estes Park opens up, blowing snow obscures the peaks of the high mountains. Rocky Mountain National Park encompasses several different ecozones; no matter how light the snow-cover in lower locales like Moraine Park and Beaver Meadows, the higher altitudes of Bear Lake and Glacier Gorge and the mountains beyond them will already be deep in snow and Trail Ridge Road across the top of the Park unplowed and closed until spring.

I pass quietly through empty Estes Park and on the way past the Beaver Meadows Visitor Center notice half a dozen browsing mule deer. Ahead of me, elk are crossing the road. As I slow to let them clear the pavement, I realize that more are moving up out of a low meadow on the south side of the road and clambering up the roadbank into a cluster of cabins on the higher ground to the north. I park and try to be unobtrusive as I step near a sparse stand of trees up the embankment. The cabins may have occupants but I see no sign of other people. For now I am alone in the winter wind and the morning sun, watching the elk flow past, listening to the steady clump of their hooves. At least seventy elk go by before I lose count. Some elders are slow and watchful, some youngsters occasionally canter, but the rest move forward at a stately, even leisurely, pace. They wear their heavier winter coats, thick dark ruffs below their necks and around their shoulders, summer antlers still perched above their heads. I wait until the last of them has crossed the road and passed my position before I retreat out of the biting wind to the car.

A pickup truck that stopped in the middle of the road pulls up next to my sedan. One of the two women inside asks me what those animals are and, when I tell her, she says, "I thought they'd be bigger." Elk can be over five feet tall at the shoulder, over six feet long, and generally weigh between 500 and 700 pounds. I suggest that they're plenty big enough when you get closer to them. I start my car and follow the women on up toward the park entrance.

We go less than a quarter-mile before their pickup slows and then halts in the center of the lane. Beyond it, I glimpse more shapes in the road and ease to a stop. Eight coyotes emerge from in front of the truck and lope across the pavement into the field on the passenger side of our vehicles. A few pass within a dozen paces of my parked car but give no overt sign that they notice it. Their red-gray fur ruffles in the wind and they blink at an occasional gust, but they trot nonchalantly along the shoulder of the road and then angle up into the trees without a backward glance. I move on, following their example.

The roads in the park are icy and snowpacked in places. I wend my way cautiously down into Moraine Park and turn off toward the trailheads beyond the meadows. Near the roche moutonnée, now partly snow-covered, the Big Thompson appears to be frozen. I swing around into a familiar pull-off where I've parked before to contemplate crossing the Big Thompson only to be dissuaded by its icy swiftness. Now I step down to the river's edge and gingerly try the strength of the ice. It seems solid but also flawlessly smooth and highly slippery. To cross, I shuffle and slide rather than step or stride. Only as I reach the opposite bank do I hear a crackling response to my weight. A trail of boot-prints, hoofprints, and scattered elk droppings meanders in the direction of the roche moutonnée; instead of fol-lowing it, I veer off on a direct line and quickly reach its base. It's more massive than it appears from the road. The brief climb to the top is steep, and arrival gives me both sat-isfaction and disillusionment. I'm standing on the roche moutonnée at last but it seems like less of an accomplish-ment than I imagined it would.

This little jaunt feels like a postscript to my Moraine Park excursions, the overdue final outing. The Moraine Park meadows look especially flat from this perspective, and the snow against the grass reveals regular routes taken by the elk, the paths etched by their filing out toward bountiful grazing. From this position, I hardly notice cars on distant Bear Lake Road and the White cabin seems small and insignificant. The small, scruffy trees on the roche mou-tonnée offer little shelter from an icy wind rolling down the canyon from the mountains, retracing the path of the Thompson glacier. I pull up my hood and tighten the fas-tenings on my parka. I'm not likely to come out to the roche again, certainly not any time soon, so I take my time dropping off the rocky hillock and wandering back to the Big Thompson. This time I cross at a snow-covered elbow where many tracks confirm that others have already tested their weight. It only takes a moment to follow the river-bank back to the warmth of the car.

Midmorning. I wind my way up Trail Ridge Road to the point where it's closed for the season. At the end of a wide paved lot at Many Parks Curve, where only a single car is parked, a low metal gate is locked in place. The roadway beyond the gate is deep in snow. Only a single set of fresh ski tracks mars the surface. I put on my snowshoes and slip the carrying strap for the tote bag over my head and chest. Then I head up the first long stretch of the highway, trudging through the snow with heavy steps. On my left, the road cut has created a partly denuded slope beneath an extensive forest of subalpine trees; on my right, the forest continues down a steep slope to the valley from which I came. Ahead, the road is merely open white space to a distant point where it curves out of sight around the mountainside and the trees thin out for a clear view across the valley.

Rounding that curve, I approach a dry spot in the road. Off to the side a woman is bent over, adjusting or refastening her skis. When she notices me she moves farther off to a low wall of square stones on the outer rim of the curve, above the meanders of Fall River in the valley far below. Coming abreast of her, I joke about the sudden appearance of bare pavement and she tells me that snow-covered and clear patches of road alternate all the way to the head of Hidden Valley, as far as she's gone up Trail Ridge Road today. I remove my snowshoes and clomp over wind-cleared pavement until I reach another curve where snow cover takes over again. Below, across Horseshoe Park, I can see traces of the flood of 1982, when the dam at Lawn Lake gave way and the Roaring River stripped clear a section of forest and spread an alluvial fan of debris out across the valley floor. The path of the debris is clearer from this perspective, the extent of the flow more apparent, than from the site itself on Fall River Road, where I've driven on and walked around that alluvial fan.

With snowshoes back on, I walk another long stretch of road, then encounter another clear patch and take them off again. This dry section goes a long way and when I come to another snowy section where I can tell the cover is lighter, I simply stomp through to the third long dry patch, which disappears beyond another curve. The wind is strong, biting, and hits me head on. I don my face mask and tighten the hood of my parka, leaning into the wind as I walk. The road curves a great deal and it's often hard to predict how long a snow-covered or snowless stretch will last. A gleaming patch of bright blue sky shines through a tear in a gray scrim of thick blowing snow lifted by the wind above the far side of the mountains. At the end of this clear section, the snow is a little more mounded up and the road ahead arches into a long switchback that eventually rises up the other side of the narrow valley. The woman's ski tracks are the only blemish on the surface. I ease over to the low stone wall and look down on Hidden Valley. Below, near a large shack in the center of the "snow play area," people are walking and children are sledding, light activity in open spaces. When I look ahead at the sky, the blue patch has vanished and the blowing snow has darkened; the wind remains persistent. I decide to turn back. Lacy wisps of snow writhe down the pavement ahead of me. With the wind at my back, bullying me forward, it takes less time to retrace my steps to the trailhead. Except for that one woman, I have seen no one on Trail Ridge Road, just as I was alone at the roche moutonnée.

Stowing my gear in the car, I stroll over to a long arc of wooden walkway and railings hanging off the side of Many Parks Curve, where a few people are taking pictures of one another. The walkway looks down on Beaver Meadows and Moraine Park, roughly 1,200 feet below. It takes me a moment to orient myself, but I soon locate the roche moutonnée and the South Lateral Moraine, the wriggling bed of the Big Thompson through the meadows, Eagle Cliff Mountain rising at the far end of Moraine Park. I think I'll never quite comprehend the sweep and scale of the terrain that Rocky Mountain National Park encompasses. From here, reaching the roche moutonnée doesn't seem like much of a feat.

Driving down the highway from Many Parks Curve, I gaze constantly at the billowing clouds above Longs Peak and its neighbors. I marvel at the way the clouds cling to the mountains at times, crawling over the summits, unable to rise above them. In almost the same section of sky, though, other swirls of cloud, their patterns as clear as needlepoint, their colors running through several shades of blue and gray, curl high above the mountains; in the center of one pattern a small distinct dab of gray cloud stands out, like a separate independent sphere of smoke. The mountaintops relentlessly give up their snow cover or are covered with snow swirling over their peaks. I can't always see the summits of the highest mountains to the west and the north, though often the bare tundra of lower mountains extending just beyond treeline are visible, starkly windswept and only slightly snow-laden. The sky and the skyline are everchanging, and it's a privilege, one charged with shifting amounts of trepidation and awe, to be able to climb so near to them and to spend the day watching how dynamically they interact.

Leaving the park, I review the day. I'm not surprised to feel fulfilled after a day in the mountains, even when much of what I encounter is, by mountain standards, commonplace. The radiant dawn, the elk, the coyotes, the roche moutonnée, the snow-covered and impassable road, the solitude, the serenity, the contentment on a par with rapture. I revel in them as if they were completely unpredictable. How many days like this—days spent collecting mountain commonplaces—could you have in a row if you spent the winter here? I'm thrilled to have arrived at a destination I hadn't anticipated.

I've gone all day without thinking of my companionable authors, the voices of Colorado past and present; I haven't been wondering what they would make of what I behold. It strikes me then that, without knowing when the transformation took place, I no longer consider myself a flatlander. Nor do I see myself as someone still in search of Isabella Bird's Colorado. Instead, I've been immersed in familiar terrain, the landscape to which I feel most connected. I've spent the day rambling a Colorado of my own.

Departure

The last evening came. I did not wish to realize it, as I looked at the snow-peaks glistening in the moonlight. . . . The last morning came. I cleaned up my room and sat at the window watching the red and gold of one of the most glorious of winter sunrises, and the slow lighting-up of one peak after another. I have written that this scenery is not lovable, but I love it.

Isabella Bird, Letter XVII

Isabella Bird's final letter is datelined "Cheyenne, Wyoming, December 12, 1873." The heading suggests a balanced closure to her life in the Rocky Mountains. She had come down to Greeley on the train from Cheyenne in September and barely three months later took the train from Greeley into Cheyenne where she would connect with the eastbound train and return to Scotland. Her final stay in Estes Park lasted a little over three weeks.

On December 9 she packed her belongings, said her farewells to Kavanaugh, Buchanan, and Allen, and rode with Evans up to Nugent's cabin. The two men were cordial to each other, Isabella observed, but in a footnote reports that "some months later 'Mountain Jim' fell by Evans' hand." She makes no judgment about the event, except to say, "The tragedy is too painful to dwell upon." Nugent and Bird rode down to a cabin owned by a man named Miller and stayed the night. The next day they rode slowly onward, burdened by Isabella's luggage, stopping only once at a house where they could warm themselves.

Isabella was now emerging onto the plains for the final time. Her description of the Rockies, evoking as she often did a phrase from the Book of Isaiah alluding to heaven, hinted at both her sense of loss and her reverence for the place she was leaving.

> I never saw the mountain range look so beautiful—uplifted in every shade of transparent blue, till the sublimity of Long's Peak, and the lofty crest of Storm Peak, bore only unsullied snow against the sky. Peaks gleamed in living light; canyons lay in depths of purple shade; 100 miles away Pike's Peak rose a lump of blue, and over all, through that glorious afternoon, a veil of blue spiritualized without dimming the outlines of that most glorious range, making it look like the dreamed-of mountains of "the land which is very far off," till at sunset it stood out sharp in glories of violet and opal, and the whole horizon up to a great height was suffused with the deep rose and pure orange of the afterglow.

They rode on through "the sunlit solitude" to Namaqua, the stage stop on the Big Thompson, and then went three miles farther to an inn in the settlement of St. Louis (both communities were later absorbed into present-day Loveland). Jim was on his best behavior and the trip was quiet and uneventful.

On the morning of December 11, they woke to a frigid landscape. "That curious phenomena called frost-fall was occurring, in which, whatever moisture may exist in the air, somehow aggregates into feathers and fern leaves, the loveliest of creations, only seen in rarefied air and intense cold." Somehow, her description of the phenomena reminds us of her sense of loss at leaving Estes Park: "One breath and they vanish. The air was filled with diamond sparks quite intangible." A man whom she identifies as "Mr. Fodder" (but whose real name was William Haugh) and whom she notes was the one who later instigated Evans's firing on Jim, was a passenger on the stage, and she introduced him to Nugent. They made a striking contrast, one dressed in "grotesque rags and odds and ends of apparel," the other "dressed in the extreme of English dandyism . . . [his] small hand cased in a perfectly-fitting lemon-coloured kid glove," but Isabella thought Jim's "gentlemanliness of deportment brought into relief the innate vulgarity of a rich *parvenu*."

The stage left and her prattling companion distracted her, though her description of what she was distracted from suggests an image deeply etched into memory: "I never realized that my Rocky Mountain life was at an end, not even when I saw 'Mountain Jim,' with his golden hair yellow in the sunshine, slowly leading the beautiful mare over the snowy Plains back to Estes Park, equipped with the saddle on which I had ridden 800 miles!"

And then she writes, as the final paragraph of the book, "A drive of several hours over the Plains brought us to Greeley, and a few hours later, in the far blue distance, the Rocky Mountains, and all that they enclose, went down below the prairie sea." She never returned.

In recent months, inevitably, I've been contemplating her departure, aware that I have reached the end of my travels in her path and that we too approach a parting of the ways. I've covered all of her routes and run out of occasions to consult her about where I am. Because her book is also the limit of her conversation about the region—she went on to wander other landscapes and write other books about them, without much looking back to earlier travels—I've gotten all the mileage, in a very physical sense if not an intellectual or metaphorical sense, that I'm likely to get from using *A Lady's Life in the Rocky Mountains* as a template for my own exploring. No matter how much I tried to match my footprints with hers, or with those of her near contemporaries, she and I wandered different Colorados across time, and by now Isabella Bird and I have both put her Colorado behind us.

Isabella Bird came to Colorado on the recommendation of friends, found more than she expected as she passed slowly through, and, except for some memories and correspondence, moved beyond it. She never expected her life here to be more than transitory. That she was able to write a book of lasting, enduring value about it is a tribute to her considerable talents. What travel books currently available will people read 132 years from now?

The Colorado that Isabella Bird rode through was rugged and challenging but most of the terrain she traveled, except for remote Estes Park, was familiar territory to the settlers, ranchers, and miners who had come west to exploit undeveloped land. That she so often was on the fringes of the wild, the edge of the frontier, is due in large part to her deliberate avoidance of the settled and more or less civilized parts of the territory. (I suspect that, if she hadn't made those choices, I wouldn't have followed her very far.) We can credit her, as Ernest Bernard does, with being an incipient environmentalist, someone who prefers a wild landscape above a cultivated one, and see her as a prototype, in Colorado at least, of the "green" tourist of our own time, but still we have to recognize that she wasn't much inclined to go beyond the fringes, into real wilderness, the terrain in which mountain men and trappers and explorers immersed themselves.

The Rocky Mountains of her title are really the Front Range—she reached the Continental Divide only once and then only at Boreas Pass, near South Park, rather than just beyond Estes Park to the west. The Front Range, the stretch of mountains running from Wyoming south to Cañon City and also synonymous with the stretch of urban development between Fort Collins and Colorado Springs and centered on Denver, is now the most extended metropolitan area in the inland west—it's the area that most resembles East Coast and West Coast megalopolises and least resembles the Colorado of Isabella Bird's sojourn; I find it the least Coloradoan aspect of Colorado. This megalopolis may, in the end, determine the quality of my time in the West, but I have a hankering to know more of the Colorado that neither Isabella nor Denver can show me.

We all need—or ought—to know where we are, not merely the address but the nature of the place. While, for some, it may be a comfort and a reassurance to live in an environment that replicates others all across the country, for others—for myself—the high-speed blending of our regional identities into one cultural smoothie is a travesty. The landscape itself reminds us of how diverse ecology can be. I long to identify the distinctive qualities of a place and learn how its histories—natural, cultural—intersect with my own history and with the moment in which I encounter them.

I believe that Isabella Bird shared some of those feelings and that they were part of her motive in locating herself in new settings. But her experiences in the Rockies seem to have altered her sense of herself. All along, she'd been independent and capable of meeting the unpredictable demands of travel, but in the American West circumstances demanded more of her physically and revealed levels of resourcefulness she hadn't known she'd had. Her compelling need to be in motion, rather than to remain in one place, kept her in motion, with memorable results, all of her adult life, especially when the deaths of her parents and her sister and her husband removed her attachments to familiar places; it was Colorado (and Hawaii as well) that confirmed her confidence in her ability to stay in motion. As memorably as she was able to preserve her Colorado for us, it wasn't Colorado she took with her when she departed, but rather a new sense of herself.

Isabella Bird's Colorado was the landscape of her aspirations, her desire to be unfettered and uncommitted. Here she found the retreat she sought from a regulated life of responsibility and obligation and social constraint. She didn't aspire to a secure, settled life, the life sought by homesteaders she encountered, or to status within a stable society, the life of a clergyman's daughter or a physician's wife. In some sense her travels allowed her to be a visitor in the very society in which she was raised. In Colorado she was attracted to the remote places set far away from the settlements that hoped to achieve the size, complexity, and prosperity of eastern cities. As a consequence, the parts of Colorado that today most resemble the Colorado of Isabella's day are the places where weather and altitude and inhospitable terrain and preservation foresight and failed exploitation have limited growth and development. My travels after Isabella have gotten me in touch with those places, at least intermittently, to the extent that they were visible through the scrim of time.

My aspirations have been simpler than hers; I've merely wanted to know where I am and to learn who to be while I'm here. In the process I've often gone beyond the limits of Isabella's experience—I've had more time and greater mobility and even better weather than she had; I've gone higher and deeper and farther than she went—and I realize that, in doing so, I've far extended the limits of my own experience, achieved a Colorado of my own.

My Colorado is one where I am continually, instinctively, engulfed in the natural world. It's a place of vista and altitude, of boundless plains and limitless mountains, of encompassing forest and exposed tundra; it's a place of parks and valleys and canyons. Here I have an overwhelming sense of immeasurable time, of unimaginable geological forces, of the transitory nature of existence—not merely of human life or culture but also of the very earth beneath my feet. Here I've felt my spirits lift in tandem with the gain in altitude, soar effortlessly each time I rise above treeline, like an eagle or hawk riding a thermal, hovering serenely in the elevating currents of the tangible transcendent.

Unlike Isabella Bird, who left and never returned, I am, for now at least, here to stay. I like who I am while I'm here, like finding myself vibrating in sympathetic tuning with the harmony of this portion of the universe. As a migrant flatlander, I've felt the world expand during my time in Colorado; as a novice Front Ranger, I would feel the world contract, close in around me, if I were to leave for anywhere else.

I can imagine moving on. I can't imagine letting go.

Acknowledgments

A ny book that explores the past relies heavily on the kindness of strangers, by whom I mean, in the case of this book, librarians and archivists at the Denver Public Library's Western History and Genealogy Collection, the University of Colorado at Boulder Libraries, the Boulder Public Library Carnegie Branch, Estes Park Public Library, Auraria Library, and Colorado History Society's Stephen H. Hart Library. I am also grateful to Rocky Mountain National Park and the Rocky Mountain Natural History Association for the opportunity to serve as a 2004 Artist-in-Residence and to reside briefly in the William Allen White cabin in Moraine Park. I especially thank Park Ranger and Artist Coordinator Jean Muenchrath and volunteers at the Moraine Park Museum. I also thank Dave Turk and the other members of the Colorado Mountain Club whom I accompanied on a hike up Longs Peak, an important trek for this book and for me as an emerging Coloradan. I need to thank as well Susan Schiller, who first introduced me to Estes Park; Reg Saner, Elizabeth Dodd, David Gessner, Mary Beth Pope, Elizabeth Sawin, Linda Peterson, and Jean Harper, for their involvement in that Estes Park conference and subsequent conversations about writing; and Steve Wingate and Shari Caudron, who keep me in touch with the world of writing. Special thanks to Sarah Dickerson for reading and commenting on the manuscript and offering valuable suggestions. Thanks as well to Matt Bokovoy for his insights into the manuscript, without which this would be a profoundly different book, and to Elizabeth Dodd and Natalia Rachel Singer for perceptive and supportive reading of the book. Encouragement for this project came as well from the opportunity to share the Front Range with my children, my sons-in-law, and my grandchildren; thanks and love to Tom Root, Becky, Paul, and Louie Schauer, and Caroline, Tim, Zola, and Ezra Disz. My wife, Sue Root, has been on most of the trails and highways this book travels and knows what it has meant to write it. My love and gratitude have traveled with her.

Notes

The quotations from *A Lady's Life in the Rocky Mountains* throughout this book are taken from the American third edition, published 1880 by G. P. Putnam's Sons. I cite the chapters (Letter I, Letter II, etc.) rather than pages since readers may have access to one or more modern editions with different pagination. Quotations from her transcribed personal letters are taken from *Letters to Henrietta*, edited by Kay Chubbuck (Boston: Northeastern University Press, 2003) and cited by date rather than page number. The third source used throughout this book is *Isabella Lucy Bird's "A Lady's Life in the Rocky Mountains": An Annotated Text*, edited by Ernest S. Bernard (Norman: University of Oklahoma Press, 1999).

The Plains

Isabella Bird's comments on Greeley, Fort Collins, the plains, and Longmont are in Letters III and IV. Grace Greenwood, in *New Life in New Lands*, talks about the plains and her first experience of Greeley in her August 10 entry of "Colorado"; her August 29 entry (opening with the sardonic line "feeling in need of a little dissipation, I ran up to Greeley") celebrates the community at some length. Bayard Taylor discusses antelope in Chapters III and IV of *Colorado*, the prairie dogs at the end of Chapter III. Rose Kingsley's remarks are on p. 36 of *South by West*. Mary Taylor

Young's chapter "Black-Tailed Prairie Dogs" is on pp. 55–67 of *Land of Grass and Sky*. Merrill Gilfillan drives north to Cheyenne in Chapter 6 of *Magpie Rising*.

The Canyon

Halka Chronic is my guide to all things geologic in Colorado. She discusses Big Thompson Canyon on pp. 30–38 of *Time, Rocks, and the Rockies: A Geologic Guide to Roads and Trails of Rocky Mountain National Park* and on pp. 149–52 of *Roadside Geology of Colorado*. Willis T. Lee's early report, *The Geologic Story of the Rocky Mountain National Park Colorado*, is also valuable. David McComb writes of the canyon in *Big Thompson: Portrait of a Natural Disaster*; see Chapter 1 in particular.

The Park

Platt Rogers's version of the climb up Longs Peak was first published in *The Story of Estes Park, Rocky Mountain National Park, and Grand Lake* by Enos Mills. Willis Lee covers the approach to Estes Park from Lyons on pp. 41–42 of *The Geologic Story of the Rocky Mountain National Park Colorado*. Halka Chronic describes the route in *Time, Rocks, and the Rockies* on pp. 25–30. William Allen White's story of his own life is told in *The Autobiography of William Allen White* and his writings, including "Mary White," are collected in *Forty Years on Main Street*.

The Peak

Isabella Bird's account of her ascent of Longs Peak was first published in *Out West* in the December 1873–January 1874 issue. Bird apparently wrote to Henrietta about the climb but hung onto the letter to use it as the basis for her article. The account in the book, Letter VII, is expanded from the article and also uses material that must have been in the letter. At any rate, her original account of it for her sister hasn't survived. A variant version told long afterwards by Platt Rogers was written and published in 1905 in *The Story of*

Estes Park by Enos A. Mills, himself a Longs Peak guide and frequent climber and the man generally credited with achieving national park status for the area. William Byers's accounts of the ascent by John Wesley Powell's party and the ascent by Ferdinand V. Hayden's party appear in editions of the *Rocky Mountain News*. Anna Dickinson tells her version in *A Ragged Register*. James Pickering covers much of this ground in *"This Blue Hollow."* Stories about the deaths of Carrie Welton and Agnes Vaille are retold in *Rocky Mountain National Park* by Curt W. Buchholtz, and also in *Longs Peak: The Story of Colorado's Favorite Fourteener* by Dougald MacDonald. Reg Saner's "Longs Peak Labor Day Weekend Parade" appears in *The Dawn Collector: On My Way to the Natural World*.

The Tour: Southern Circuit

Isabella's correspondence with her sister has not been completely preserved. Louisa Ward Arps published an article excerpting the existing Colorado letters, and those transcribed in Chubbuck's edition of *Letters to Henrietta* date only between October 23, 1873, and December 4, 1873, and the ending of the final letter is missing. Eliza Greatorex's travel book, *Summer Etchings in Colorado*, is illustrated by her. Helen Hunt Jackson writes about Manitou Springs in "A Winter Morning at Colorado Springs" in *Bits of Travel at Home*. Information on the Long expedition may be found in *The Natural History of the Long Expedition to the Rocky Mountains 1819–1820* by Howard Ensign Evans. The history of Perry Park comes from *Fading Past: The Story of Douglas County, Colorado* by Susan Consola Appleby. William Henry Jackson's photograph of Perry Park and a corresponding recent photograph by John Fielder can be seen in *Colorado 1870–2000 II* (pp. 16–17).

The Tour: Mining District

The Foss General Store has closed since this chapter was written. Harriet Martineau's comments are in *Society in America*; she traveled eastern America over forty years before Isabella Bird came to Colorado and Martineau's comments on the prairie were evoked by her visit to Illinois, the farthest west she went. Bayard Taylor visits Golden in Chapter VII of *Colorado: A Summer Trip* and Black Hawk and Central City in Chapters VIII and IX. Helen Hunt Jackson's account of her visit to the area in *Bits of Travel at Home* appear in the essays "Central City and the Bob-Tail Tunnel" and "Georgetown and the 'Terrible Mine.'" Samuel Bowles passes through the region in Chapter 4 of *The Parks and Mountains of Colorado* (or, *The Switzerland of America*). Grace Greenwood recounts her travels in the September 4 entry and the September 20–22 entries of the Colorado section of *New Life in New Lands*. As a further footnote to the dangers of canyon passage, I should mention that, on May 11, 2006, two days after I drove up the canyon again to check out details, a casino bus and a utility truck collided head-on, injuring the drivers and several bus passengers, as well as a motorist and a motorcyclist who crashed trying to avoid the other vehicles. The highway was closed for hours as the collision was investigated, the vehicles towed away, and the debris cleaned up on the highway.

The Last Canyon

Helen Hunt Jackson's essay, "Bowlder Canyon," is in *Bits of Travel at Home*. The presence of mountain lions in populated areas is being confirmed regularly. In early 2006 the local news was showing video of a cougar in a fenced-in backyard on Boulder's University Hill. In April a seven-year-old boy was attacked by a cougar on Flagstaff Mountain, behind Boulder, while he was walking on a busy trail with his family and holding his father's hand. The very day I drafted these remarks a yearling lion was trapped in a Boulder neighborhood after killing a pet cat and transported to a relocation facility and the next day, as I typed this, I read an article of more sightings in populated areas near where I live. The issue will not go away anytime soon. Reg Saner's essay, "Lions in the Streets," is in *The Dawn Collector*; his title essay is the source of the quote about the sunrise. The Don Kroodsma quote is an epigraph to Don Stap's fine book, *Birdsong*.

Bibliography

Appleby, Susan Consola. *Fading Past: The Story of Douglas County, Colorado*. Palmer Lake, Colo.: Filter Press LLC, 2001.

Arps, Louisa Ward. "Letters from Isabella Bird." *Colorado Quarterly* 4 (Summer 1955): 26–41.

Bird, Isabella L. *Isabella Lucy Bird's "A Lady's Life in the Rocky Mountains": An Annotated Text*. Edited by Ernest S. Bernard. Norman: University of Oklahoma Press, 1999.

———. *A Lady's Life in the Rocky Mountains*, 3rd ed. New York: G. P. Putnam's Sons, 1880.

———. *Letters to Henrietta*. Edited by Kay Chubbuck. Boston: Northeastern University Press, 2003.

———. "Long's Peak." *Out West* 1:6–7 (December–January 1873–74): 21–24.

Bowles, Samuel. *Across the Continent: A Summer's Journey to the Rocky Mountains, the Mormons, and the Pacific States, with Speaker Colfax*. Springfield, Mass.: Samuel Bowles & Co, 1865.

———. *Our New West: Records of Travel Between the Mississippi and the Pacific Ocean*. Hartford: Hartford Publishing Co., 1869.

———. *The Parks and Mountains of Colorado: A Summer Vacation in the Switzerland of America, 1868*. Edited by James H. Pickering. Norman: University of Oklahoma Press, 1991.

———. *The Switzerland of America: A Summer Vacation in the Parks and Mountains of Colorado*. Springfield: Samuel Bowles & Co., 1869.

Buchholtz, Curt W. *Rocky Mountain National Park: A History*. Boulder: Colorado Associated University Press, 1983.

Byers, William N. "First Ascent of Long's Peak." *The Trail* (October 1914): 21–23.

———. "The Hayden Expedition," *Rocky Mountain News*, September 24, 1873, 2.

———. "The Powell Expedition," *Rocky Mountain News*, September 1, 1868, 1.

Chronic, Halka, and Felicie Williams. *Roadside Geology of Colorado*. 2nd ed. Missoula, Mont.: Mountain Press, 2002.

Chronic, Halka. *Time, Rocks, and the Rockies: A Geologic Guide to Roads and Trails of Rocky Mountain National Park*. Missoula: Mountain Press, 1984.

Dickinson, Anna E. *A Ragged Register (of People, Places, and Opinions)*. New York: Harper & Brothers, 1878.

Dixon, William Hepworth. *New America*. London: Hurst and Blackett, 1867.

Evans, Howard Ensign. *The Natural History of the Long Expedition to the Rocky Mountains 1819–1820*. New York: Oxford University Press, 1997.

Gilfillan, Merrill. *Magpie Rising: Sketches from the Great Plains*. Boulder: Pruett, 1988. Reprint, Lincoln: University of Nebraska Press, 2003.

Greatorex, Eliza. *Summer Etchings in Colorado*. New York: G. P. Putnam's Sons, 1873.

Greenwood, Grace. *New Life in New Lands: Notes of Travel*. New York: J. B. Ford & Co., 1873.

H. H. [Helen Hunt Jackson]. *Bits of Travel at Home*. Boston: Roberts Brothers, 1890.

Jackson, William Henry, and John Fielder. *Colorado: 1870–2000: Then and Now*. Englewood, Colo.: Westcliffe, 1999.

———. *Colorado: 1870–2000*, Vol. II: *Historical Landscape Photography*. Englewood: Westcliffe, 2005.

Jones, William C., and Kenton Forrest. *Denver: A Pictorial History from Frontier Camp to Queen City of the Plains*. Boulder: Pruett, 1973.

Kaye, Evelyn. *Amazing Traveler: Isabella Bird*. Boulder: Blue Penguin, 1994.

Kingsley, Rose. *South by West, or, Winter in the Rocky Mountains and Spring in Mexico*. Edited by Charles Kingsley. London: W. Isbister & Co., 1874.

Lee, Willis T. *The Geologic Story of the Rocky Mountain National Park Colorado*. Washington, D.C.: Government Printing Office, 1917.

Leonard, Stephen J., and Thomas J. Noel. *Denver: From Mining Camp to Metropolis*. Niwot: University Press of Colorado, 1990.

MacDonald, Dougald. *Longs Peak: The Story of Colorado's Favorite Fourteener*. Englewood, Colo.: Westcliffe Press, 2004.

Martineau, Harriet. *Society in America*. 3 vols. 1837. Reprint, New York: AMS Press, 1966.

McComb, David. *Big Thompson: Portrait of a Natural Disaster*. Boulder: Pruett Publishing, 1980.

Middleton, Dorothy. *Victorian Lady Travelers*. New York: Dutton, 1965.

Mills, Enos A. *The Story of Estes Park, Rocky Mountain National Park, and Grand Lake*. 4th ed. Estes Park: pub. by author, 1917.

Norton, Boyd, and Barbara Norton. *Backroads of Colorado*. Stillwater, Minn.: Voyageurs Press, 1995.

Pickering, James H. *"This Blue Hollow": Estes Park, The Early Years 1859–1914*. Niwot: University Press of Colorado, 1999.

Rossiter, Richard. *Boulder Climbs North*. Denver: Chockstone Press, 1988.

Saner, Reg. *The Dawn Collector: On My Way to the Natural World*. Santa Fe: Center for the American West, 2005.

Stap, Don. *Birdsong*. New York: Scribners, 2005.

Stoddart, Anna M. *The Life of Isabella Bird (Mrs. Bishop) Hon. Member of the Oriental Society of Pekin, F.R.G.S., F.R.S.G.S.* London: John Murray, 1906.

Taylor, Bayard. *Colorado: A Summer Trip*. Edited by William W. Savage, Jr., and James H. Lazalier. Niwot: University Press of Colorado, 1989.

White, William Allen. *The Autobiography of William Allen White*. New York: Macmillan, 1946.

———. *Forty Years on Main Street*. Compiled by Russell Fitzgibbon from the columns of the *Emporia Gazette*. New York: Farrar & Rinehart, 1937.

Young, Mary Taylor. *Land of Grass and Sky: A Naturalist's Prairie Journey*. Englewood: Westcliffe, 2002.